P9-ARS-294

PROFILES IN FAITH

GLENN D. KITTLER

PROFILES IN FAITH

INTRODUCTION BY CATHERINE MARSHALL

Coward-McCann, Inc. New York

Library of Congress Catalog

Card Number: 62-10948

MANUFACTURED IN THE UNITED STATES OF AMERICA

TO EDWARD A. MOLLOY, C.Ss.R.

Contents

CONTENTS

Introduction

On occasion many of us have wished for a collection of short biographies of some of America's interfaith religious leaders for our reference shelves. Here is such a volume.

To some readers, the choice of the men and women for this book may seem strange. The religious convictions and practices of some are at odds with the convictions and practices of others. For that matter, there are personalities here whose beliefs are at sharp variance from my own. And knowing Glenn Kittler personally, I am aware that he has written about persons whose theology is far afield from his.

Yet the fact remains that each of these individuals made a constructive contribution to American life. That such contributions were made by obviously imperfect creatures may surprise some readers, perhaps even shock others.

But this is nothing more or less than the grace of God in action. Most of us are loath to accept the notion of grace. It means that not a one of us can earn God's blessings for ourselves or others. It means that the Creator can and does use imperfect, sometimes blundering instruments to carry forward His creative processes.

This glorifies God and not man. It follows that some favorite human idols may fall from pedestals—even in the religious field. Most challenging of all, we begin to suspect that since God requires willingness and not perfection, He can use any one of us.

For given man's willingness to be used, difficult circumstances do not frustrate God's purposes: neither that of being born into slavery—like Richard Allen; nor the wretched health of someone like Francis Asbury; neither poverty nor discouragement—such as that of Joseph Krauskopf; nor what might have been the greatest obstacle of all—the wealth and overprivilege of Catherine Drexel.

Actually, the dawning discovery of the grace of God through a book like *Profiles in Faith* should delight us. Without that grace, organized religion would not have survived and made its great contribution to an ongoing America. With it—whether in religion or politics or the international arena—we can take heart and a new grip on hope.

CATHERINE MARSHALL

Chappaqua, N. Y.

PROFILES IN FAITH

CHAPTER

ONE

The Lion of the Lord

THE young man was visiting his married sister one afternoon and he noticed a new book on the living room table. He picked it up. "Did you just buy this?" he asked.

Rhoda Green glanced up from her sewing. "A salesman left it the other day," she said. "He said if we like it we could buy it; otherwise he'll take it back."

The young man flipped through the pages. "Looks like the Bible. Have you read it?"

"No, not yet."

"Has John?"

"No, he hasn't had time," said Rhoda. "But you know how preachers are, always so busy. I'm lucky to have him home for supper more than once a week."

He put the book down. "I'd better get home to fix our own supper."

Rhoda got up and followed him to the door. "How's Miriam?"

"The same. The doctor stopped by the other day to have a look at her. He said she'll never be really well again."

Rhoda shook her head slowly. "That's a shame. Well, I guess that's the way it is with tuberculosis in these parts. Give Miriam my love."

"I will."

"And the children."

"All right."

He climbed into his wagon, took up the reins and gave the horse a soft slap with them and rode away. At home, he prepared dinner for his invalid wife and their two young daughters, then went out to finish the evening chores on his small farm. This done, he returned to the house to help his wife and children get ready for bed. This done, he sat down at the table, put a match to the oil lamp at his elbow, and began to read.

The only book in the house was the Bible. He had learned to read from it when he was a boy and he had seldom read anything else. Every night, when he was alone like this, he read a few pages. And yet he did not claim to be a religious man. He was well aware that he lacked the extreme fervor the rest of his family possessed. His sister had married a Methodist minister; his father and brothers occasionally acted as lay preachers when there were no ordained men around. The atmosphere of his boyhood had been sternly fundamentalist: no smoking, no drinking, no harsh language, family prayers and Bible reading every day, and when visitors came the talk was always of a religious nature.

Somehow little of it rubbed off on him. When the family attended revivals, which was as often as revivals were held, he found some excuse to stay away. He was twenty-one before he finally joined the Methodist Church, and then he joined mostly because Miriam wanted him to. There was a time, when the children were infants, when he did not go to church at all, volunteering readily to stay home with the babies so that Miriam could go. And after she fell ill, he used her condition as an excuse to stay home on Sunday mornings more often than he went to church. He frankly admitted that he derived little spiritual fulfillment from the services. He admitted, too, that he was puzzled by the various denominations that surrounded him: if Truth were singular, then only one of them could contain the truth but he could not decide which one did. And he also admitted that although he read the Bible daily much of it confused him to the point that he was not sure what he believed.

But he continued to read the Bible. And he said his nightly prayers, mostly for Miriam's recovery.

About a week after he visited his sister's house, he went to see his father, and he found the old man sitting on the porch, a book in his lap. He recognized the book, and he asked: "I saw that at Rhoda's house the other day. Did you borrow it from her, Pa?"

"No," said the old man. "Your brother Phineas brought this copy over. He bought it, too."

"Must be pretty good, if the whole family's reading it," the young man said.

The old man regarded his son seriously. "I think," he said in a soft, firm voice, "that this is the greatest book I've ever read, including the Bible."

The young man could just say: "Well."

His father said: "I want you to read it. Take it home with you and read it carefully."

That night, after he had finished his chores and put his wife and children to bed, the young man sat down as usual at the kitchen table and lighted the oil lamp. It was then, on a memorable summer night in 1830, that Brigham Young, twenty-nine years old, read for the first time the stirring words of the Book of Mormon.

2

That same night, just a few miles away, another young man sat at a kitchen table and read the Book of Mormon, but to him the book was nothing new. In fact, he was distinctly responsible for its existence, and this had come about in a most unusual way.

Joseph Smith claimed that when he was a boy of fourteen on his father's Upstate New York farm, two personages appeared to him and identified themselves as God the Father and Jesus Christ. They discouraged him from joining any of the existing religious sects and urged him to wait until a messenger came to him with special instructions. The messenger arrived four years later, on the night of September 21, 1823, and greeted Joseph with the words:

"I am Moroni, an angel of God. God has work for you to do." Then Moroni told Joseph this story:

In the year 600 B.C., there arrived on the American continent the family of Lehi, a Hebrew prophet, along with the Jaradites, a Babylonian clan. Quarrels broke the Lehi family into two factions—the Nephites and the Lamanites. God favored the Nephites and gave their holy men many prophecies regarding the future of this new land where they had made their home. It was here, God said, that the new Zion would be built, here that Jesus would eventually come to rule the earth in peace and glory, and the spiritual heirs of the Nephites would be His chosen people. God, on the other hand, did not like the Lamanites, and as punishment He darkened their skin, turning them into what became known as the American Indian.

After Jesus's resurrection, Moroni said, He appeared to the Nephites and they accepted Him as the Messiah. He told them that soon after the deaths of the Apostles a great apostasy would occur among Christians in the Old World and their churches would become heretical. But one day there would be a restoration, brought about by the builders of the new Zion.

Moroni further related that by the year A.D. 421, the Lamanites had succeeded in exterminating practically all of the Nephites. It was then that Mormon, the last Nephite prophet, wrote the history of his people on gold plates. Moroni said to Joseph:

"The book is in a stone box and is buried on the hill called Cumorah, which is near here. God wants you to find the book and translate it, for it contains the fullness of the Gospel as delivered by the Saviour." He added that buried with the book were optical instruments which would enable Joseph to translate the hieroglyphics.

Joseph located the hill and found the book the next day, but when he was about to carry off the book, Moroni appeared to him again and said Joseph must leave the book there. "God wants you to return to this hill on this date for the next four years," Moroni said, "and if you do so, He will permit you to take the book on your fourth visit."

Joseph did as he was told. Meanwhile, he moved to Harmony, Pennsylvania, where he married Emma Hale, his landlord's daughter, and supported himself by a series of odd jobs. He never made a secret of his experience; his family believed him, so did a few neighbors at his boyhood home at Manchester, New York, and so did a few at Harmony. Most people, however, suspected that he had made it all up.

In 1827, Joseph, now twenty-two years old, returned from his annual trip to the hill called Cumorah with, he said, the gold book, and ordered now by God to show it to no one. With Emma's help, he went to work immediately on the translation. For secrecy, Joseph strung a blanket across a room, then sat on one side of it as he translated aloud to Emma on the other. The work was slow and difficult. Martin Harris, affluent farmer, businessman and believer, replaced Emma, and when he also proved too slow he was replaced by Oliver Cowdery, a schoolteacher.

During their work, so Joseph Smith and Oliver Cowdery reported, John the Baptist appeared to them and conferred upon them the priesthood of Aaron. Later the Apostles Peter, James and John appeared and elevated the two men to the higher priesthood of Melchizedek. It was now clear to Joseph that his destiny was to assume full authority as High Priest over the revived faith of the Nephites, which, according to the Prophet Mormon, was the only true Christianity extant in the world. As such, Joseph himself would become a prophet.

In June, 1829, Joseph, Emma and Oliver Cowdery moved to Fayette, New York, to the home of Peter Whitmer, a believer, who had offered to support their work in its final months. As the end neared, Joseph came upon a reference in the book directed to him: he was to show the book to three witnesses to prove its existence. He chose Cowdery, Harris and David Whitmer. The three men later signed statements that, as they knelt together, Moroni appeared to them, turning the pages of the book. Moroni displayed the book a second time, to Joseph's father, his brothers Hyrum and Samuel, four Whitmers and their brother-in-law Hiram Page, and then the angel took the book to heaven. These men, too, signed statements that they had seen the angel and the book, and although most of these men subsequently broke with Joseph, they never denied the experience.

The Book of Mormon, 275,000 words long, was published in March, 1830, at Palmyra, New York. Martin Harris sold his Harmony farm to pay for the five thousand copies. To repay the debt, Joseph's father and brothers undertook a house-to-house selling trip through New York and Pennsylvania. It was Samuel Smith who, one day that summer, left a copy of the book at the home of Rhoda Green in the town of Mendon, New York, and another copy at the farm of her brother, Phineas Young. Phineas loaned his copy to his father, and thus it was that John Young came to place the book in the hands of his son Brigham.

3

Brigham Young was a cautious man who weighed new ideas carefully before making decisions about them, and this trait prevented him from rushing into the new religion of Joseph Smith as eagerly as did the rest of his family. To those who believed Joseph Smith, the religion was not new: it was the revived Christianity of the ancient Nephites, whom the resurrected Christ had personally converted into the only true Christians. When, in April, 1830, shortly after the Book of Mormon was published, Joseph Smith instituted his church, he called it the Church of Christ of the Latter-Day Saints, thereby emphasizing the historic link with the Nephites. Joseph's converts referred to themselves as Saints; nonbelievers were called gentiles. Because of the importance the Saints put on the Book of Mormon, ranking it with the Bible, gentiles soon began calling them Mormons and their religion Mormonism. The Saints resented this at first, but the terms became so popular that the Saints eventually accepted them.

A vital factor of Mormonism was the requirement that all Mormons must work as missionaries for two years at their own expense. From the start, then, bands of inspired converts left their homes to spread the exciting news that America was to become the second Zion, that one day Jesus Christ would rule the world from here. Many people who heard the news had been born during the Revolution that won America its independence; many others had fought in its battles. Nationalism was almost a religion in itself, so that the promise that Jesus Christ had chosen America as the place of His Second Coming was certainly credible. Reactions ran high, and they soared when reports arrived that God had granted Joseph Smith extraordinary faculties—the gift of healing, the gift of prophecy, the gifts of revelations and visions. At Mendon, the Youngs were anxious for baptism in the new religion. But Brigham held out.

He continued to read the Book of Mormon and to discuss it with his family. When five elders of a Mormon group in Pennsylvania visited Mendon to hold services, Brigham attended and asked many questions. Still unsure, he went to Canada to consult with his brother Joseph, a Methodist minister, and his sober concern so impressed Joseph that he returned to New York to investigate Mormonism himself. Even after Joseph became a Mormon, Brigham still stood aside. He considered going to Fayette to meet Joseph Smith, then discarded the idea when he learned the Prophet had gone to Kirtland, Ohio, to head a fast-growing Mormon colony there. Instead, Brigham went to Pennsylvania to question the elders again. Still he held back.

It was not until April, 1832, his two years of doubts now resolved, that, on the fourteenth of the month, Brigham allowed himself to be baptized at Mendon by one of the Pennsylvania elders. This proved to be the most important baptism in the history of Mormonism.

Immediately he began his required missionary work. With his brother Joseph and his friend Heber C. Kimball, a potter by trade, he toured the Finger Lakes district of New York, preaching Mormon doctrine. Unlike his Methodist-trained brother, Brigham was a quiet speaker, reserved, direct, brief, his tense sincerity occasionally lightened by a joke. But he was effective, much more effective than his two partners. Listening to him, his audiences recognized that he had not come to overwhelm them with a dramatic new message: he was there simply to state what he believed. And they could believe.

They believed in the Bible, for example, and they also believed that the Book of Mormon was equally the word of God. They considered the Holy Trinity to be three separate personages united in principle and purpose. They believed in justification by faith, remission of sin by baptism by immersion, the transmission of the gifts of the Holy Ghost through the laying-on of hands, and they maintained that God continued to reveal Himself regularly to the chosen of the believers.

They also believed that man came into being at the same time God did and that souls underwent a premortal period of spiritual progression during which they proved themselves worthy to take on human form for the final test that would determine their level of joy in the realm of eternal glory. There were two important aspects to this particular tenet. First, it assured Heaven (and an immortal body) to every Saint, with his portion of joy to be measured by his human conduct. Second, it encouraged the Saints to have big families in order to provide bodies for the worthy premortal beings.

The tenet also produced the basis for Mormon plural marriages. Who could tell how many millions of premortal beings still awaited the opportunity to pass through the human state in order to earn the highest heaven? It was the Mormon duty, then, to provide the opportunity: any Mormon who was remiss in this duty might well be in sin. Therefore, all Mormons should marry, and if there was a surplus of women—which there always was—Mormon men who could afford it should take more than one wife. Certain questions arose from this, but Joseph Smith had the answers.

He said, first, that he himself was struck by the polygamy of Abraham, Jacob, Solomon and David, and he asked God if these great men had actually committed adultery or had merely done what He wanted of them, and God answered: "Go, therefore, and do the works of Abraham; enter ye into my law and ye shall be saved." Through subsequent revelations, God gave Joseph the concept of plural marriages, thus:

A virgin a man married remained his wife throughout eternity; she and any children she bore him would join him in the next world. Like Abraham, a man could marry as many virgins as he could afford, as long as his other wives approved. They and all his children would be with him in Heaven. When the man died, his widows would be free to marry other men, although the second husbands might already have other wives. The children resulting from the second marriage nevertheless belonged to the first husband and, with their mothers, would join him after death.

Sexual hunger was not the excuse for the plural marriages: providing bodies for the premortal beings was the purpose. Faithful Mormons found this theologically understandable and morally acceptable. But there was the matter of family economy and because of it, despite outrageously exaggerated accounts to the contrary, less than five percent of the Mormon men actually engaged in plural marriage during the period it was reported to be rampant, because they couldn't afford it.

Joseph Smith took his second wife, a twenty-year-old virgin, while he was heading the Mormon colony at Kirtland, Ohio. Brigham Young knew nothing about this when he finally met Joseph because Joseph had not as yet enounced the doctrine.

Even so, Brigham would have approved it, just as he approved everything Joseph did. For Brigham, the strength of Mormonism was in absolute faith in Joseph, God's elect in reviving the true Christianity of the Nephites. Without that faith, Brigham was to argue repeatedly in years to come, there could be no Mormonism at all.

While on his first mission tour, the summer of 1832, Brigham developed a great desire to meet Joseph Smith, the man who had so vividly changed his life. Returning home in September, Brigham disclosed his plan to move to Kirtland to join Joseph. But he saw there was small chance of it. Miriam was weaker than ever before. She could not go with Brigham and he would not go without her. He had just about resigned himself to this when, quite suddenly, Miriam died. Vilate Kimball offered to take Brigham's two daughters as her own.

He was free now. He could go to Kirtland.

4

There were both remarkable similarities and differences between Brigham Young and Joseph Smith. They had both been born in Vermont, just a few miles apart, Brigham four years before Joseph. They were both the sons of farmers who seemed unable to make their farms pay and who gradually migrated westward, on almost the same route and at almost the same time, settling finally in Upstate New York just a few miles apart. Neither boy had much formal education; after acquiring the rudiments of learning from their families, they both proceeded self-taught. Both came from extremely religious families, but as teen-agers they were both discontent with the religions they knew. It was Mormonism that at last provided them with the religion they wanted and eventually brought them together. When they met, Brigham was thirty-one; Joseph, twenty-seven. Joseph was tall and lean and handsome; Brigham was short, stocky, swarthy. Joseph had the delicate air of the dreamer, the thinker; Brigham was clearly a practical man, a realist, a doer. Despite his ability to attract people, Joseph lacked the qualities to hold close friends: men like Martin Harris and Oliver Cowdery, who had helped him so much in the beginning, eventually broke with him. For Brigham, on the other hand, loyalty was a treasured virtue: he inspired it in others because he gave it himself. Loyalty proved to be the basis of his importance to Joseph Smith and to Mormonism.

Joseph Smith had moved to Kirtland, Ohio, in January, 1831, as a result of the many conversions there and the missionary zeal that brought in more converts from Ohio and Pennsylvania. In two years, Kirtland had swelled from a hamlet of a hundred and fifty people to a bustling city of three thousand. Many of the new arrivals still lived in covered wagons and everywhere there were signs of a building boom. There was also some dissension over the Mormon concept of communal effort. The more zealous converts felt the Church should own everything, even their clothes, and provide for the Saints according to their needs and efforts. Conservative Saints, although ready to support the Church and help the poor, were not so eager for the sudden extermination of private enterprise.

Joseph had been summoned to Kirtland to solve the problem. He chose the middle road. He introduced tithing, the giving of ten percent of his earnings by every Saint, from which the Church could derive a working capital. He also set up agencies from which those who had money could loan it to the poor for the purposes of buying property and building houses. And he organized cooperatives for business and farming, with the provision that a share of the profits should go into a church fund for the community good. Further, he stressed the importance of education for the young by opening schools, and he instituted recreational and cultural programs for people of all ages. His presence had such a calming effect on the community that he decided to stay. His family followed him.

Joseph had specified that there was to be no professional clergy in the Church, which meant that everybody, even the high-ranking church officials, had to find his own means of livelihood. Like most of the others, Joseph chose farming. He acquired land a short distance from town and, when Brigham Young arrived from Mendon in the fall of 1832, he was busy with his relatives building a barn.

There was no indication when the two men met that they perceived the importance they were to become to each other. Joseph Young and Heber Kimball had accompanied Brigham. After they had all introduced themselves to Joseph Smith, they told him of their missionary successes in central New York. He told them how well the movement was progressing in Ohio, and he was especially enthusiastic about a surge of conversions that was taking place in Missouri.

From their conversation, Joseph and Brigham discovered their similarities of background, and this both amused and pleased them. Joseph said, "This evening some of the brethren are meeting at my house for worship and discussion. Would you like to join us?"

"Yes, very much," Brigham replied.

A dozen people gathered at Joseph's house that night. For the first part of the evening, Joseph answered questions about Mormonism. Brigham was deeply impressed: never before had man's relation to God been made so clear to him, so logical. When the questions were over, the group sang hymns. Then Joseph asked, "Brother Young, would you please lead us in prayer?"

Brigham lowered his head a moment to collect his thoughts, and when at last he spoke there was a gasp in the room: he was speaking in tongues. This unusual faculty was not uncommon among the frontier fundamentalists whose excessive religiosity sometimes drove them into an emotional and mental disbalance that caused them to jabber unintelligible words that they took to be the divine gift of ecstatic prayer. Joseph was aware of this spreading abnormality and had frequently denounced it. This time, however, he listened in silence until Brigham finished.

When the people rose from their knees they gathered around Joseph. "You heard him," a man said. "He spoke in tongues."

"It was the pure Adamic language," Joseph said.

"But you've always been against this sort of thing," the man reminded. "Aren't you against it this time?"

"No," said Joseph. "It is of God."

Joseph's approbation deepened Brigham's faith. In New York, Brigham still had affairs to settle, his house to sell, and he wanted to complete his second year as a missionary, so he left Kirtland, returning in July, 1833, this time to stay. He easily found work as a carpenter in the fast-growing town; the following February he married again, to Mary Ann Angell, a twenty-eight-year-old convert from Rhode Island.

By now, Joseph had organized the Church into a neat, well-functioning unit. The First Presidency, comprised of himself as High Priest and Prophet and two advisers, constituted the absolute authority. An important advisory board was the Quorum of Twelve Apostles; Brigham was appointed to the position of third seniority in it. Also in the higher echelon were the Patriarch, assistants to the Quorum, the First Council of Seventy, their assistants, and certain Melchizedek priests and elders. Kirtland was established as a stake (diocese) and divided into wards (parishes), with bishops and Aaronic priests to administer it. Any worthy boy of twelve could become an Aaronic priest, thus carrying the Church into every Mormon home in the community. A second stake was set up in the thriving Mormon colony in Missouri; ordinances provided for other stakes throughout the world as soon as the Mormon population allowed.

The only trouble with this plan was its powerful influence upon a community, to the extent that gentiles found themselves being socially, economically and politically overwhelmed. From the start, Joseph had insisted on respect for all religions and respect for law and lawmakers, but this did not always work. Imbued with zeal, Mormons associated only with Mormons, they did business only with Mormons, they elected Mormons, and the elected Mormons worked to enforce Mormon law. Gentiles didn't stand much of a chance in any sphere. This was unfortunate but it was also inevitable. Concerned as Mormonism was with premortality, mortality and postmortality, plus a favored position in the world of the Second Coming, Mormons simply did not have room in their great plan for anybody else. It was not surprising, therefore, that the warm welcome the Kirtland gentiles had at first extended to the arriving Mormons was gradually replaced by resentment. In Missouri, the change of heart was accompanied by violence.

Slavery and denominational competition added to the Missouri predicament. Missouri had entered the Union as a slave state on the 1821 compromise that brought in Maine as a free state, thereby sustaining the balance of power on the slavery issue in the Senate. Missouri Mormons, coming almost entirely from free states, were sternly abolitionist. They said so in their newspapers and they invited Negroes to join their church. This disgusted Missouri gentiles. Missouri law forbade Negroes to enter the state without certificates of citizenship as free men in other states, and this disgusted the Missouri Mormons. The growing Mormon voting power gave evidence that the law might be changed, and this aroused the gentiles. Also arousing them were the sermons of gentile clergymen who, losing followers to the zealous Mormon missionaries, denounced Mormonism from their pulpits. Open conflict was thus unavoidable. Contributing to the matter was the divine revelation disclosed by Joseph Smith that when Jesus Christ returned to earth He would rule the world from Independence, Missouri, which by then would be entirely Mormon. The gentiles didn't believe this, but they were nevertheless afraid of it.

One day the Independence gentiles issued an ultimatum, forbidding further emigration of Mormons, demanding the discontinuance of the Mormon newspaper and ordering Mormons out of the county "within a reasonable time"—or else. Mormon leaders were given fifteen minutes to respond to the ultimatum, and when they did not, gentiles wrecked the newspaper plant, set fire to Mormon homes and fields, and shooting broke out with men killed on both sides.

Infuriated, Joseph Smith formed a Mormon army in Ohio, with Brigham Young as his first lieutenant, and marched off to fight for the Mormon cause in Missouri. He claimed that Mormons were being persecuted because of their religious convictions. As true as this implicitly was, it was a truth that won little sympathy elsewhere: the subject of civil rights was already too delicate throughout the country for anyone to risk an explosion by speaking for the Mormons or against them.

The Mormon army of two hundred and five men was doomed from the start. The long six-week march to Missouri withered the fighting spirit of the men, it gave the Jackson County gentiles time to rout the Mormons who remained there, and it brought out the well-equipped Missouri militia. Then just when the Mormon army was ready to line up for battle, cholera struck, decimating the ranks.

Unable to fight on the fields, Joseph was determined to fight in the courts. He hired lawyers for a battle that was to last for months. Brigham was sent back to Kirtland to represent Joseph in the normal operations of the Church, and he was there when the decision finally arrived. Mormons were to remain in Missouri, but they were to leave Jackson County and move to Caldwell County, in the empty northwest corner of the state, where they could have their own laws, their own militia, their own way of life undisturbed. Many Ohio Mormons felt Joseph had showed weakness in accepting the compromise. What about the lost homes, the lost farms, the lost businesses, the lost investments? Was there to be no reimbursement for these? The dissension grew.

Before returning to Ohio, Joseph led his refugees to their new Missouri colony and he remained there several months. He gave hope to them by announcing that it was here that Adam and Eve had settled after their expulsion from the Garden of Eden: in a way, then, the resettled Mormons were starting the human race over again. The Kirtland Mormons were still dissatisfied. It became Brigham's job to calm them. For months he argued with individuals, families, wards, the whole stake, to convince them that Joseph was right, that he had to, as Prophet, be right: God would not misguide him. Slowly the majority came to believe him, but there were many apostasies and a discouraging exodus. By the time Joseph got back, however, there was peace at Kirtland, the people busy both at their private enterprises and the construction of the first Mormon Temple, a magnificent, three-story structure that grew into the biggest skyscraper west of the Alleghenies, and Joseph had no idea how close he had come to losing his leadership over his first followers.

But his troubles were not over. The great Depression of the 1830's was working its way west. Many Mormon business dealings had been underwritten by the Church—by Joseph, in effect—on loans granted by banks and industries elsewhere that accepted as collateral land titles held by the Church and the promise of future tithes. But now the tithes were not being paid. Now Kirtland businessmen, already operating on over-extended credit to outside customers, were unable to pay the interest on their loans. Banks and industries demanded either payment or the collateral. In an effort to forestall disaster, Joseph formed a bank and, as was the custom then, issued his own paper money, backed by the land titles and investments the Church still held. When the outside banks and industries received the money they immediately returned it and demanded United States currency. Joseph had none. His entire Kirtland empire collapsed.

There was no place to go but Missouri. In December, 1837, having sent his family ahead, Joseph Smith left Kirtland on horseback for the cold journey across the country. Sixty miles out of town he encountered Brigham Young and his family who, traveling by covered wagon, were spending the night at the side of the road. Joseph joined the tiny caravan.

Even in this desperate hour, Joseph Smith was not downhearted. "We are going to the new Zion," he said to Brigham. "That is where we should have been all along."

And even in this desperate hour, Brigham Young remained steadfastly faithful. He said: "Yes. The new Zion."

It was only a matter of time until the new Zion produced the old problems. About ten thousand Jackson County Mormons had moved to Caldwell County; another ten thousand migrated from the fallen Kirtland. Inevitably, many of them overflowed into neighboring counties. At the same time, thousands of gentiles were pouring into Missouri, settling in the neighboring counties. The familiar frictions began to flare up.

On August 8, 1838, a state election was scheduled. In adjoining Davies County, a group of Mormons arrived to vote and found a barricade of gentiles who jeered: "Mormons and niggers ain't allowed to vote here." Undaunted, the Mormons broke through the barricade and left a dozen gentiles strewn unconscious on the ground. From this there could come only chaos. Nightly skirmishes erupted. Young Mormons formed a shock troop called Danites, named after the Genesis reference: "Dan shall be a serpent by the way, an adder in the path, that biteth the horse's heels so that his rider shall fall backward." The war was on again.

Once more, Joseph sought to avoid open battle through negotiation, but when he went to the militia camp to negotiate he was arrested on charges of treason and jailed. A few days later, through his brother Hyrum's friendship with a militia guard, he sent word to Brigham to move the Mormons out of Missouri.

"To where?" Brigham asked.

"To Illinois," said Hyrum. "Joseph says we have friends there who will help us."

Moving out twenty thousand Mormons was no overnight chore. Completing it required from November to April of the next year. Eager to display its free-state liberality, the Illinois legislature granted a town charter to the Mormons in Hancock County on the banks of the Mississippi. The task was almost completed when Hyrum's friend, at the risk of his own life, was persuaded to provide horses for Joseph's escape. Joseph was therefore back with his people as they once again began to build a new world.

Joseph named the new settlement Nauvoo, which he explained meant "beautiful plantation" in Hebrew. Nauvoo did not start out so beautifully. Using Missouri property titles as collateral, Joseph bought almost a hundred thousand dollars' worth of land at Nauvoo and across the river at Montrose, Iowa. Brigham was among those who chose to live in Iowa. It then turned out that the agent from whom the land was acquired had no authority to deal in Iowa property and only questionable authority to operate in Illinois. When Joseph took action against the man, he disappeared. In desperation, Joseph sent Brigham and others to the East to raise funds among Mormons there and their success saved the project. Brigham and the others in Iowa moved over to the Illinois side of the river.

From then on, Nauvoo flourished. In two years it was the biggest town in Illinois, bigger than Chicago. It had its own schools, its own militia, its own laws, and its people had the prerogative of habeas corpus in other juridical areas.

Now Joseph wanted to concentrate on the foreign missions. In January, 1840 he sent Brigham, whom he considered his most effective missionary, to England where, in twenty months, Brigham baptized over eight thousand converts and convinced a thousand of them to migrate to Illinois. Hard work and loneliness finally led Brigham to ask Joseph for permission to return home, with the understanding that he would not have to travel any more. Joseph agreed. Reaching home, Brigham discovered two things that upset him. First, he saw that his wife and children were still living in the rugged log cabin outside town where he had left them when Joseph sent him abroad before he had time to build a good home. He complained, and Joseph gave him the money to build a house, then appointed him a member of the Town Council, of which he himself was mayor.

Second, Brigham discovered that the plural marriages which Joseph until now had kept secret (he had managed to hide the existence of six wives) had become common knowledge, and that Joseph was encouraging similar unions among his followers. There was uncertainty about the idea among some Mormons and considerable complaint among the gentile neighbors; but after Joseph defined the doctrine and disclosed God's approval of it, Brigham, with typical loyalty, accepted it and defended it. He took his first polygamous wife in 1842, a girl half his age; in 1843, he took two more.

By now, Nauvoo was the most vital political factor in Illinois, courted by both the Whig and Democratic parties. As Nauvoo went, so went the state, a fact that inevitably incensed Illinois gentiles. Joseph became so impressed by his political influence that, in 1844, he decided to run for President of the United States, principally on a platform of freeing slaves with federal funds acquired through the sale of public lands. Several apostles were dispatched to various parts of the country to sample public opinion regarding Joseph's candidacy. Brigham was sent to New England.

While this was going on, Joseph had a falling out with William Law, a Canadian convert who had risen fast in the Church, and Law apostatized. On June 7, Law brought out the first edition of a new paper, the *Expositor,* in which he accused Joseph of polygamy, of conniving to create his own empire and of misuse of public funds. Joseph retaliated by ordering the Nauvoo police to destroy Law's printing plant. Immediately the cry went up from publishers all over the country that Joseph was trying to stifle the free press. Law escaped to Carthage, the county seat, where he swore out a warrant against Joseph on charges of attempted murder. By exercising his right of habeas corpus, Joseph managed to elude arrest. However, anti-Mormon feelings in the state were now running too high for him to remain free for long. The state militia was called out; in return, Joseph called out the Nauvoo Legion. Then, unwisely, he sought personal safety by crossing over to Iowa, accompanied by Hyrum and two top aides. Hyrum was distressed. Convinced that Joseph could prove his innocence, Hyrum urged him to go back and face his accusers.

"Very well," Joseph said, "let us go back. But I warn you we shall die."

They went to Carthage and surrendered to Governor Thomas Ford, who was there in an effort to restore peace. Joseph was charged with inciting a riot and treason. He put up bail of seventy-five hundred dollars and was about to leave for Nauvoo when he was arrested again on the treason charge and held, with Hyrum and the two aides, without bail. They remained in jail a week but were allowed Mormon visitors, several of whom came with plots for Joseph's escape, which he declined, and one of whom slipped him a revolver, which he accepted.

On the afternoon of June 27, the four prisoners heard the approaching rumble of a mob outside the jail, and through the window they saw a gang of armed men, their faces hidden under layers of mud. Seconds later, bullets splattered the wooden door of the cell. More bullets crashed through the window. Hyrum was struck full in the face and fell dead. One aide was hit in the thigh and chest. Using his revolver, Joseph fired at the door as the attackers pushed it open, then backed to the window. From both directions came a storm of bullets. Joseph, losing his balance, fell through the window, crashing to the ground below.

He cried, "Oh, Lord, my God!" And he died.

5

Brigham was still in New England. When the news reached him, he sank back in his chair for a stunned moment and then let the tears flow. The men with him waited in silence until he seemed ready to listen to them. Finally one asked, "What do we do now, Brother Young?"

"We go home as quickly as possible," said Brigham. "We must find out if Joseph has taken the keys of the kingdom with him from the earth."

En route to Nauvoo, Brigham remembered that Joseph had often said: "When I die, the First Presidency ceases to exist. The keys pass to the Quorum of Apostles." This meant, Brigham decided, that the Apostles were to elect the new ruler of the Church—from among themselves, if they wished, or any man they considered worthy. So the Church was still alive.

There were others who were struggling to keep it alive, for their own advantage. When Brigham reached Nauvoo, he found it a turmoil of ambitious men, each arguing for his own ascension to Joseph's empty throne. It appeared that God had been exceedingly generous with His revelations: each contender vowed that God had specifically instructed him to take over. Brigham was willing to grant that God could reveal Himself to anyone He chose, but the confusion of claims made him suspect that there had been no revelations at all. For himself, he did not want the job. His only desire was to return to his family, work his farm and serve the Church in some minor capacity. He felt, however, that the Church would survive only if its new leader's sentiments absolutely reflected Joseph's. In the herd of aspirants, Brigham could not see one such man. In fact, most of them had opposed Joseph at one time or another. Brigham alone had unswervingly upheld him in all things. It was on this basis that one day Brigham sent out word that he wished to address the Saints, and the crowd that arrived to hear him was so big they had to move out to a meadow to have room enough for all. He wasn't sure what he would say; his first words came like cannon fire:

"Attention all!"

The startled crowd caught its breath, then leaned forward to hear Brigham. He spoke slowly, firmly, with greater eloquence than ever before, and what amazed the crowd was that, quite definitely, it was the voice of Joseph Smith that came from the mouth of Brigham Young. In a long speech, Brigham argued that the Church must remain as Joseph had constituted it or it would not be the same church and thus would never fulfill its purpose. When he finished, he left the meadow quickly, leaving the people to think about what he had told them. That afternoon, the Quorum met and elected Brigham to the awesome dignity of High Priest and Prophet of all the Mormons.

The people were not unanimously happy. Disappointed contenders collected their coteries and left Nauvoo, settling elsewhere in schismatic groups. Others announced they would wait a few months to see how Brigham functioned in the high office before deciding whether or not to impeach him. But for the most part there was satisfaction, a readiness to follow Brigham as Joseph had been followed.

Brigham had no time to fret about dissenters. The shock of Joseph's death had plunged Nauvoo into such disorder that Brigham was kept busy night and day with the struggle of restoring peace and calm and productivity. He was everywhere, into everything, at every church and social level, suggesting, cajoling, advising, instructing, commanding, forceful, firm.

The Nauvoo paper described him as "the Lion of the Lord."

Skirmishes with the gentiles continued. An effort was made to bring Joseph's assassins to justice, but when the men were finally rounded up and brought to trial the courts decreed that no Mormons could serve on the jury: the suspects were acquitted. Now the gentiles grew even more arrogant. By the summer of 1846, two years after taking office, Brigham faced the fact that there could be no peace for Mormons in Illinois, that it was time for them once again to move on. He disclosed this conviction to his advisers, and the truth of it could not be denied. But where could they go?

"West," Brigham said. "I have been shown the place in a dream. When I see it I shall know it."

With that, Brigham became a second Moses, leading a persecuted people on the long search for a promised land where they could be left alone to live as they pleased. All Nauvoo agreed that this had to be done. Overnight the town became one big factory, building covered wagons, stockpiling food, clothes, medicines, furniture. For twenty thousand Mormons to travel in a single caravan was unthinkable; so vast an exodus would be unmanageable. Besides, no one knew Brigham's destination, not even Brigham himself, and no one knew how long it would take to get there. How would the wanderers support and feed themselves on the road?

In answer, Brigham ordered that the people would move out in groups of a few hundred, that every fifty miles or so each group would settle down to plant a crop which would be harvested by another group coming up from behind while the planters moved on. The first group moved out in June, 1846, and by the end of the year there were fifteen Mormon settlements stretching from the Mississippi shores of Iowa to the western limits of Nebraska. The main body spent the winter on the site of the future city of Omaha, building a fragile city of their own of tents, covered wagons and lean-tos. As organized as the trek was, there were unavoidable hardships. Temporary dwellings provided scant protection against the winter cold, there was no sanitation, frequently no water, so there was much disease and many deaths. And there were Indians who, if they did not fight, threatened, harassed and stole.

In April, 1847, Brigham led his headquarters caravan ahead of the others, crossing Nebraska into Wyoming, to Fort Laramie, covering the six hundred miles in six weeks. Here the trail turned north to Oregon; Brigham decided to go south, breaking a new path across the plains to the Continental Divide, then ascending into the great mountains. Malaria broke out and Brigham fell victim to it, but he insisted on proceeding, supervising the advance from a cot in the wagon of his old friend Heber Kimball.

On July 24, scouts returned and reported that on the other side of the mountains was an enormous valley that swept away to a great lake. Brigham asked Kimball to drive the wagon to the mountaintop so that he could see the valley for himself, and when he saw it he said, "Yes. This is the place. Drive on."

They called the valley Deseret, a word from the Book of Mormon that meant Land of the Honeybee, and the city they built they named after the enormous lake, Salt Lake. When the Mormons arrived, the vast, unoccupied territory still belonged to Mexico, and from this the people took hope that they would not be subject to the political resistance they had encountered in an America torn by political strife on the slavery question. But already the first battles of the Mexican Wars were being fought in the Southwest, and it was only a matter of time until the Mormons once again found themselves confronted with American opposition. This time, the Mormons wanted to be ready, strengthened by overwhelming numbers. Mormon immigration therefore was stressed: in the next thirty years, eighty thousand converts trekked across the vast plains and over the mountains to Deseret, coming from all parts of the world, six thousand of them losing their lives along the way, due to cold, heat, storm, drought, exhaustion, disease and Indians.

No hardship was too great for the determined people. The winter of 1847 was unusually severe. Food ran out and it was impossible to get supplies over the snow-blocked mountains. Many died, and more died when spring floods swept down from the mountains and across the valley. In June, just when the valley was rich and green and the people were once again full of hope, the four-inch crickets of the mountains suddenly increased by the millions and cascaded across the valley, devouring all growing things. There was nothing the people could do but pray. Then, with equal suddenness, great flocks of sea gulls came like clouds from the lake and swooped down on the crickets, destroying the army of them in a few hours. It was a miracle: every Mormon believed that.

They found it hard to believe, however, after all they had gone through, that the America where most of them were born and which all of them wanted to love would not, even here in the valley they had pioneered and built into a new Eden, let them live alone in peace. In 1849, Brigham petitioned the Congress for statehood. His intentions were obvious in Washington: he hoped, while the Mormons were still overwhelmingly in the majority, to place them in state offices before gentiles grasped command. The petition was refused. Instead, Congress created the Territory of Utah, and although Brigham was named governor, practically all public offices were filled by Washington appointments. Most of the appointees were anti-Mormon for any number of reasons and often irrationally so. Two associate justices, for example, reported to Washington that the general records of the Utah supreme court had been stolen and destroyed by Danites on Brigham's orders. If true, this was treason. Brigham's second term of office was to expire at this time. President James Buchanan refused to reappoint him, then sent the Army into Utah to investigate the treason charge. A blizzard blocked the Army at the mountains, but the following spring when the troops marched into Salt Lake City they found the records where they belonged and in perfect order.

But the bitterest anti-Mormon sentiments focused on the doctrine of plural marriages. At Nauvoo, Brigham had four wives, and after Joseph Smith's death he married six of the Prophet's widows. During his thirty years in Salt Lake City, the number of his wives increased to twenty-seven, with an estimated forty children not counting those brought into his home by the widows he married. He could afford them. At the time of his death, he was worth almost a million dollars, derived from investments in a hotel, sawmills, a shipping company and real estate. Even so, Brigham's financial qualifications to practice his religious beliefs made no difference to those who opposed him.

In 1862, Congress passed a bill which made polygamy illegal in the territories but not, oddly enough, in the states. Mormons argued that they were not engaging in illegal polygamy but in religious plural marriages in which legality was not involved. Further efforts were made at this time to ban the Mormon marriages but President Abraham Lincoln, who as an Illinois legislator had voted for the Nauvoo charter, warned Congress that he would veto any bill that struck him as a possible infringement of the religious prerogatives of any particular denomination.

President Ulysses S. Grant felt differently. In 1869, he supported a bill that granted the vote to women in the territories, the hope being that Mormon women, loathing their harems, would, armed with the ballot, vote themselves out of them. The bill backfired when the Mormon Church, confident of its women, enthusiastically endorsed the bill. It was dropped. Triumphantly, the Utah legislature passed its own bill giving women the vote, thus making the territory the first political area in the country to do so.

Then President Grant backed a bill that would require polygamists throughout the country to put aside all but their first wives. This aroused the fury of apostate Mormons, some of them influential men in the East, who had plural marriages they wanted to continue, and their pressure on their senators brought sudden death to the bill.

Numerous attempts were made to embarrass Brigham personally. A gentile rural saloonkeeper charged that Brigham had ordered the Danites to assault him, destroy cases of whiskey and wreck his saloon, and he sued Brigham for sixty thousand dollars. Brigham was arrested, refused bail, and put under house arrest for five months while the case worked its way up to the United States Supreme Court, where it was thrown out.

Meanwhile, Brigham's twenty-seventh wife, Ann Eliza Webb, goaded by Brigham's enemies in Salt Lake City, complained that he had refused to support her parents and sued him for divorce, demanding over two hundred and fifty thousand dollars in settlements. The first court decision was in her favor, but then Brigham's lawyers argued that if, as Congress had decreed, the plural marriages in Utah were illegal, a court of law therefore could not very well dissolve one of them by legal action. The case dragged on for ten years and was finally resolved in Brigham's favor, but by then he could foresee that the days of plural marriages were numbered. By then, too, Ann Eliza had written a book about life in Brigham's home, grossly exaggerating and distorting the facts, and adding to the gentile feelings that were mounting against him.

Resigned, Brigham turned his full attention to the Church. Now in his seventies, he realized he did not have long to live. More than anything, whatever the fate of plural marriages, he wanted to shore up the church he had served all his adult life against any other threats that might come against it. Some of the Mormon concepts he crystallized during this period proved to be forerunners of what became American ideas of good government. Based on the precept that Mormons should take care of each other, the welfare of the dependent young, the ill, the aged and the unemployed was provided for. Brigham said each Mormon ought to see to these things himself, but if the demands, due to famine, pestilence, or depression, grew too widespread, then it was the Church's responsibility to step in. Through investments of tithing surpluses, the Church prepared itself by erecting granaries, building schools, hospitals and orphanages, supporting industries and helping individual farmers and businessmen. The time was still to come when governments at every level would recognize their responsibilities in these spheres and adopt the ideas that Brigham Young developed during his thirty years as leader of his church.

On the morning of August 23, 1877, a Thursday, Brigham indicated to others in his office that he felt ill. He thought he was going to vomit, he said, and he complained of unusual pains in his arms. He remained at his desk, and he was there the next day, but on Saturday he could not rise from bed. His pain increased. Monday, he lapsed into unconsciousness and he did not speak again until a few minutes before his death on Wednesday, August 29.

He said: "Joseph, Joseph, Joseph."

In his will, he left instructions for his burial and he insisted that there be "no crying or mourning with anyone, as I have done my work faithfully and in good faith."

He had—even though a town, a county, a state and the entire country stood against him. It was in 1890 that the Supreme Court upheld the constitutionality of antipolygamy laws passed after Brigham's death, and that same year the Church issued a manifesto forbidding Mormon plural marriages thereafter. But a positive result of his defeat was, in 1896, the admission of the Territory of Utah into the Union as the forty-fifth state, which Brigham had wanted for almost fifty years.

Without doubt, Brigham Young built the state of Utah, but he built something else more important. By his own faith and fortitude, he built dignity, honor, respect and acceptance for the unwanted, despised, heaven-hungry people who followed him across a continent in search of God's peace.

CHAPTER

TWO

Bishop on Horseback

THERE was no intention among those who first called themselves Methodists to initiate a new denomination. On the contrary, their only wish was to become more devout Anglicans. They were, at the beginning, a handful of Oxford University students who were disturbed by the growing atheism, the spreading materialism, they saw around them, and they hoped that by their own return to the clearly defined discipline of the Established Church they might provide a bulwark against the rising tide of indifferent Christianity they perceived in their fellow students. In a group, they received the sacraments every Sunday, and Sunday evenings they held Bible-reading and discussion sessions. They fasted on Fridays, later adding Wednesday fasts to their schedule, and they observed the feast days of major British saints. Soon they were holding their prayer sessions nightly. So methodically did they carry out the requirements the Church of England imposed on its members that other students derisively started to call them Methodists, and by their sincerity they brought honor to the name.

The founder of the Oxford Methodists was a young poet named Charles Wesley, son of an Anglican minister and himself destined for the ministry, but the group did not take on scope and depth until Charles's older brother John, already a minister, returned to Oxford on a fellowship. More experienced, more astute, more perceptive, and with the added faculty of ordination, John Wesley attracted more men to the group. In a short time, the Oxford Methodists expanded from four or five students to twenty-five. Even so, quantity was not the group's aim; personal sanctity within the Anglican sphere was.

In 1735, John and Charles Wesley sailed to the New World, to Georgia, as Anglican missionaries, and this was the journey that changed Methodism from a club to a movement.

Aboard the ship were several of the Moravian Brethren, a Bohemian sect which for three hundred years had suffered persecution from both the Protestant and Catholic churches. Twice they were almost exterminated. In 1722, they had found haven on the private property of Count Nicolaus Ludwig Zinzendorf, in Saxony, and the Count hoped to draw the Brethren closer to his own Lutheran Church. The Brethren, however, wanted to restore their own ministry and to revive their traditional evangelism. To satisfy the Count, they declared that their religious tenets were basically Lutheran, and then, under his protection, they set out to establish new Moravian colonies throughout Central Europe, in England, and finally onward to the New World.

John and Charles Wesley were deeply impressed by the stern simplicity of the Moravians, by their sober denunciation of all worldly pleasures, by their extreme reliance on the Holy Spirit, by the cyclonic enthusiasm of their preachers. The Moravians, it appeared, were Methodists of much greater austerity. In Georgia, the Wesleys gave less time to the conversion of the Indians than to efforts to instill some of this austerity into the High Churchmen living there. They failed. Two years later they went back to England convinced, as the Moravians were, of the total depravity of man.

By exposure to them, John Wesley had assimilated the fiery manner of Moravian preachers. At home, his verve won him a certain popularity and he was often invited to be guest preacher at Anglican churches. But what he had to say proved startling. He violently denounced drinking, dancing, card playing, horse racing, parties, even laughter, and people began drifting out of churches wondering if they were doomed to hell simply by being alive. In the summer of 1738, John visited the Moravian colony in Saxony and returned even more ablaze with his crusade of self-denial for the sake of salvation. Astonished Anglican pastors stopped inviting him to speak in their churches. Undaunted, he took to preaching in the streets, sometimes even on the steps of the churches whose pastors rejected him. The following year he bought an abandoned building in Moorsfield and established his first church, formally declaring Methodism to be a movement to return the Anglican Church and the world to their apostolic purity. But the man who was to lift Methodism to its eventual greatness as a specific religious denomination had yet to be born.

2

On a small farm near the village of Hampstead Bridge, four miles from Birmingham, England, lived Joseph and Elizabeth Asbury. Their first child, a girl, had died in infancy, an event which plunged Elizabeth Asbury into religion on a frantic search for consolation. A devout Anglican, she nevertheless failed to find her peace in her church, so she began to attend the religious sessions, called classes, that were conducted in the homes of her neighbors by men who called themselves exhorters and identified themselves as local delegates of John Wesley's Methodism. From them she learned the doctrine of suffering and she came to suspect that her daughter's death might actually be an occasion for her own purification. She became an avid Bible reader and a fervent singer of hymns that stressed suffering, the worthlessness of man and the sinfulness of comfort and pleasure.

In 1745 she discovered she was pregnant again, and she revealed to her friends that God had appeared to her in a vision and told her that the son she would bear would rise to the heights of church leadership and convert the heathens. Before the boy was born, she was convinced he would become the Archbishop of Canterbury, which was as high in religion as an Anglican could hope to go. He was born on August 20. He was named Francis.

The first sounds Francis heard were his mother reading the Bible to him and singing Wesleyan hymns. Before he could sit up, she taught him how to fold his hands in prayer. By the time he was six, he had so completely absorbed his mother's dread of both sin and pleasure that he was considered a misfit at school, frequently ridiculed and beaten, and finally sent home. For the next seven years he was educated by his parents. With his mother, he attended Anglican services every Sunday. During the week they went to revivals held in the area by various evangelists. And when his mother's friends conducted their religious classes at the Asbury home, young Francis was brought in to read the Bible, to interpret it and to give brief sermons. At thirteen, he was apprenticed to the local maker of shoe buckles, in whose house he lived for two years and where his piety was admired and encouraged. He then returned home, and for the next six years he spent his days at his trade and his evenings traveling anywhere in the county where he could find groups to listen to his sermons.

By 1760, the Wesleys had divided England into *circuits*—or dioceses usually on a county level—and assigned to each a qualified lay preacher—circuit rider—who traveled the circuit on horseback continually, conducting nightly revivals for crowds brought out by the local exhorters. Francis attended his first bona fide Methodist revival that year. He was so impressed that he wrote to London for available literature and thereafter his own sermons reflected the Methodist idea entirely. He got to know the various circuit riders who worked in Staffordshire County during his own years as an unofficial exhorter, and in 1766, when Francis was twenty-one, a rider named Orp asked him to give the main talk at a Methodist revival. He was a great success; Orp took him on as a full-time assistant, a position he held for the next year without pay. Eager to become a full-fledged circuit rider, Francis went to London in 1767, presented himself to the Wesleys, underwent their series of examinations, passed and was assigned as a rider in the north counties. So at last he was officially a preacher, although not ordained; he was formally affiliated with an established movement, although not an established church. But he was on his way, and his mother was very happy.

He was ambitious. Reports of his effective sermons began to reach London. To be effective, the sermons had to stir such emotional penitence in the congregation that they shouted their sorrow for their sins at the tops of their voices and frequently went into convulsions. Francis consistently left half his listeners writhing on the floor. To assure his effectiveness, Francis later called at the homes of professed Methodists to see to it that their private lives reflected the proper austerity.

But there were other reports that were not so glowing, these from other circuit riders. As the newest and youngest preacher, Francis should have been the most amenable, but other preachers complained that he was not only telling them when and where to preach but also what and how. Orp, his mentor, once wrote him: "I could not but be surprised to hear you had turned dictator." Whether this trait was natural leadership or merely a grab at it was impossible to determine, but it remained a sore point among Francis's co-workers for the rest of his life. John Wesley heard of it and was displeased, but he recognized the importance of Francis's ardor and hoped one day to be able to apply it properly. The day came in 1771 when Wesley announced that missionaries were needed for the New World. Francis was among the score who applied; he was one of the two chosen.

3

Of the two and a half million people then living in the colonies, some four hundred were Methodists, attracted by exhorters and preachers who had moved to the New World more as settlers than as missionaries. There were seven such men in the country, at New York, Philadelphia and Baltimore, each spending a few months a year evangelizing his area. The Church of England was the established church of the colonies, but less than two hundred thousand people belonged to it. New England was predominantly Congregationalist; the middle colonies were Presbyterian and Quaker; the South was Baptist. There were Catholics in Maryland and a scattering of Jews in major cities, but both groups were banned by law and conducted their services in secret. By Methodist standards, all denominations, particularly the Anglicans, were shockingly dissolute. There was much work to be done. Most of the urban Methodists were Anglicans who still attended their church, but in rural areas, expecially in the South, were nondenominational clusters, with no ministry of their own, that responded enthusiastically to the hellfire sermons of the Methodist itinerants. Rural life was already rugged enough, and the Methodist assurances that these hardships—and more—would guarantee a glorious hereafter in a golden heaven made the ordeal easier to bear and thus provided fresh fields for Methodism. The entire country was, then, ripe for a man like Francis Asbury.

Francis landed at Philadelphia on October 27, 1771, located the Methodists and that night attended his first service in America. The next night he preached his first sermon, stunning his audience with his fervor. The fact that he had been put in charge of American Methodism by John Wesley himself gave him an added aura of divine authority, which he demonstrated in a sermon so loud and reviling that the devout Methodists suddenly suffered new guilts for their old sins and threw themselves on the floor in fits of traumatic reconversions. To Methodists, such displays were miracles: God was inside the penitent wrestling Satan, which caused the acrobatics, and the peace that finally came over the sinner was evidence that God had won. During his two weeks in Philadelphia, Francis kept God in constant combat—and always victorious.

He then left for New York. On this trip he established the pattern of living he maintained for forty-five years. He arose at four in the morning and spent an hour at prayer and Bible reading. At five, he preached his first sermon of the day, usually to the people in whose home he was staying, often to the one or two men who traveled with him. After a light breakfast, he mounted his horse and was ready to depart. While riding, he read to occupy himself. In this way and despite his own meager education, he taught himself Latin, Greek and Hebrew. Five or six times a day, he stopped to preach—to farmers in a field, to hunters, to others on the road, in towns and hamlets, and each evening he held a revival meeting. Before retiring, he made entries in his journal and wrote letters, then read the Bible for another hour.

He cared nothing for personal comfort. Most homes where he stayed lacked beds for visitors: he slept on the floor. Often nightfall found him miles from a house or inn: he slept on the ground. On such occasions he was usually without food: he ate whatever wild fruits he could find or he went without food entirely. He disliked inns: they were always so noisy at night with drinking and merriment. Sometimes he would rush at the rowdies, shouting damnations at them, but when he lacked the strength for this he went out to the barn and slept with the horses. As he grew older, he was almost always ill. Summers, he suffered from skin diseases that made him a mass of boils and blisters. Winters, he was never without a cold, usually bronchitis. Throat and stomach ulcers kept him in constant pain. Nevertheless, he refused to pamper himself and would grow violent if anyone suggested he needed a few days of rest. To him, illness was merely another form of austerity to endure. A lean man, five feet nine, a hundred and fifty pounds, his physical resistance did not match his moral resistance and so there was always one illness or another he had to endure.

Even so, he managed to travel between five and six thousand miles a year, practically all of it on horseback. He toured every state from Maine to Georgia and westward beyond the Alleghenies. He once claimed that he had preached in every existing county in the country; he might well have added that he had preached in every town. He was said to be the best-known man in the nation. The time came when John Wesley could write him: "Frank Asbury, America," and the letters invariably reached him. So imbued was he with his cause that he never married, he never had a home of his own, he never possessed more than he could pack in his saddlebag, he never earned more than eighty dollars a year—and most of this he gave to the poor. There were men who for a while literally revered him, but he warily discouraged these influences and friendships, and often, because he could be so stubborn, so political in his leadership, his closest associates turned bitterly against him. His deep-set, piercing, pale blue eyes, buried under thick brows, gave the uncomfortable feeling of penetrating into a man's mind; he had a large nose and mouth which, when he was dissatisfied or in pain, blended into a forbidding snarl that gave strangers on the road the impression that he was a mean old man.

He was, on the contrary, dynamic and magnetic, generous and outgoing, thoughtful and benign, yet all this without involving the least sentimentality, affection, charm or personal warmth. He cared only for his cause, and because of him it flourished. The four hundred Methodists and seven preachers in America on his arrival expanded in his lifetime to two hundred and fifteen thousand Methodists and two thousand ordained ministers, and he ruled them all. He never became, as his mother had wished, the Archbishop of Canterbury simply because he never returned to England, but for success, power and influence there was not another churchman in America in his time who could match him.

4

The nature of American Methodism directly affiliated it with the Church of England. First, the Wesley brothers, its coleaders, were both Anglican priests; second, the purpose of Methodism was to restore Anglican spiritual vitality; third, all English Methodists were members of the Church of England and so were most of the Americans. These circumstances were to create serious problems in America. At the time that American Methodism was enjoying its first successes the early grumblings of the American Revolution were being heard throughout the colonies. Even devout American Anglicans resented the fact that King George III, the head of their church by law and tradition, was now burdening them with taxes. Many Anglicans indignantly stopped going to church or joined other churches. But the Methodists could not do this. One of their aims was the fervent return to Anglican sacraments, sacraments they believed to be valid by the process of apostolic succession which they felt the Church of England retained after its sixteenth-century break with Rome. As good Anglicans, the Methodists believed that none of the other Protestant sects possessed valid sacraments, with the exception of baptism and marriage, and thus they could not bring themselves to leave their church. Furthermore, none of the Methodist preachers in the colonies, including Francis, had the sacerdotal faculties to provide the vital sacrament of the Lord's Supper. There was nothing the Methodists could do, then, but continue to attend Anglican churches. Passionate revolutionaries did not understand this, and they charged that continued Methodist adherence to the Church of England likewise indicated pro-British sympathies.

Inevitably, the perscution of Methodists erupted in the colonies. Francis Asbury foresaw it and was caught in the crossfire. His own political sentiments were unswervingly pro-American. Four years in the country had convinced him of the righteousness of the American cause and assured him of its victory. He wrote John Wesley that, for the good of the American Methodists, some way must be found to break the tie with England, with the Church of England. Wesley furiously refused. When the war broke out, seven of eight British-born and -trained Methodist preachers went back to England, leaving Francis the only qualified man in the country. Then most of the Anglican clergy left the colonies, thereby creating a serious double shortage for Methodists of both preachers and priests.

Francis ran into a new problem. Most of the colonies passed regulations that required clergymen affiliated with "foreign churches" to swear an oath of allegiance to the new country. Methodism forbade the taking of oaths; it also supported men who felt they could not in conscience participate in armed conflict. To the revolutionaries, this was evasion and disloyalty. In Maryland, local authorities confronted Francis with the choice of taking the oath or getting out of the state. He crossed over into Delaware, where the oath was not enforced, and although he had freedom of movement within the state he was virtually a prisoner in Delaware for almost two years. Then a letter was uncovered in which he had, before the war, expressed his confidence and hopes in America. This was enough to lift all suspicions from him. He applied for and received citizenship in Delaware and was once again free to travel.

He had, during his restriction, managed to establish forty-three new circuits attended by eighty-three new preachers, mostly in the North. Now he sounded out the men on the idea of severing relations with England and establishing American Methodism as an independent movement, with him at its head. The preachers responded that they would support him, whatever he decided. He decided, however, to do nothing. In the South was growing evidence of a schism and Francis feared his own break with England might encourage it.

The southern controversy had two bases. First, the departure of the Anglican clergy had left southern Methodists without the sacraments. The people were clamoring for them and begged their preachers to find some way to provide them. Second, a faction of southern preachers, headed by James O'Kelley, considered Francis to be too dictatorial in matters of discipline and appointments and they took steps to set up among themselves a presbyterian-type of leadership which they felt would be more democratic and more to their own advantage. By doing so, they could, they believed, declare their own ministry and thereby be in a position to meet the growing demands for the sacraments by the people.

Always a sensitive politician, Francis perceived that it would be dangerous for him to try to assert his authority over the southerners at this point. Instead, he relied on northern friends to calm the southerners and urge them to defer any action for the present. Francis then besieged John Wesley with pleas to find some solution to the problem of the sacraments.

Wesley himself was beginning to recognize that something had to be done. He knew he could not ask the Church of England to ordain the American preachers for the simple reason that they were not properly educated for it. For that matter, he realized that the Americans did not want to be part of the Church. He found his answer in his own interpretation of church history. He observed that in the first Christian years a bishop was elected by the elders—the priests—of an area, that only later were bishops elected by other bishops, later still when they were appointed by popes, and later—in England—that they were appointed by the archbishops of Canterbury. It seemed to Wesley now that apostolic succession, which was so important to him, was actually in the hands of priests, not bishops or archbishops or popes, and he felt that the Church ought to return to this process. Well, he was a priest, and he knew there were other Anglican priests in England who trusted his judgment fully. He decided to ask them to join with him in electing a bishop for America, a man who could then ordain the American preachers into the ministry and thus equip them with sacramental faculties. It seemed simple enough. Charles

Wesley disagreed and argued that the act would be heretical, but John did not think so. He decided to go ahead.

By rights, Francis Asbury should have become the first bishop, but John Wesley distrusted Francis's ambition and saw in Francis's pleas for a separation from the Church of England the hint of a separation from himself. Instead, he chose Dr. Thomas Coke, an Anglican priest and zealous Methodist missionary. Coke was duly elected bishop and consecrated by the laying on of hands by John Wesley's Anglican confreres. Coke was then sent to America for the purpose of consecreting Francis as his assistant bishop (Wesley preferred the title "general superintendent"), and together they were to ordain ministers who could provide the sacraments. That, Wesley felt, would settle the entire American problem while still keeping American Methodism in his own hands.

Francis did not agree. He had no intentions of taking second place in American Methodism to anybody, so he devised his own plans. When, late in 1784, Coke arrived in Philadelphia with his news, Francis was properly impressed, properly humble, but he insisted that he could not accept such extreme responsibility, such extreme authority, without the expressed approval of the American preachers, and he urged Coke to summon the circuit riders for a vote. Unaware of the threatening schism in the South, Coke was moved by Francis's democratic gesture. A general conference was announced, to be held in Baltimore during Christmas week. This was a time when the circuit riders were very busy, and it was therefore not surprising that the only men who showed up were those who owed Francis favors or simply liked him enough to want him to be their leader. The vote was held; Francis was approved. On December 24, he was ordained a deacon, on Christmas Day he was ordained an elder, the next day he was consecrated general superintendent (he preferred the title "bishop").

He left Baltimore almost immediately to begin ordaining the preachers, alarming most of them by appearing in a cassock, complete with the episcopal decorations of the Church of England. The preachers and the people complained that he looked too Anglican, too papal, so he put aside his robes. But he did not put aside his conviction that he was a bishop. He signed his letters and documents with that title, he referred to himself by it, and he adopted the habit of hearing people only when they addressed him by it.

John Wesley heard of all this and was furious. He wrote Francis:

> How can you, how dare you, suffer yourself to be called bishop? I shudder, I start at the very thought! Men may call me a knave or a fool, a rascal, a scoundrel, and I am content; but they shall never, by my consent, call me a bishop. For my sake, for God's sake, for Christ's sake, put a full end to this!

With that, Wesley unwittingly put a full end to his own authority in America. Thereafter, his name was seldom mentioned in the records of ministerial conferences, Francis had only the most formal and infrequent contact with him, any instructions coming from England were ignored unless they reflected American sentiments. Francis defended his position with:

"I will tell the world what I rest my authority on. First, divine authority; second, seniority in America; third, the election of the general conference; fourth, my ordination by Thomas Coke; fifth, because the signs of an apostle have been seen in me."

Thomas Coke was having his own troubles. He was so English in his attitudes and acts that the American Methodists, imbued with their new nationalism, could not stand him. Also, he was an unattractive man, small, flabby, effeminate, who, when trying to sound stentorian in his sermons, succeeded only in emitting falsetto screams that sent snickers through his audience. He had no conception of the American mentality, which so quickly formed, and he soon alienated most of the preachers with his lack of diplomacy. Francis knew this was going to happen and he avoided Coke as much as he could in order to escape guilt by association.

Coke was impatient to open a Methodist college. Francis, on the other hand, knew there were few Methodists ready for higher education and proposed instead a series of primary schools in the more heavily populated circuits. But Coke was adamant. The first college—called Cokesbury, after both of them—was built at Abingdon, Maryland, in 1787, but was destroyed by fire a few years later. A second college was built, this time in Baltimore, but it burned down within a year. Thereafter Francis took over the education program, building primary schools and academies in scores of circuits that could support them. His efforts eventually to expand into higher fields were always hampered by insufficient funds, but he nevertheless laid the groundwork for such prominent schools as Wesleyan University, Augusta College, Randolph-Macon College, Dickinson College, Drew Theological College, and Allegheny College. In 1784, Francis opened the Methodist Book Concern in Philadelphia; the office subsequently moved to New York, its sales volume increasing steadily to, at present, twenty-five million dollars a year.

At the general conference of 1789, Francis proposed that a statement of congratulations be presented to George Washington, whose first inauguration had taken place a month before, adding that the statement include the Methodist approbation of the Constitution and a profession of allegiance to the new republic. The proposal was approved; Francis and Coke drew up the statement and presented it jointly to Washington in New York on May 29. The presentation made the Methodists the first religious group to pledge support to the American Government, a gesture that won wide and favorable publicity. Out of that support, however, Francis suffered his worst defeat and deepest heartache.

5

By nature and by conviction, Francis Asbury was opposed to slavery. His first trips through the South left him sad and shocked. Early in his American career he exclaimed: "O Lord, banish the infernal spirit of slavery from thy dear Zion!" During a trip through South Carolina he recorded in his journal:

> My spirit was much grieved at the conduct of some Methodists who hire out slaves at public places to the highest bidder, to cut, skin and starve them. I think such members ought to be dealt with. On the side of the oppressors there are law and power, but where are justice and mercy to the poor slaves? What eye will pity, what hand will help or ear listen to their distresses? I will try, if words can be drawn swords, to pierce the hearts of the owners.

He tried. He wrote letters and pamphlets against slavery. After preaching against it in Virginia, an angry crowd approached. He recorded that he considered himself fortunate to get away "with whole bones." He continued to try.

At the general conferences he repeatedly tried to get Methodism to go on record against slavery. In 1780, he succeeded in having included in the conference minutes an agreement that circuit riders would release their slaves and attempt to persuade other Methodists to do the same, but the agreement had little effect. Three years later he managed only to have the conference record show that the question of slavery would be discussed sometime in the future.

Unable to push through concrete abolitionist declarations in the general conferences, Francis acted outside them. Wherever he traveled, north or south, he argued his position with preachers and politicians, feeling that if he could not give his crusade national scope he might at least get results on the local level. It would be impossible to measure his effectiveness, but there were signs of it in the emancipation of slaves in Massachusetts in 1783, in Connecticut and Rhode Island in 1784, and the Congressional Act of 1787 that prohibited slavery in the Northwest Territory.

Francis attacked broadly in 1785 by instructing all circuit riders to circulate petitions against slavery, which were then to be submitted to state legislatures. He personally submitted the Virginia petition to George Washington at Mount Vernon. Washington admitted that he was against slavery, adding that other Virginia leaders knew his sentiments. He felt, however, that in his own position he could not sign the petition. "But," he said, "I shall write a letter to the Virginia Assembly clearly defining my stand against slavery, if you think it will help your cause."

Francis had little hope for Virginia. "I am brought to conclude that slavery will exist in Virginia perhaps for ages," he wrote in his journal.

Devereaux Jarrett, a Virginia Anglican minister, once said to Francis: "I suggest that the Methodists restrict their devotions to white souls."

Francis replied: "In Heaven all souls will be white, regardless of the color of the human bodies that once housed them."

Francis could have avoided a serious schism had he been willing to put aside principle for the sake of popularity. But he refused. Records of the 1796 general conferences indicated his continued efforts for a united antislavery stand by the Church. In 1800, he tried again to stir some enthusiasm for the petition to legislatures. Evidence of his losing battle occurred four years later when North Carolina, South Carolina, Georgia and Tennessee refused to take part in the petition program. The next clue was equally discouraging. South Carolina copies of the Form of Discipline—the compilation of Methodist ordinance—omitted all references to slavery.

In despair Francis exclaimed, "If the Gospel will tolerate slavery, what will it not authorize!"

He did not live to see. He died in 1816; four years later his episcopal edict urging regional conferences to promote antislavery laws was dropped. At a subsequent conference, a southern majority managed to have the subject of slavery banned from future general conferences. This was something northerners would not tolerate. As a result, the first schism on a racial basis took place in 1843 when twenty-five thousand northern Methodists broke off to form the Wesleyan Methodist Church.

The great schism occurred the following year, growing out of the fact that Bishop James O. Andrew, successor to Francis, married a slaveholding wife. Northern Methodists feared this would result in proslavery jurisdiction at the top level and worked futilely for the bishop's suspension. Hard feelings created an impasse that could not be resolved: the only agreement was that the two sides should go their separate ways. That year, the Methodist Episcopal Church, South, was formed, producing the biggest schism in American history by cutting off almost half a million people from the parent organization.

During the early battle over slavery, Francis witnessed another schism, a smaller one and one with different grounds. Francis did not agree with John Wesley that a bishop was merely a chairman of the board of elders, director of them but not superior to them. Although he had accepted consecration on these terms, Francis later argued: "There cannot be a perfect equality between a constant president and those over whom he presides." Besides, Francis liked being a bishop, and he wanted to be one in the traditional sense. A bachelor and probably a misogynist (he once revealed that he had never found women attractive and had never been involved with any), he tried at first to extract vows of chastity from the ministers he ordained, which would have given his episcopacy even more authority, but the effort failed. The most outspoken critic of Francis's despotic leadership had long been James O'Kelley, who had opposed him from the start. Oddly enough, Francis and O'Kelley were enjoying a brief period of friendliness at the time of Francis's consecration and O'Kelley had voted for it. But when Francis then tried to fill the role as he thought it should be, O'Kelley again became a vitriolic opponent.

This situation, plus the demands for sacraments and the slavery issue, drove the two men irreparably apart. In 1792, O'Kelley led the first Methodist schism by setting up in Virginia what he called the Republican Methodist Church, thereby riding on the popular tail of political Republicanism which opposed the growing centralization of government power. The Republican Methodist Church had a short but active life: in ten years it attracted a hundred thousand members, collapsing eventually because of its own loose structure. Many of the members returned to Francis; others joined the Congregational Church.

But the seed of increased lay authority in Methodism had

been planted. Francis's strongest defender during the battle with O'Kelley was Nicholas Snethen, who debated with O'Kelley in a series of pamphlets. Years later, however, Snethen found himself on the opposite side of the fence and was instrumental in establishing the Methodist Protestant Church.

It was not until 1939, the Civil War far behind, that Methodists—South, North, Wesleyan, Protestant—were able to resolve their differences and reunite into a single Methodist Church, constituting the largest Protestant denomination in America. Still remaining apart was the majority of Negro Methodism, schisms which evolved out of the Civil War racial question and which deferred reunion until racialism would no longer be a question. In view of subsequent developments, this day seemed hopefully imminent.

6

There was no question that for forty-five years Francis Asbury was the personification of Methodism in America. Stubborn, ambitious, dictatorial though he was, he was nevertheless a man of unwavering conviction, devotion and service. He was incapable of indifference: what he was for, he fought for; what he was against, he fought against. Whether he won or lost was not as important to him as the fact that he got the battle started. This was true of slavery. It was also true of drinking. He was violently against it. Under his pressure, the general conference of 1780 denounced drinking as evil, and just as Francis went to politicians about slavery so he went to them about the sale of liquor. Dr. Benjamin Rush, a signer of the Declaration of Independence, was one of his strongest supporters, and there was scarcely a governor, mayor or congressman who did not hear from Francis on the subject throughout his long life. Francis preached and wrote so much against alcohol that he left an indelible imprint on Methodism. It was therefore not surprising that Carrie Nation, the famous saloon buster, was a Methodist; that James Cannon, Jr., who made the Virginia Anti-Saloon League such a national influence that it led directly to the Eighteenth Amendment, was a Methodist bishop; and that after repeal of the Amendment the sale of alcohol remained under severest control in Methodist strongholds in the Midwest and South.

Francis's intractability weakened men who were close to him. Although Thomas Coke was his episcopal superior, the man knew it was Francis who actually dominated Methodism in America and Coke soon gave up efforts to control it himself. Within a few years, he returned to his first love—missionary work—and though he occasionally returned to America for general conferences he spent most of his time out of the country, dying in 1814 on a boat to Ceylon. Wesley was also dead: the link with England was now definitely broken.

At that time, Francis was seventy, himself near death, but he refused to give up his travels. Despite age and illness, he would not ease his long day, which still began at four with morning meditation. There were times when he had to be helped on and off his horse and held up while he preached, but he did not care. He would not stop. The white hair, bent figure and wrinkled face that came with the years gave him a commanding dignity: people spontaneously rose to their feet when he entered a room or a church. It was the sort of thing his mother would have loved. With typical presumption, he merely felt this was the way a bishop ought to be treated.

He began to realize, however, that he did not have long to live. He made out a will, leaving everything he had—two thousand dollars that others had bequeathed to him—to the Methodist Book Concern, saying: "Let it all return and continue to aid the cause of piety." By now he had consecrated other Methodist bishops to serve as his assistants in remote corners of the country. In the autumn of 1815, as he prepared for another trip, he admitted that perhaps he should resign his office in favor of one of them. He was denied the occasion.

The trip that proved to be his last took him from New York to Ohio, then on to South Carolina. His plan was to work his way northward again on a series of revivals that would bring him to Baltimore the following May, where he intended to preside over another general conference. It was winter, bitter cold. In South Carolina, Francis suffered an attack of bronchitis and influenza, and those with him expected him to rest there until he recovered. But in two days he insisted on resuming the trip; he also insisted on preaching three or four times a day as he traveled.

On March 24, he reached Richmond, Virginia, and though illness forced him to enter the city by cart instead of on horseback, he brushed aside efforts to cancel his preaching engagement that night. His friends could see that death was near and tried in vain to make him rest. Instead, he ordered them to put him back in the cart and continue the trip. Four days later, the caravan arrived at Spottsylvania, Pennsylvania, and Francis was invited to stay at the home of George Arnold. He was too weak to sit up and had to be put to bed.

The next day he could not speak, but on the next, Sunday, March 31, he asked that the Bible be brought to him and he instructed the Arnold family to gather around his bed so that he could preach to them. He opened the Bible to the twenty-first chapter of Revelation and began to read aloud: ". . . And I saw a new heaven and a new earth: for the first heaven and the first earth were passed away, and there was no more sea. . . ."

Suddenly he raised his hands high, and then he died.

In many ways he had been responsible for a unique new earth. In the new America that was born during his first years here, he had worked hard for all that was good and worked hard against all that was evil. He had been specifically responsible for the development of a religious body which, despite conflict and controversy, friction and feud, evolved into a mighty force for morality, equality, spiritual welfare, education, peace and social justice. There could be no more magnificent heritage.

In Washington, D. C., on October 15, 1924, President Calvin Coolidge unveiled a statue of Francis Asbury on horseback, the sight that thousands of early Americans had come to know, respect and love, and the President said:

"A great lesson has been taught us by this holy life. It was because of what Bishop Asbury and his associates preached, and what other religious organizations through their ministry preached, that our country has developed so much freedom."

CHAPTER

THREE

Shepherd of the Unwanted

THE boy had murdered his father. One night the man had come home drunk, as he did so often, and as he always did on such occasions he had beaten his wife into unconsciousness and then turned on his son. The boy was sitting at the kitchen table; a carving knife was at his elbow. As his father approached, the boy picked up the knife and held it in front of him and let his father walk into it. The man screamed and fell to the floor. The boy stepped over him and went into the bedroom to his mother. She lay strewn on the bed, blood pouring from her nose and mouth. The boy fetched a damp cloth and patted her face gently. When she opened her terrified eyes and looked at him, the boy said, "I think Pa is dead."

Nobody in town was surprised. The family had a bad reputation. The father seldom worked, and when he did he spent most of his income on liquor, returning home to take out his rage against the world on his wife and son. When she was well enough, the mother cleaned house for other families, and there were rumors that when her husband was away on one of his sprees she went to the bus station or to the hotel bar to seek out men from whom she could earn a few more dollars. The boy had heard the rumors and suspected they were true, but he would not concede it openly and so he was often in fights with other boys who taunted him with it.

The town had marked the boy for doom. It was known that he had stolen candy and toys and clothes from shops. To keep the boy out of reformatories, the father had to pay for these things—which the man remembered with fury when he was drunk. Also, the boy was a frequent truant from school. A sullen refusal to study had put him three grades behind his age group. He had run away from home twice, once getting as far as Denver where he was caught stealing a loaf of bread in a supermarket.

So the town was not surprised by the murder. People merely wondered why it hadn't happened sooner. And they wondered why he hadn't killed his mother, too. She certainly was no better than the old man.

There was no need for a trial. The boy was held in jail for two weeks while the legal preliminaries were carried out, then he was brought before the judge in an almost empty courtroom, admitted to what he had done and glumly accepted his sentence of life imprisonment.

Then a clear, firm voice broke the courtroom quiet. "Your Honor, may I address the court?"

The judge looked up and recognized the Catholic priest standing in the aisle. "You're Father Flanagan, aren't you?"

"Yes, I am."

"I heard you were in town."

"I've come about the boy," Flanagan said. "I want you to let me have him."

The judge almost smiled with pity. "You can't do anything for this kid, Father," he said. "He's bad, that's all, just bad."

"There is no such thing as a bad boy," said Flanagan.

"I know you feel that way," the judge admitted, "but I've always thought you were being unrealistic. I've seen too many of this type. You wouldn't want to turn a kid like this loose in Boys Town."

"I've done it before."

"Murderers?"

"Murderers," said Flanagan, "and bank robbers and car thieves and prostitutes and shoplifters and housebreakers and muggers and— You name it, Judge."

"And you've had no trouble with them?"

"Nothing serious."

"I can't believe it."

"Come and see for yourself."

The judge thought about it. "What's your secret, Father?"

"No secret," said Flanagan. "I simply give the boys something they never had much of before."

"And what's that?"

"Love."

2

With the uncomplicated therapy of love, Father Flanagan had, in over forty years, salvaged thousands of boys who were marked for doom. For doing so, he was made a monsignor, an honorary position which, as a domestic prelate, made him a member of the papal household, but always he was referred to as Father because that was precisely what he was to the battalion of boys who needed one. He had the Irish habit of affectionately calling the boys "dear," and although this startled some of them at first and deluded others into thinking he was going to be a pushover, they gradually realized that he meant it. It was a new experience for them.

All that Father Flanagan knew about boys he learned from the boys themselves. And the most important thing he knew was that no boy will get into serious trouble who comes from a home where there is love—the right kind of love: spiritual love as well as human love. Most of the boys came from broken families, from poor homes, from orphanages, sometimes via reformatories. But others had fathers who were professional and financial successes; two or three had been the sons of millionaires. Solvency, then, didn't guarantee proper love in a home any more than it guaranteed good health.

Once a famous editor, on leaving his son at Boys Town, offered the boy: "If you behave yourself while you're here I'll give you a new car for yourself when you come home."

Annoyed, Flanagan said, "You've just ruined any chances I had to do some real good with the boy."

"By promising to reward him for good behavior?"

"He will behave here because he will be happy here," Father assured. "And he will be happy because we shall pay some attention to him."

It was an indictment against millions of parents, a valid indictment.

Over the years, the fiction arose that, confident in the efficacy of love, Father Flanagan never resorted to physical punishment with any of his boys. On the contrary, for years he had a stern rule that he would be the only adult on the staff to use a paddle on a boy when the situation warranted it. When the Boys Town civic structure included a court and a misdemeanor was serious enough to merit the sentence of the paddle, it was Father who carried it out, believing that if a boy understood why he was being punished he would accept it with a good heart, albeit with a stinging bottom.

On the other hand, he loathed senseless extremes of punishment: he knew that most boys got into trouble because they already had too much of that, at home or out of it. When he became a recognized leader in the training of boys, he was often appointed to committees to inspect reformatories and other such institutions. He saw boys in solitary confinement, others in chains, others on bread and water, others who had been viciously beaten. This always sickened him. Once while inspecting a Japanese institution he asked why five boys were in solitary confinement, and he was told: "They're new. We always lock up new boys for a week so they will know what will happen to them if they misbehave later."

"Release them," Father ordered, then continued his inspection. At the tour's end, Father was invited to address the inmates. Waiting for the boys to assemble, he asked about those he had seen in the cells and was given an evasive answer. When the moment came for him to speak, he refused to step to the microphone. The puzzled officials introduced Father a second time, then a third, but still he would not move. Then the officials understood. The confined boys were sent for and led to the first row in the audience. At the sight of them, the other boys cheered and applauded. Only then did Flanagan go to the microphone.

Such experiences brought Father back to Boys Town even more determined that his boys would not be subjected to excessive discipline, and sometimes he acted unwisely in this regard. Returning from a tour, he summoned his boys for one of the Sunday morning conferences he gave whenever he was home, and he told them of some of the horrible things he had seen. Then he said: "My dears, I promise you this—if any man on the staff here lifts a hand to you, I want you to tell me and that man will go."

A purr of triumph rose from the boys. Boys Town had grown to a population of five hundred; raising funds kept Father frequently away, and he had a staff of seventy-five adults as teachers, counselors and administrators. The morning after the promise, the high school principal, who had a paddle the boys autographed before becoming better acquainted with it, went to Father. "Here is my paddle," he said, "and here is my resignation."

Father said, "Keep both."

"Very well," the principal said. "I just want you to know that I've never used the paddle unless I've had to, but I'd lose all control over the boys if they thought I'd never use it at all." It was a clear axiom that every parent could approve, but an axiom that was approved only with distaste by the man who had enough love in him to be a parent to thousands.

3

Edward Joseph Flanagan was born on July 13, 1886, on his father's farm across the Suck River from the town of Ballymoe, Ireland. Of the four sons and seven daughters born to John and Nora Flanagan, he was the frailest, and for awhile his parents feared he would not live. He announced in his childhood that he was going to become a priest, the fulfillment of which was to prove particularly difficult for him because of weak lungs that kept him extremely sensitive to climate and sudden changes in it. He studied first under his older brother Patrick, and when Patrick went off to the seminary in Dublin he was taken on as a student by the pastor in Ballymoe. He completed his preparatory education at the national school at Drimatample, five miles away. Excellent tutors and a natural brightness put him three years ahead of his age group, and when he entered Summer Hill College, at Sligo, on the northwest coast of Ireland, he was, at fourteen, the youngest member of his class, and he was soon at the head of it.

His four years at Summer Hill left a deep mark on Flanagan.

It was a good school, its standards held high more by discipline than morale. The students' attitude, like the old buildings themselves, was damp and cold. Flanagan eventually left the school with the unusual distinction of being the only boy during his years there who had never been whipped by a teacher, a distinction he did not enjoy because it put him apart from his friends and a distinction which his friends tried to overcome by suggesting pranks for him at which he had the dubious luck of never being caught. Graduated in 1904, he was ready now for the seminary. That same year, Patrick Flanagan had finished the Dublin seminary and was ordained. Because of the plethora of vocations then in Ireland, young priests usually had difficulty obtaining assignments near home, so they often offered themselves to American bishops who needed them, expecting to return to Ireland someday when the older priests had died off. With Patrick Flanagan, there was one difference: having been accepted by the Omaha diocese, he intended to stay there. Also that year, Nellie Flanagan, the oldest daughter, returned from New York, where she had moved, and she raved about the wonders and opportunities of America.

"You ought to go to the seminary in America, Eddie," she told her young brother. "I'm sure you'll love it, and maybe, like Patrick, you'll want to stay."

He was easily convinced. The last winter at Sligo had been severe for him. The land of sunshine and roses that Nellie spoke about sounded irresistible. Thus when Patrick and Nellie left for the United States, Eddie was on the boat with them. He found a land of sunshine and roses, to be sure, but only in the New York parks. Along the narrow streets he found poverty and hunger and juvenile crime—the results of heavy immigration. He supposed the poverty and hunger would fade as the newcomers learned the language and developed roots, but he was appalled by the juvenile crime and he wondered why nothing was being done about it other than jailing the boys occasionally.

He presented himself to Archbishop John Farley as a candidate for the priesthood. To his surprise, Summer Hill had not prepared him fully for the archdiocesan St. Joseph's Seminary at Dunwoodie, thirty miles north of the city, and it was necessary for him to attend Mount St. Mary's College, at Emmitsburg, Maryland, for two years to acquire the proper bachelor's degree. At last, in 1906, he entered the seminary. He felt he was on his way.

With a vigorous determination to make up for lost time, he threw himself at his books as though they were demons he had to conquer. Once again, he was quickly at the head of his class. As part of his training, he was required to visit New York hospitals to comfort the sick. Tuberculosis was then raging in the city, especially among the poor, and many of the seminarians were reluctant to enter the TB wards. Flanagan went in. He discovered that many patients were Irish immigrants, too weak to write home; he wrote the letters for them. Meantime, the rest of his family had moved to America. Nora Flanagan worried about her son's visits to the hospitals, reminding him of his own weak lungs, but he refused to be dissuaded.

On Christmas morning, 1908, the Flanagan family attended Mass together at St. Patrick's Cathedral. The service was long; the church was stifling hot. Outside, a blizzard stormed. When Flanagan walked out into it he felt a stabbing chill cut across his back. The next day he was not well. By the time he returned to school he was, he knew, very ill. He went to the infirmary, where the doctor diagnosed double pneumonia. He was put to bed and he remained in bed for six months.

He soon wearied of the inactivity and asked for his books.

One of his professors, Father Francis Duffy, later the famed chaplain of the Fighting 69th, volunteered to tutor him. At the term's end, Flanagan was able to pass his examinations, but the faculty suspected he still was not strong enough to resume the arduous course of studies and recommended he take a year or two off to recuperate in a climate where dry air would mend his lungs. There was only one place he could go—to Omaha, where his brother's country parish was fast being engulfed by the growing city. His parents and three sisters said they would move West with him. The prospect of living in a home again with his family provided a certain joy for him, but it was his only joy. He was now twenty-three years old, an age when most seminarians were anticipating the end of their studies, and he had scarcely started his.

Frustrated, he loafed for weeks in the burning Nebraska sun, letting his mother stuff him with her cooking. Gradually his cough stopped and he began to put on weight. By the end of summer, he was confident that he could take on his studies again, but he realized the chances of re-entering the New York seminary were slim. He said so to the Omaha prelate, Bishop Scannell.

"That's probably true," the bishop agreed. "And most likely it would be true of any American seminary. Your health record would be against you. But there is a place you can go. Rome."

"Rome!" said Flanagan. "How I would love that. But I can't afford it."

"If you're willing to enter my diocese, I will pay the bills for you," the bishop offered.

So he was on the way to Rome. But Rome was no kinder to him than New York. In November, he was back in the hospital with a recurrence of pneumonia. The following January, he was traveling back to Omaha.

This seemed like the end. He rested until summer had passed, then he took a job as a bookkeeper for a meat packer. As far as his family knew, he had put the priesthood out of his mind. He said nothing about it for almost a year, occupying himself with his job, a few friends and reading. Then one day he received a letter from the University of Innsbruck, in the Austrian Tyrol, and after reading it he revealed to his family:

"I wrote Innsbruck a few weeks ago, asking if they'd take me on as a student for the priesthood. It's in the Alps and the air is cold and clear; I should be all right there. They're willing to accept me; they've sent the application forms. All I have to worry about now is the expense."

The family assured him they would help. So now he was on his way to Austria, and when he returned three years later, in 1912, he was a priest. Overjoyed, he exclaimed, "I never thought I'd live to see the day!"

4

His first assignment was in O'Neill, Nebraska, about two hundred miles west of Omaha. For a year he was a busy country curate, working around the clock, then he was transferred to St. Patrick's Church in Omaha, on the fringe of what was becoming the city's Skid Row.

Omaha had grown too fast. Situated in the heart of the wheat belt, it had become a railroad center overnight; its stockyards flourished; its meat-packing industry was second only to Chicago. While it was able to offer jobs to skilled laborers, it was also the victim of thousands of migrant workers who flocked into the city between harvests. A rich city, Omaha nevertheless suffered a steadily increasing impoverished element of unemployed farmhands it could not absorb. Winters, hundreds of men loitered around the freight yards or walked the downtown streets panhandling, and when they were desperate enough for money and food they shoplifted, robbed and mugged.

What he did not see of all this for himself, Father Flanagan read in the papers. One night he told his pastor, "We must do something for these men."

"I've thought of that often," said Father John T. Smith, "but what can we do? There are so many of them."

"The worst are those with families," said Flanagan. "I saw a family the other day who've been sleeping in their car all winter."

Father Smith nodded. "This winter is the worst yet. The harvest was bad; few men made any money at all, and there are no jobs for them in town."

"Maybe we can't find jobs for them all," Flanagan conceded, "but we should do something. Feed them, at least."

"Do you know how many there are?" asked Smith. "An army. It would cost a fortune to feed them."

"Will you give me permission to see what I can work out?"

"Of course," Smith consented, "but I warn you now it's a big job. You'll never be able to do enough."

He had to try. Next day, he made the rounds of butchers and grocers of the parish, asking if they would be willing to donate their leftovers every day for a soup kitchen at St. Patrick's. They were reluctant at first, afraid that their generosity might only attract more drifters to the city, but the young priest persisted with them and he won them over. From parish clubs, he was able to solicit funds to buy cooking equipment. But who would do the cooking? He put the question to his family one afternoon; immediately his mother and his sister Nellie volunteered. In a few days, then, Father had his soup kitchen established. News of it traveled fast. Every noon a long line of the migrants, some with their wives and children, formed at the rectory back door for soups and stews, the only food they could obtain without begging or stealing.

Father derived consolation from being able to do this much, but at night, when he was warm in his own bed, he would think of the men sleeping out in the cold, under sidetracked freight cars, in doorways, in roadside ditches, and his own comfort would be destroyed.

"We've got to open some sort of hostel for the men," he announced to Father Smith one morning.

"What next?" Smith joked. "An athletic club?"

For the next few days, Father Flanagan wandered the Omaha streets looking for a building he might use for his hostel. He found it on the corner of Eleventh and Mason streets, an abandoned two-story building that had once been the Burlington Hotel but now looked ready to collapse. He located the agent and asked about the monthly rent: it was precisely the amount he had in his pocket. With no idea where he could get the next month's rent, he signed the lease. The building needed a lot of work. The owner was willing to repair the leaky roof, but painting and plastering had to be done by the lessee—by Father. Once again his family came to his aid, to paint, to plaster, to sweep out tons of dirt, to scrounge for cots, furniture, rugs, linen. Just as the first wintry blasts of 1915 came in off the Nebraska plains, the hostel was ready for guests.

At first, nobody came. The migrants and the bums could not believe anybody would care for them to such an extent and they feared there was a catch to it. Then one man came, then two and three. The second week, there were over fifty.

"This is not," Father assured them, "your private club. You can stay here without charge, but you've got to do chores."

This did not go down too well with some of them, but most were willing to do their share. They kept the building clean;

those with trade skills made repairs. The hostel had its own barber, a tailor shop, and Father opened an employment agency. When Omahans recognized that Father had indeed established a hostel and not a flophouse, they were more ready to give what aid they could. Food and clothes were offered and part-time jobs were created.

Spring came and the migrants left to seek summer jobs. Now Father had time to appraise his efforts. One thing was certain: the hostel was too small. He would have to find a bigger place. A few months earlier this prospect would have terrified him, but records of the past winter had shown a distinct drop in crimes attributable to migrants, and city authorities readily credited Father Flanagan and his hostel for the happy change of events. Thus when Father let it be known that he wanted a bigger building, he found new friends on all sides who were ready to help him. When autumn, 1916, arrived, the new Workingman's Hotel on Thirteenth Street had its doors open. Now there was room for hundreds—and they came.

In addition to the farmhands who came merely to have a place to sleep until they could find temporary jobs there was a new element—drunks, dope addicts, hustlers who came merely to loaf or to avoid the police. Now there were fights in the hotel. Now there were complaints from the farmhands that worthless derelicts had confiscated their beds. Perhaps Father would have been justified in throwing the derelicts out, but the sheer helplessness of them prevented him from doing so. He talked with them, trying to find out where they had gone wrong. A pattern appeared: poverty, alcoholism, incompatibility in their childhood homes; then split families, further destitution, a shuttling among indifferent relatives, perhaps orphanages; then crime, immorality, arrests, reformatories and jails.

"Nobody ever cared."

Father heard that repeatedly. It might have been a sign of weakness in men, but these were men talking about when they were boys. Realizing this, Father recognized that he might be too late to do much for the men except to keep them from hunger, disease and more crime by letting them remain at the hotel. But . . .

He began to frequent the juvenile courts.

Day after day, he saw the boys being brought in, he listened to their brief trials, he watched them being marched off to reformatories, to jails if they were old enough. He remembered what the men had told him: in reformatories and jails they had learned everything they knew about crime that they hadn't known when they went in. Now day after day Father watched new pupils go off to the cruel schools.

One day he could stand it no longer. As another prospect for serious crime was being led off to his training grounds, Father called out: "Your Honor, would you consider paroling that boy to me?"

The judge asked: "Who are you?"

"I'm Father Flanagan, of St. Patrick's parish. I run the Workingman's Hotel."

"What do you want to do? House the kid with the rest of your drifters?"

"The boy has a home," Father pointed out. "That was disclosed during his hearing."

"What good has it done him? It hasn't kept him out of trouble," the judge said.

"I know, sir, but maybe I can."

"How?"

"By being his friend," said Father. "I'd be grateful if you'd parole him to me for, say, six months. That will give me time to find out if I can do anything for him."

"Six months?" the judge scoffed. "He'll be back here in six days."

"If he is, then I will have failed, Judge, but I would appreciate the chance to try."

"You've got it."

And so it began. First one boy, then three, then six, then seven, all of them boys from Omaha homes, homes of the kind the men at the hotel had described, homes without love, homes without God. They were a strange assortment of boys, ranging in age from eight to fourteen, most of them with police records, all of them categorized as incorrigible; they had different religious and nationality backgrounds, different reasons why their home lives were shattered, different incentives down the wrong road. One thing they had in common: they all needed an adult who cared for them.

Father saw each boy privately at least once a week for a personal talk; two evenings a week and on Sunday he brought the group together for baseball or picnics. He saw to it that they went to church—any church. And when school opened in the fall he saw to it that they were all there. To be sure, the boys did not become saints overnight, but each day their arrogance mellowed more until they could settle for venting their young angers in the boxing matches Father arranged for them.

The major negative factor in Father's program was that the boys had to return every evening to the homes that had bred them into what they had become. Father could only hope he might steel them sufficiently to withstand the destructive influence of their own families. Each week they remained out of trouble was further evidence that Father was succeeding. But he could just love and guide them; the basic strength they needed could come only from God, and for this reason he urged—even commanded—them to practice their religions. True, faith could not be injected into the boys, like some wonder drug, but they had a good chance of acquiring faith by assimilation, if nothing else, as long as they frequented the places where it was preached.

At least they had homes. In courts, Father discovered there were many boys who did not, some of them orphans who hit the streets rather than enter institutions, some the sons of migrant families they had abandoned or which had abandoned them, others the unhappy escapees from miserable homes, in Omaha or elsewhere, which they put out of their minds by denying that they had them. These were the boys who most seriously concerned Father Flanagan. He wondered if he would still be around when, as men, the homeless boys would come stumbling into the Workingman's Hotel, drunk, diseased, their veins throbbing with narcotics.

"A boy should have a home," he repeatedly insisted to everybody who would listen to him. It was while he was privately meditating on the need one day that he realized he must be the one to provide it.

On the corner of Twenty-fifth and Dodge, he found a two-story Victorian house, sturdy and roomy, that was available for a ninety-dollars-a-month rent. He had to borrow the money. On December 12, 1917, he moved in with five boys, three of them orphans consigned to him earlier in the week and the other two parolees he had picked up at juvenile court that morning. Three nuns appointed at the request of Archbishop Harty were awaiting the pioneers when they arrived, as was Nellie Flanagan.

"Well, boys," said Father, as he led the youngsters through the door, "you're home."

5

There was no place like it in the country. For the first time, there was an institution where boys would go not as a punishment but as an opportunity. The five boys who moved in with Flanagan were all under ten years of age, and although they had lived many places in their few years, this was to be their first home. It was, to be sure, a corrective institution, but it differed from others in many important ways. No boy had to go there unless he wanted to, no boy had to remain any specified length of time, any boy could leave whenever he wished simply by walking out the door. Both the boys and Father freely took on definite responsibilities: if the boys wanted to stay, they had to obey the rules; if Father wanted them to stay, he had to provide the closest possible resemblance to a real home, the kind the boys had always desired but never had. The challenge was equal on both sides. Most unique about it was the fact that wayward boys, previously treated like criminals, were now to be treated as human beings, worthy of as much respect as they earned. It was up to them now to prove or disprove Father's adage that there were no bad boys, just bad environments and bad adults. In their circumstances, they could not hope for a better environment; in Father, they could not hope for a better adult.

Within the first week, the home's boy population soared from five to twenty-five, most of them boys who had walked in off the street to ask if what they had heard about the place was true. The unexpected arrivals brought about a rule that became symbolic of Father Flanagan: the door was never to be locked. Whatever the hour, any boy who had decided to live there should be able to enter the moment the decision struck him. The open door would assure him that he was both welcome and wanted.

From the start, it was clear that the home would develop into a full-time job. Father was released from his parish duties and he withdrew from the Workingman's Hotel. When he was away from his boys, it was only to find money to feed and clothe them. At first, this was not too easy. When school opened after the first Christmas the boys had together, Father tried to enroll them, but there was an uproar from parents who did not want their children exposed to young tramps. So he started his own school in the house and taught the classes himself. At every turn, Father faced a similar opposition, and at every turn he had to find his own way around it. People simply would not believe that any good could come of the boys and they could not see the sense in donating to a doomed cause. Months had to pass before Omahans perceived that, as with the men, a roof, a bed and a meal were the best deterrents to crime; that if the boys were indeed to come to any good they needed some good people to help them to it. A few good people, curious, came to see for themselves. A short time later, a Mothers Club was formed, with members visiting the home every day to cook and sew and supervise. Several businessmen formed a committee to see to it that there was always enough food in the house, enough coal, enough athletic equipment, and that somehow the rent would be paid.

In six months, the house was too small. Clearly, any house would eventually be too small: there seemed to be enough homeless boys in the country to fill a town, and now they were all heading for Father Flanagan. In June, 1918, he found himself again scouring Omaha for a suitable dwelling place. On South Thirteenth Street, within the pungent horizon of the stockyards, he came upon a long, two-story building surrounded by spacious playing fields, and it was all for rent. When he discovered the low cost, he asked: "Is anything wrong with it?"

"Oh, no," the renting agent said. "Everything's in good shape."

"Then why are you practically giving it away?" Father asked. "There's a war going on. Housing space is at a premium."

"That's just the point," the agent said. "This place used to be the headquarters of the German-American Society, which is worse these days than being haunted."

So the boys moved in with the enemy. The additional room allowed for a hundred boys; the number was getting too big for Father to handle alone. Fortunately, his nephew, Patrick Norton, arrived from Ireland and needed a job. He went to work with Father as business administrator, a position he was to hold for the rest of his life. The volunteer program also came under his jurisdiction, and from this work he was able to detect the needs for better public relations. If people knew more about the home, he said, they would be willing to do more for it. Father agreed. Out of this discussion came the idea for a publication about the home. But what to call it? The word "home" had an unpleasant connotation in many circles, implying a haven for life's rejects.

"What we actually have here is a town," Father said, "a boys' town." When the first edition of the home's publication came out, it was called the *Boys' Home Journal,* but under Father's new attitude it was changed to the *Boys' Town Times.*

By 1921, over a thousand boys had passed through Father Flanagan's care. The postwar unrest produced countless more boys who needed a home. It was soon evident that Father would have to make another move, but this time merely a bigger house was not the answer. Instead of searching in the city, Father went out into the country. About ten miles west of Omaha was Overlook Farm, ninety-four rolling acres with a couple of barns and chicken coops, a one-car garage and a small house. The place was for sale.

Father had enough to make the down payment, but this did not console the owners. "The rest will come in," Father assured. "Every issue of our newspaper brings in money from the readers."

"We can't do business on that basis, Father," the owners said. "What kind of security can you put up?"

Father answered confidently: "The future of the thousands of boys who will become men here."

So they moved again. Compared to what they had in town, the farm facilities were primitive. The boys had to work hard to make their new home livable, but nobody minded. They were out in the country, they had a place of their own, now they could really be a town. The chicken coops and barns were converted into dormitories for the boys; the small house became part convent for the nuns and part school; Father moved into the garage. Paths were laid, land was cleared for vegetables, a tool shed was turned into a trades school.

And the boys kept coming.

Father had three good friends in town: J. D. Davidson, a prominent Mason; Morris Jacobs, the B'nai B'rith leader; Francis Matthews, active in the Knights of Columbus. Father told them: "I want to get the boys out of the barns and the chicken coops. Winter is coming. We ought to put up a good building for them."

"What sort of building do you have in mind?" Davidson asked.

Father showed them a sketch. It looked like a hotel.

"That'll cost a fortune," Matthews said.

"I suppose," Father conceded. "But I must have it if I'm to raise the boys properly."

The three men waited warily.

"You three are important businessmen," Father said. "You know everybody in town. I was thinking that if a fund drive could be organized . . ."

They raised two hundred and fifteen thousand dollars by forming a battalion of door-knockers who rapped at every house and shop in the city. In March, 1922, the building was in operation—four floors of dormitories, classrooms, offices, staff quarters, a clinic.

And the boys kept coming.

They would always keep coming.

6

The sad truth was that in good times or bad there would always be boys who needed a Father Flanagan, someone who cared for them and who would see that they would have a place to live, food to eat, an education, and that they would be raised to love God and their country. The boys who needed these things most were usually those in the worst trouble—or on the brink of it. Boys nobody wanted. Father Flanagan wanted them, and he pioneered in a training program for them that was to revolutionize America's approach to boys at the crossroads of life. Others were to follow. During Boys Town's early days, Floyd Starr founded the Commonwealth for Boys, near Albion, Michigan. Later, Cal Farley established Boys Ranch, Texas, at Amarillo. In Denver, Judge Ben Lindsey began his Junior Republics and Boys' Brigades. In time, practically every state—in some areas, every county—would have its duplicate of Boys Town, institutions without walls, without bars, without armed guards.

But there would never be anything like Boys Town itself. Its population grew, first two hundred, then five hundred, then upwards of a thousand. Obviously, Father Flanagan could no longer give individual attention to each boy and it became necessary for him to acquire a staff of dedicated men and women who, like himself, believed that working with the boys was not a career but a vocation. To repair the damages of thoughtless parents required a host of well-trained, high-minded, full-hearted adults who were willing to work around the clock, in the classrooms, the craft shops, on the farm, at sports and music, and in the quiet of their quarters late at night with a troubled boy who just wanted to talk. A popular symbol of Boys Town was a sketch of a small boy carrying a smaller and crippled boy on his back and saying: "He ain't heavy, Father. He's my brother." A true incident similar to this had inspired the effective sketch. Among Father's staff—these men and women who were qualified for top salaries in government-supported institutions but who preferred Boys Town with its moderate financial rewards—a popular joke was: "It ain't heavy, Father. It's my pay envelope." But they stayed on because the rewards of being part of Boys Town were far greater than whatever they might bank.

The rewards were intangible. One day a disgruntled counselor admitted to Father Flanagan: "I've been here a year and I can't be sure I've accomplished anything."

Father said: "I've been here thirty years and I can't see what I've accomplished."

No one could tell. This much was sure: of the thousands of youngsters who came to Boys Town to stay, not one subsequently got into trouble with the law. This was accomplishment enough. Moreover, a high percentage of them went on to success in the professions, in business, in the trades, and several of them entered the clergy. It would be safe to say that none of these successes would have occurred had the boys not been given a home, friendship, love and education when they needed it most. The boys themselves, many of them today fathers, even grandfathers, steadfastly assert this.

But from the start the purpose of Boys Town was not to be an assembly line of future pillars of the business and social worlds. Instead, the purpose was to give unfortunate kids a break. Over the years, the ratios have been constant. Only about twenty percent of the boys had criminal records; the rest were on the brink of them because of environmental circumstances. Also, the population remained about evenly divided between Catholics and Protestants, with Jews rarely constituting more than five percent. Chapel services twice a week were made available from the beginning for Christians; Jewish boys were taken into Omaha on Fridays to attend services with Jewish families.

As Boys Town took on more of its own character, the boys became more like citizens of it than residents in an institution. Boys Town was awarded its own post office in 1934, making it a definite municipality. Twice a year the boys elected their own mayor, commissioners and assistant commissioners. The law of the town was simple: Be where you're supposed to be, do what you're supposed to do. They would be good laws for anybody anywhere.

It would be unrealistic to attest that every boy was happy every moment he was at Boys Town. The boys were normal. They got lonely even for the families that did not want them or could not keep them. They sometimes resented authority, even from boys they had elected into office. They grew bored with their lessons and with their chores; they were occasionally restless and rebellious. Some even ran away, wandering back later on their own or telephoning from a distant city for a ticket to Omaha. It was all a part of their wanting to be individuals, and the longer they remained at Boys Town, advancing to their high school graduation, the more they realized that, for them at least, Boys Town was the best place to become precisely that. Graduating, they left, many to go into the Armed Forces, others to go to waiting jobs they were now trained to do, others to go to relatives who could accommodate them now that they were no longer waifs, others to accept scholarships from universities. Importantly, they were not public burdens or social threats, as they might have been had it not been for Boys Town. That was enough for Father Flanagan; any outstanding successes were a bonus.

Gradually Boys Town developed into a multimillion-dollar operation. It had to be maintained; it had to be ready to grow. This necessitated the endless job of finding money, all of which had to come through donations. A direct-mail solicitation was set up; the Boys Town Choir, the Boys Town Band and Boys Town athletic teams went on tours. But without question, the most effective fund raiser was Father Flanagan himself. Now the recognized leader of boys' training in the world, he had access to the offices of wealthy businessmen, he could address clubs, conventions and conferences, he could approach government officials at every level, and invariably he came away with a check. Invariably, too, he came away with at least one boy, presented to him by a destitute widow, a deserted father, a frustrated aunt or uncle, a worried judge.

World War II expanded his horizons. In every foreign country there were new crowds of orphans, new crowds of wayward boys on their own. Governments and private groups asked Father to come and show them how to do what he had done. So he went to Japan and Australia and throughout Europe, leaving a trail of new Boys Towns behind him, not only instructing how they should be operated but injecting the vital spirit of his own Boys Town that would provide stability and permanence.

In 1948, he was called abroad again. Starting in Italy, he and Patrick Norton traveled northward, conferring, lecturing, examining sketches and properties, inspecting, interviewing, meeting boys and getting to know them. May 14, in Berlin, was a particularly busy day. Father wanted to go to bed early because of the heavy schedule facing him the next morning. He retired at nine-thirty. At midnight he awoke and called across the room to Norton, "I have a pain in my chest. Get a doctor right away, Pat."

The doctor recognized the symptoms of a heart attack. Father was taken to a hospital. "I want a priest," he said as he was put to bed.

An Army chaplain was summoned, and after the man had heard Father's confession, Patrick Norton was allowed back into the room. He stood aside as the chaplain gave Father Flanagan the last rites of the Church. Listening, Father kept his eyes open, occasionally brushing his eyebrows thoughtfully. The prayers finished, he said: "Amen." Then he died.

He was taken home, home to the place he had made a home for thousands of boys whose lives had been changed because of him. He was buried in the chapel he had built there. Inscribed on his sarcophagus were the words:

FATHER FLANAGAN — FOUNDER OF BOYS TOWN
LOVER OF CHRIST AND MAN

CHAPTER
FOUR

There Is No Death

THERE were mixed feelings about Mary Baker Eddy. Some people considered her to be an absolute saint, but there were others who felt she was a cantankerous, despotic old woman who was getting rich off a weird idea. Both factions were wrong. If she was controversial it was simply because she refused to have any part of controversy. Her aloofness thus struck some people as a sign of her patience and charity, while others took it to be a clue to her intractability. And her idea, however strange it seemed to many, was clearly grasped by thousands who claimed it had made them better human beings, better Christians, and this was all she wanted. True, she was rich, but this was the natural result of having written a book that rated second as a best seller only to the Bible, and few people knew how much of her income she gave away. It was estimated, for example, that during the fifteen years she lived at Concord, New Hampshire, she put almost half a million dollars into local charities and community projects. An accurate determination of her philanthropy would be impossible: she invariably specified that her contributions be kept secret. It was only after she had passed on that hints of her generosity began to appear, and these from people who broke their silence in an effort to overcome the continuing criticism against her. She would have disliked that. Criticism never bothered her, but a broken promise was a personal wound, and she had suffered more than her share of wounds.

She was born in Bow, New Hampshire, near Concord, on July 16, 1821, the last of the six children of Mark and Abigail Baker. Mark Baker had a small farm about a mile from town; he was also a justice of the peace, he was on the school board and he was a deacon of the Congregational Church. Of moderate means, he was able to send his sons to Dartmouth College. Sternly religious, he saw to it that all his children were firmly trained in what he considered proper fear of the Lord. Here he encountered opposition from his youngest daughter. Even at twelve, Mary could not bring herself to believe in a vengeful God; at that age, she and her father had a heated argument on the subject, which ended when Mark Baker exercised his parental prerogatives and sent Mary to bed.

There were many arguments in the Baker household. All the children had quick minds and strong wills, and no debatable statement by anyone was allowed to pass without some degree of combat. The effects of such tension on Mary were significant. Frail at birth, she developed in childhood a chronic fever and a spinal disturbance that both grew worse during family quarrels. There were times when her pain was unbearable; doctors could do nothing for her. One day after hot words with her father, Mary's temperature soared dangerously. Putting her to bed, Abigail, always the peacemaker, suggested: "Lean on the love of the Lord." Mary began to pray. Immediately her temperature dropped. She never forgot the incident; years later she was able to explain it.

She was a bright child, small, with blue eyes and brown hair. Her self-confidence appeared at an early age. She was four when someone asked her what she was going to do when she grew up. "I am going to write a book," she announced. And she meant it. At five, she could read, and she was so pleased by this that whenever she saw others reading she would appropriate the book or newspaper and say, "Here, let me read to you." Any words she didn't recognize she skipped. Only her mother could endure this habit without annoyance. Abigail was Mary's first teacher; the girl was also tutored privately by Congregational deacons; she attended the public school at Bow and the academy at Tilton. Always her major interest was in writing, in words, and although she eventually developed a style that was both majestic and lucid she never overcame her deficiencies in spelling, grammar and punctuation. Years later, when her works were appearing, she was irritated by complaints from friends about these shortcomings, and she asked her publisher testily: "Why don't you hire a good copy-reader?" One was hired, but he went too far in that he not only corrected her errors but also rewrote her sentences. Infuriated, she put everything back the way she had written it and warned the man that he was a copy-reader, not her collaborator.

Mary's first writings were published in her late teens. Her education finished, she supported herself by teaching younger children, and in her free time she wrote poems and articles that appeared in the New England press. Her work was mostly religious in nature, as was her reading. She read the Bible every day, marking passages that particularly impressed her; the family had a good library of spiritual books, which Mary likewise read thoroughly and marked. She was also keenly interested in politics and the slavery question, and she wrote on these subjects too. She was very serious about her career, so serious that, at twenty-two, she announced to a friend that she had no intentions of marrying until she was established in it. But then George Washington Glover came along.

Mary had met Glover first when she was ten and he was twenty. It was at the wedding of her brother Samuel to his sister Eliza. Glover took Mary on his knee and asked how old she was, and when she told him, he said, "I'll come back in five years and marry you." Startled, she slid off his knee and locked herself in her room.

He was back in five years, this time to attend the wedding of Mary's sister Abigail to Alexander Tilton, a manufacturer, after whom the town of Tilton was named, but this time there was no mention of a marriage. Glover and Samuel Baker were co-owners of a contracting firm in Boston. A year after Abigail's wedding, Glover moved to Charleston, South Carolina, and went into business for himself. One day in 1843, Mary was walking down a street in Tilton when she saw ahead of her a man she thought was her brother George. She caught up with him, slapped him on the back and said, "Oh, you're so dressed up!" It was Glover.

He laughed heartily at her embarrassment, then asked: "Say, didn't I once tell you I was going to marry you?"

"Yes," said Mary, "but I didn't say I would marry you."

"Well, you will," he assured her. And she did, on December 10.

On their honeymoon voyage to Charleston, a severe storm struck that threatened to sink the ship. In their cabin, the newlyweds knelt in prayer when the storm was at its height. Instantly the storm subsided. The amazed captain discussed the odd event with his passengers, and when he learned that the Glovers had been praying for help the very moment the storm ended he insisted that a miracle had occurred.

Life in Charleston was stormy in another way for Mary. She

later disclosed: "The people were kind and hospitable, so long as the question of slavery was not raised." Firmly abolitionist, Mary raised the question repeatedly. Glover owned a few slaves, and Mary was always asking him to free them. He was willing to do so, but he feared that the public reaction to it would harm his business. Under a pseudonym she used for Glover's sake, she wrote a stinging antislavery letter to the Charleston newspaper which stirred scores of other readers to urge the editor to "tell that Yankee to go home."

She was to go home much sooner than she expected, and in sad circumstances. In June, 1844, when she was six months pregnant, she accompanied Glover on a business trip to Wilmington, North Carolina, where a yellow fever epidemic was raging. Glover fell victim to it and died in a few days. He was buried in Wilmington. She found he had left little money and that his only negotiable assets were his slaves. She refused to sell them; instead, she gave them their freedom. And then she went home.

Her baby, a son named after his father, was born on September 12. The delivery was so difficult that Mary almost died. She was months in her recovery. During this period, her mother fell ill. A nurse had to be brought in for the two of them. When, months later, Abigail Baker died, Mary was still too weak to take over the household. Mark Baker was married again a short while afterwards, to Elizabeth Patterson Duncan, a woman with a mind of her own who did not enjoy having another grown woman in the house. It was soon evident that Mary would have to move. She had no money. The only place she could go was to the home of her sister, Abigail Tilton, but there was a problem there, too. Abigail had a small son, and knowing that she would have to be a nurse to Mary most of the time, she did not feel that she could also be a nurse to Mary's baby.

It was therefore necessary for Mary to find someone who would take the boy. She finally placed him with the woman who had been her nurse when the baby was born. He was never to be hers again.

The nine years Mary lived at her sister's house were bleak years, full of loneliness and heartache. The two sisters did not get along well, which added strife to Mary's other pains. Childbirth had left her internally damaged; her back was worse, and she developed a stomach trouble which forced her to live mostly on fruit, graham bread and rye pudding. When she was strong enough, she took in students or substituted at the academy or tried to write, but most of the time she had only enough strength to sit on the porch swing and read. She went to church when she could, and when she was called upon to lead a prayer or make a short speech she effused a spark of vitality that almost made her seem like her old self. Two or three men expressed an interest in her during these years, but none was willing to take her son into his home, so she rejected them all. Then she met Dr. Daniel Patterson, of Franklin, New Hampshire, a dentist and her stepmother's cousin. He was a tall, handsome man and an ardent suitor who, when Mary told him about her son, said he would be delighted to have the boy live with them. They were married in June, 1853, and settled in Franklin. Mary quickly made arrangements to send for young George, then living with his foster parents at New Groton, forty miles away, but Patterson asked her to wait. His practice was bad; he could not afford the boy for awhile.

Mary waited three years. Patterson had hoped that moving out of Abigail Tilton's house would improve Mary's health and attitude, but if the belligerent environment of Abigail's home had contributed to Mary's condition, the lethargic environment of her new home in Franklin had a worse effect. Patterson had few patients, and the patients he had, rarely paid him. He was thus always in debt and often there was nothing to eat. However, poverty did not bother him. He had lots of friends—many of them women—at whose homes he was always welcome, and he never hesitated to go alone. Sometimes he stayed away for a few days. He openly admitted that he had wearied of his invalid wife; Mary naggingly admitted that she had wearied of his slothfulness. She accused him of having deluded her regarding her son, which was apparently true, and she insisted that if the boy could not live with them, then they must move near him. Finally, Patterson agreed to move to New Groton, but more to escape his increasing Franklin creditors than to appease Mary. In New Groton, too, his dental practice failed to provide sufficient income. He took a job supervising a sawmill, but he was so frequently absent on his visits to friends that it scarcely paid.

Then Mary suffered another disappointment. Although she sent gifts to her son on his birthday and at Christmas, wrote him regularly and contributed to his support when she could, she had seen him only occasionally over the years. Living near him now, she was able to visit with him more often, but the visits were not very happy. Young George had developed into a bit of a brat. Not knowing his mother well, he had little affection for her, a sad state he displayed by his sullen resistance to her love for him. His sense of rejection had turned him into a noisy ruffian and arrogant prankster who was blacklisted by all other mothers in the community as an unfit companion for their sons. Mary thought she could mellow him, especially if they could live together, but late in 1856 the boy's foster parents announced they were moving to Minnesota and told George he would have to decide whether he would go with them or remain with his mother. He chose Minnesota. Mary did not see him again for over twenty years, in which time he had not changed much.

Mary's husband did not change much, either. At New Groton he sank deeper into debt each month and each month he spent more time away from home. Mary had to borrow from her sister Abigail, a humiliating experience for her in view of their brittle relationship. Nevertheless, the mortgage holders on her house foreclosed and she was dispossessed. She and Patterson boarded briefly with a family at Rumney Station, then rented a small house. The Civil War broke out; Patterson promptly volunteered and was promptly captured. He wrote Mary that she was not to worry about him because he had "found very gentlemanly officers and friendly gentlemen as fellow prisoners." He said he would like to send her some money, but because his letters had to be left unsealed for censorship he was afraid somebody would steal it; so he didn't send her any. Mary had to move back with Abigail.

Her health now was shattered. In Portland, Maine, there was a man named Phineas Parkhurst Quimby, a former clockmaker who had earned a reputation as a mental healer. Mary wanted to go to him, but Abigail would not hear of it. Abigail considered Quimby to be a quack, and she insisted that Mary go to Dr. Vail's Hydropathic Institute at Hill, New Hampshire, for the water cure. Since Abigail was paying the bills, Mary had to submit to her, but at the Institute she saved as much as she could from the weekly allowance Abigail allotted her and in the autumn of 1862 she took the train to Portland.

There was wide interest in the varieties of mental healing that were being practiced at this time. Some practitioners used hypnosis; others exercised a form of mental suggestion. Quimby had devised a method of diagnosis somewhat like psychoanalysis. A perceptive, quick-minded, strong-willed man with a firm, paternal attitude, he uncovered through interviews whatever negative relationships his patient might have had, attributed illness to them, then counseled along positive, religious lines. As part of his treatment, he massaged the patient's head with wet hands, which he claimed restored the normal flow of an electricity that was essential to good health. In twenty years, he treated over three thousand cases with enough success to make himself a leading figure in his field.

Quimby had little trouble detecting enough negative relationships in Mary's life to account for her run-down condition. She was so weak when she went to see him that she had to be helped up the stairs to his office. But she responded quickly to his treatments, and within a few days she appeared to be in perfect health. Amazed and intrigued, she stayed on in Portland and carefully studied Quimby's methods with the intention of becoming a similar practitioner herself. Her grasp of his techniques, her tremendous faith in them and her superior religious knowledge so impressed Quimby that, perceiving she would surpass him, he made the remarkable comparison to her: "As I see it, I am John and you are Jesus."

Three weeks later, Mary returned to Tilton apparently a cured woman. Abigail was deeply impressed. She sent her son Albert to Quimby to be cured of alcoholism, but Quimby failed with the young man. Mary charged it was Albert who failed: he lacked enough faith. To Abigail, however, the fault was Quimby's and she resumed calling him a quack, triumphantly increasing the accusation as Mary's ailments gradually returned. But Mary's faith in Quimby remained steadfast. Her illness, she said, was returning because she had returned to the environment that had originally sickened her and she was not yet sufficiently spiritually insulated to resist it. That remark put an end to the armistice between the two sisters. Mary went back to Quimby, again with temporary success, but even so she remained in better health than she had been for years. She also began to make trips throughout New England to treat others with Quimby's therapy, which both provided her with a small income and established her as a personality in metaphysical circles.

Patterson wrote occasionally. In one letter, he said that he could be released from his Confederate prison for a ransom of thirty dollars and he asked Mary to get it. She had to borrow it from his brother. Patterson was freed in 1864; with the hope of salvaging their marriage by a fresh start, he and Mary moved out of New Hampshire and settled in Lynn, Massachusetts. But he soon reverted to his old self, and after two years of a losing battle he ran off with a married woman in 1866 and never came back. Mary waited until 1873 to divorce him on grounds of adultery; he died in a Maine poorhouse in 1896. Deserted, Mary was once again on her own.

3

She moved into a boardinghouse where she was permitted to conduct classes for students who wished to become Quimby practitioners, and from their small fees she was able to earn enough to pay her rent. Unfortunately, many of them were more interested in the promise of personal profits from the treatment than in the philosophy behind it, and they rushed out to practice before they were properly equipped. Their subsequent failures reflected not only against themselves but against Mary as well. Quackery gossip began to spread about her, discouraging some of her sincere students to the point where they quit. Co-tenants grew suspicious of her and her landlord was annoyed. Mary soon found it necessary to move frequently to avoid hostility and because, lacking enough students, she often fell behind in her rent.

One evening Mary was returning from a meeting of the Good Templars when she slipped on an icy street and was seriously injured. She was carried to a nearby house and a doctor was summoned. He diagnosed severe internal injuries and gave her a small quantity of narcotics to ease her pain. The next day she was moved to her own room. Her pain was intense and she required more narcotics. The next night, to distract her mind from her pain, she reached for her Bible and opened to Matthew and began to read. In the ninth chapter, she read how Christ had cured a palsied man. She had read this before, but now she seemed to be reading it for the first time.

Christ had first told the sick man that his sins were forgiven, and when this stirred the watching crowd to call Christ a blasphemer, Christ then displayed His power to do all things by telling the man to get up and walk, which he did. Meditating on this, a question occurred to Mary. Was there a link between sin and sickness? To Mary, God was the All Good, the Perfect, the Creator whose Mind was the source of all things that existed; and now she wondered if being the All Good and the Perfect, God could create anything that was imperfect, less good, than Himself. She concluded that He could not. From this she deduced that if God could create only perfections, then only perfections existed, only perfections were realities. Imperfections like sickness, failure, hardships, ugliness, even sin, were negative qualities that could not have their source in God. He had not created them, therefore they did not exist. Thus they were unrealities. The Biblical passage she had just read she now interpreted as evidence of how the dynamic perfection of Christ could wipe the unrealities of sin and sickness from the mind of a man who misguidedly thought he suffered from both.

If Christ could do that once, Mary decided, He could do it again. She replaced her Bible on her night table, closed her eyes and prayed for attunement to Christ's perfection. Then she swept back her bedcovers, got up and walked around the room without an ache in her body.

As wondrous as the event was, the logic that led to it had occurred to Mary in a flash, like a divine revelation, and it turned out to be a concept that even she could not fully grasp without much more knowledge and much more spiritual development. It was therefore understandable that, at first, she occasionally fell short of the lofty ideals that had occurred to her so suddenly, so vividly. Her friends, astounded by her instantaneous recovery, nevertheless urged her to sue the city, and she agreed to do so. Within a couple of weeks her physical discomfort recurred. As the suit dragged on, Mary devoted most of her time searching the Bible for further substantiation of her new idea, and as she studied she became aware that her basis for suing the city, being contrary to the All Good Principle of God, was unreal. She dropped the suit.

The knowledge and development Mary needed were so gigantic in scope that they were slow in coming. During the first three years, she continued to teach her students, but as her own philosophy grew clearer to her she superseded Quimby's ideas with her own. For example, she instructed the students to stop massaging their patients' heads. In giving treatments, she restored more and more to her own methods. With Quimby, religion was a factor in treatment; with Mary, it was the only factor. One had to have complete faith in God, to live above all for Him, to be attuned wholly to Him, or the method wouldn't work. The major part of Mary's concept was to bring about precisely that absoluteness.

It was more than a concept; it was a science. The very name for it—Christian Science—had been given to Mary in a dream, she subsequently disclosed. And it was scientific, as neat as arithmetic. The cause could be identified and so could the effect; a believer had only to follow the rules to get the results. Mary was getting most impressive results. She had effected the cure of a man run over by a heavy wagon, she restored life to a cripple's lifeless arms, she freed a teen-age girl of tuberculosis. The power to do these things, she assured, were not reserved for her but could be obtained by anyone who believed.

In 1870, at the age of forty-nine, Mary went to work to fulfill the prediction she had made when she was four: she began to write a book. She was to spend five years at it, writing and rewriting, improving and elucidating, learning more about the science of mind as she wrote about it. They were difficult years, years marked by poverty and hardship that would have discouraged anyone who was not purposely unmindful of difficulty. The book, *Science and Health,* was finished in 1875, and then came the chore of finding a publisher. For weeks she walked the streets of Boston, calling on one publisher after the other, but all refused her because they felt there would be no profit in the book. Finally W. F. Brown & Company offered to print it for her for fifteen hundred dollars. Realizing that this was her only alternative, she borrowed the money from friends, and before the book was published the bill rose to over two thousand.

The first edition of *Science and Health* appeared on October 30, 1875. It was an immediate success—not so much, oddly enough, because of its content as by the attention it earned from the violent criticisms flung at it by clergymen and reviewers.

Curious, people bought it. Reading it, many of them came to believe.

Mary suspected that the bitter complaints against Christian Science might be justified because perhaps she had not explained herself clearly enough. Thus the first edition was just off the presses when she was making corrections for the second. For the remainder of her life, Mary was never completely satisfied with the book, even when its popularity was surpassed only by the Bible, and out of this urge for perfection she made extensive changes in each of the fifty editions that were published under her direction.

The critics remained vicious. In addition to damning her personally with every printable calumny, they rejected her Science as being even more unrealistic than she claimed evils to be. Distressed friends again urged her to sue, but she refused. She said, "A Christian Scientist is a humanitarian; he is benevolent, forgiving, long-suffering, and seeks to overcome evil with good."

The good she did was in the people she helped and those she helped to help themselves and to help others. With her first royalties, Mary fulfilled an old ambition: she bought her own house, in Lynn, and there soon began a steady parade of her readers who came to seek her aid and to share her Science. Among those who came was Asa Gilbert Eddy, a Boston sewing-machine salesman who was almost crippled with disease. After two consultations he was cured, and he became both an avid follower of Christian Science and its first qualified practitioner. His devotion to Mary was soon enhanced by love; they were married on New Year's Day, 1877.

Mary Baker Eddy had never intended to start a new religious sect. She believed that Christian Science had a place in the existing denominations, but the violent reactions to it by clergymen easily convinced her that this would never happen. Thus, in 1879, she established the Church of Christ, Scientist, and received a Massachusetts charter for it. The first services were held at Hawthorne Hall in Boston. Services included hymns, silent prayer and a sermon by Mary. These devotions were held on Sundays; on Wednesdays a testimony service was held at which members of the congregation related their personal experiences with Christian Science, both as witnesses and as guides to others. Scientists were required to abstain from tobacco, liquor, drugs and medicines; they had also to rid themselves of any attitudes, habits or tendencies that fell under the broad category of sin. Guidance along these lines was an important part of the Wednesday sessions.

Once established in Boston, Science grew rapidly. Each year it was necessary to find a bigger hall for the meetings. Moreover, branch churches were opening across the country. To maintain contact with them, Mary founded the Christian Science Publishing Society, and over the years she brought out the *Christian Science Journal,* and *Christian Science Quarterly,* the *Christian Science Sentinel* and the *Herald of Christian Science,* all of which she personally edited. She also wrote the *Christian Science Manual,* the book of worship, and meanwhile continued to revise *Science and Health,* adding to it *A Key to the Scriptures.*

She was the sole authority of the Church. Those who accepted Christian Science believed that Mary—Mother Eddy, as they called her—was God-guided, so they never questioned her. Even after her passing, the rules of Christian Science remained as she had written them—complete, practical and unchangeable in the minds of believers. To be sure, not all the believers were steadfast. Some resented her supreme authority and balked at it. Others had merely come to study with her and had then gone elsewhere to become her imitators. There was even an effort to oust her on the grounds that old age had made her incompetent: an effort that advanced into court action, but the committee that was delegated to determine her mental faculties in an interview went away convinced that her mind was keener than theirs combined. Such instances, however, resulted in bad publicity and formed in the public mind the image that she was an intransigent dictator. The wealth that accrued from her book sales gave rise to rumors that she was diverting church funds to her own account. Quite the reverse was true. When the Mother Church was built in Boston in 1892, Mary made the biggest and quietest donation for its construction.

As before, friends tried to protect her reputation by offering to testify for her in any legal action she would take, but, as before, she refused. An author wrote a book about her victory over the attempt to oust her from church leadership and sent her an advance copy. Despite the fact that it was a rare sample of favorable public notice for her, she wrote the man that she did not want to have the book released, adding:

> You will render me a statement of all expenses to which you have been put. Make liberal allowances for those who have aided you in the work. Put a value upon your own time and services while engaged on it, and when you have done this, double the value you have placed on your own work and double it again and then send me the bill.

The bill came to several thousand dollars, and she paid it rather than rake the ashes of a battle she had won and then put out of her mind.

On another occasion, after she had relinquished editorship of her magazines in order to devote more time to her own writing, she saw that her devoted successors were filling pages with praise of her. She sent off a memo to the staff:

> FIRST. Let my works and not my words praise me if I am worthy of praise.
>
> SECOND. I always detested flattery.
>
> THIRD. What is being said and written in such profusion of reference to—and praise of—me is not Christian Science and I hereby forbid its publication in the *Journal.*
>
> Practically, Christian Science is manifested by moderation, meekness and love.

4

During the years the Church was taking on its own character, Mary Baker Eddy faced three challenges to her own practice of Science. One was the death of her husband Asa in 1882, after five years of marriage. He had been the perfect mate, loving her as his wife and as the leader of his church. No one had ever brought her so much happiness. Suddenly she was deprived of him. As a Christian Scientist, she could mourn his loss but not his death, for Science maintained there was no death, merely a passing on to the rewards of the faith. Now that death had struck close to her, she had to face the experience of applying Science to it for the first time, and friends who knew how deeply she felt his loss were reassured when she told them: "Death is swallowed up in victory."

The second challenge came from her sister Abigail. Mary was the only member of the family not mentioned in Abigail's will. Certainly Mary was not disturbed about the money, but the affront was clearly a final thrust that Mary might well have resented. She said, however, "My oldest sister dearly loved me, but I wounded her pride when I adopted Christian Science, and to a Baker that was a sorry offense."

Mary's son George was the third challenge. When she began

to accumulate a little money, she located him in the West and brought him and his family to Boston, hoping that now she could make up to him for all the disappointments she felt she had caused him in the past because of her poverty and problems. He was only too willing to give her the chance. He had gone into mine prospecting, unsuccessfully, and now he had a mother who was rich enough to underwrite further ventures. At first she did; but when she saw he continued to fail, she stopped and he went home. He returned eight years later, in 1887, again with big plans. Again Mary finally had to recognize there was no filial sentiment in him for her, and she asked him to leave. She continued to send him money occasionally and in her will she left him a hundred and twenty-five thousand dollars, thus content to be a mother to her son in the only way he wished.

At the time of the Mother Church dedication, Mary announced her retirement. She was seventy-one years old, but retirement did not signify abandonment. She appointed a five-man board to supervise the Church for her, and although she warned them in stern language never to consult her but to trust their own judgments, she nevertheless assured them they would be hearing from her from time to time.

She bought the Pleasant View estate near Concord and settled down to her writing. For the next fifteen years, her output was phenomenal. Up between five and six every morning, she first did the daily Bible reading and meditation required of all Scientists. After breakfast, she spent the morning at her mail, a constantly growing chore that kept her and several secretaries busy. She lunched with her staff, then received visitors for an hour, and the rest of the day she gave to her writing. Revised editions of *Science and Health* and the *Manual* continued to appear, and Mary was still the major contributor to Science magazines. Evenings were devoted to reading. Withdrawn from the world, she managed to keep abreast of it by reading books and periodicals on all subjects from around the world. She urged all Scientists to make themselves informed on world affairs and to contribute to peace and social welfare however they could.

Because Science did not have a clergy nor engage in the usual parish activities in the fields of charity or community service, outsiders sometimes accused Scientists of lacking a social consciousness. The reverse was true, and if it seemed inconspicuous, this was because Mary had instructed that Scientists should practice charity and service on a quiet, individual basis, just as they practiced their religion. Mary also decried religious persecution against anyone. She once wrote: "I love the prosperity of Zion, be it promoted by Catholic, by Protestant or by Christian Scientist. I would no more quarrel with a man because of his religion than I would because of his art." Such tolerance at the turn of the century, when there were bursts of religious persecution in practically every country against one denomination or another, was typical of Mary Baker Eddy and, because of her, typical of Christian Science.

She grew older, but she did not seem to age. Her hair turned white, her militant manner mellowed somewhat, and she became inclined to reminisce, but there were no other signs of her years. Instead of diminishing her work schedule, she let it increase to any extent it required. In 1908, at eighty-seven, she announced that she needed a bigger house and a bigger staff, both of which she wanted closer to Boston. On January 26, she and her entourage boarded a private car and went by train from Concord to Chestnut Hill, Massachusetts; then by carriages to the new house. On arriving, Mary saw that the lawn was crowded with reporters and photographers who clamorously blocked her way.

She turned to a young man at her side and asked, "John, can you get me into my house?"

"I sure can," he said. And he swept her up into his arms, lunged through the crowd into the house and slammed the door behind him. The peals of her gay laughter reached the astonished newspapermen outside.

Although she occasionally granted interviews, Mary Baker Eddy did not hold newspapermen in particularly high regard. She had once observed in the *Christian Science Journal*:

> Looking over the newspapers of the day, one naturally reflects that it is dangerous to live, so loaded with disease seems the very air. These descriptions carry fears to many minds, to be depicted in some future time upon the body. A periodical of our own will counteract to some extent this public nuisance, for through our paper, at the price at which we shall issue it, we shall be able to reach many homes with healing, purifying thought.

Now the time had come to start such a paper. On August 8, 1908, she wrote her publishing staff in her familiar crisp way of giving orders:

> It is my request that you start a daily newspaper at once, and call it the *Christian Science Monitor*. Let there be no delay. The cause demands that it be issued now. You may consult with the Board of Directors; I have notified them of my intention.

The first issue appeared on November 25, just three months after Mary had decided on it, and it quickly developed into the country's only national newspaper. Its integrity, its high standards, its accuracy and the caliber of its staff eventually made it one of the most respected and widely read newspapers of the world.

Respect and wide popularity were Mary's, too. The concept of science of mind that had occurred to her on a winter night in Lynn had lifted her to world prominence. The Christian Scientist Association, which had held its first meeting in her Lynn home, spread to twelve hundred churches and societies in her own time. No census of Scientist membership was ever taken, because Mary was not interested in such statistics. She cared only that those who adhered to the principle should attain what she assured it offered: health, happiness, love, success, constructive purpose. Her own life, since its turning point that wintry night in Lynn, was proof of this, as was the spiritual vitality of the church she founded, a vitality that permeated every corner of the nation with its stimulating influence of hope and vigor.

On December 1, 1910, as she did daily for years, Mary went out for her afternoon carriage ride. As usual, a cluster of her devotees were at the gateway to wave to her as she departed and returned. Back in her study, she asked for a pad and pencil.

She wrote the words: *God is my life.*

They were the last words she was to write.

The next day she had noticeably failed, and the following day she was too weak to leave her bed. Her staff knew that she would not last much longer. It was shortly before midnight on December 3, as a few close friends gathered at her bedside, that Mary Baker Eddy went peacefully to her final victory.

CHAPTER

FIVE

The Man Who Believed in One

HE was a serious-minded man, so much so that people often said he utterly lacked a sense of humor. William Ellery Channing was aware of this shortcoming in himself, but he felt helpless to do anything about it. In his pulpit, he could enthrall his large congregation for two hours with his masterful control and clarity, but in his parlor he could be a bore, sinking into his own thoughts, so busy analyzing ideas aloud that he paid no attention to people. The simple fact was that Channing had never learned how to *hold* a conversation; he always *preached* one, and usually it was more for his own benefit, to crystallize his own convictions, than for his visitor's. One visitor, on leaving Channing's house, declared: "I have never met anyone to whom it was so interesting to listen and so hard to talk when my turn came." Channing admitted of himself: "I am strong before the multitude but weak before the individual." And yet it was the individual that meant most to Channing. Destined to become the spokesman for American Unitarianism, he devoted most of his life to defending the individuality of God. But the individuality of each human being was equally important to him, and he defended it with equal sincerity.

Channing was raised in an era when individuality was making its strongest impressions on the shape of the world. His grandfather had been a signer of the Declaration of Independence and a member of the first Congress. When Channing was ten, his father, a successful Rhode Island lawyer, took him to the state convention that ratified the Constitution. He was thus reared in an atmosphere that clamored for the freedom of man and his mind, an atmosphere that remained Channing's as long as he lived.

Channing himself, however, was not a clamorous individual. The third child and second son in a family of seven youngsters, he was meek and reserved from boyhood. Living as the family did at the Newport seaside, it was natural that the children should want to swim. But their mother was against it. Even so, she permitted them to go through the swimming motion on the kitchen table so that they would know the mechanics of it if they should ever be on a boat that sank. Channing was the only youngster of the family who obediently restricted his practice to that; the others tried it out in the water.

Instead of swimming, he strolled alone down the beaches and across the fields. On one such walk he came upon a nest of birds and fed them some crumbs he had in his pocket. He returned to the nest for several days, observing the growth of the chicks as he fed them. Then one day he found that someone had killed the chicks and cut them up. He wept his heart out and he never forgot the experience. Later he said it was a major reason for his abhorrence of violence of all kinds, a conviction that was to turn friends against him at times when violence seemed the only answer.

He was his father's favorite. As such, the two were often together and the boy was thus exposed to adult thinking at a period when adult thoughts were most impressive. Allowed to remain at the dinner table with guests when the other children were dismissed, young Channing heard men like Ezra Stiles, the family's Congregationalist minister and future president of Yale University, carry on at length against political and religious tyranny. He heard Dr. Samuel Hopkins, the fiery theologian, volubly denounce slavery. He heard his uncle, Henry Channing, leading minister at New London, hint that maybe Jesus Christ was not divine. Listening, he watched his father and observed the man's quiet acceptance. So the boy accepted quietly, too.

One day when Channing was still quite young, his father took him to a tent revival at which a preacher ranted violently about sin, hell and the depravity of man. The slightest pleasure meant doom, the preacher insisted. Channing was stunned by the vehemence. He searched his father's face for some sign to assure him that the preacher was exaggerating, but the elder Channing merely listened in calm attention. As they left, the boy heard his father comment to a friend: "Sound doctrine." Dazed, the boy took his place beside his father for the carriage ride home, and all the way he hoped the man would indicate that neither of them had to believe what they had heard. Although Channing knew that his father was now a district attorney, he did not realize that the man, as such, was frequently called upon to attend public events, which a tent revival was, where his presence need not necessarily indicate personal approval. It was not until they were almost home that the elder Channing began to whistle a popular tune, a lighthearted display of merriment the preacher would certainly have denounced, and from this the boy took heart. At home, Channing knew, his father would discuss the sermon if he liked it, as he customarily did with other sermons. But at home the man said nothing, and out of the understanding that had grown between the father and son this was enough to convince young Channing that what the preacher had said was not true. By his silence, the elder Channing had rejected it; in his silence, so did the boy.

A habit grew out of this incident, the habit of rejection by silence, and although it might have been enough to content a Channing there were to be others who demanded something more explicit and who considered the Channing silence to be indifference or weakness, which it never was. Nevertheless, the habit was to backfire many times before Channing learned to overcome it.

Lucy Channing was frequently ill. For quiet in the house, the children were sent to school early. Thus young Channing was being carried to day schools before he could walk. At six, he was entered in a Newport boarding school, and at ten he was ready for the tutoring that would prepare him for college. His tutor was his Uncle Henry, into whose home he moved for three years. In addition to his regular studies, Channing often listened to his uncle discuss his opinions on the trinitarian-versus-unitarian nature of God, a subject that had intrigued thinking men since the first Christian years and that was now a matter of serious debate among the Congregationalist clergymen of New England. The time was yet to come when Channing would be embroiled in it.

2

The three years at New London passed quickly. In 1793, when Channing was about to become fourteen years old, he passed his entrance examinations for Harvard College. That summer, his father died. The man had left little money, and it seemed at first as though the education of the children would have to be stopped. But Lucy Channing made up her mind against this. Francis, the oldest child, was about to finish his law studies; he would soon have an income and could thus contribute to the support of the family while the others passed through school. Meanwhile, Lucy retrenched her household operations as severely as possible, accepting financial aid from her relatives on only the most dire occasions. When fall came, Channing was on his way to Harvard.

He lived off-campus in Cambridge, at the home of another uncle, Chief Justice Francis Dana of the Massachusetts supreme court. Here again he had the good fortune of being able to listen to the finest minds of the era at dinner conversations. Despite his age, his uncles, like his father, sensed that the boy had the intellectual capacity to cope with the ideas put forth by the political and religious leaders who frequented the Dana home. If Channing's youth kept him from contributing to the conversations, his maturity equipped him to profit from them.

He profited, too, from the intensive reading required in the classical course he took at Harvard. Probing the minds of philosophers from the ancient Greeks to the contemporary British was high adventure for him, and he read much more than he had to. Throughout his reading he came upon a theme that was already his personal conviction: man is perfectible, society improves itself as a moral factor at a rate reflecting its technological development, the worthiest display of religion is in service to others. Another consistent theme that impressed him was the high regard for the individual intellect. Richard Price, Channing's favorite British scholar, had put it this way: "It is undeniable that many of our ideas are derived from the 'intuition' of the truth—or the discernment of the natures of things by the understanding. This therefore may be the source of our moral ideas." The thought appealed to Channing. It provided hope and optimism for the future of man, something vastly different from the dismal doctrine of the total depravity of mankind to which Calvinistic New England had clung for so long.

As the Harvard years passed, Channing felt himself increasingly drawn to the ministry. Two things held him back. First, ministers were notoriously badly paid; Channing thought he ought not enter a profession that would prevent him from contributing his share to the family's support. Second, he was still unsure of his own religious convictions and considered it of primary importance to make up his mind on doctrinal matters before presumptuously telling others what they ought to believe.

His tendencies, however, were clear to his friends, who often referred to him as "the little minister." And he was little. Always small and frail, a change in the weather or the slightest exertion were enough to send him to bed ill. His condition kept him off the Harvard playing fields and might have sent him through college a complete nonentity had he not possessed a neat, articulate mind which he expressed with a clarity, both in writing and in speeches, that attracted a great deal of attention. He could be a most persuasive debater, on a platform or at a bull session, and his writings, both for class and the school publications, were masterpieces of logic and sagacity. His only problem, his friends felt, was that he retreated too readily in the face of stern opposition. Though true, this was not weakness: it was evidence of his deep-rooted conviction that every man had a right to his own interpretations of any proposition and should not be pressured into submission even when stubbornness was his only defense. As admirable as the attitude was, it frequently annoyed Channing's friends who wanted him to be more aggressive. Even so, his mastery of words was enough for his classmates to elect him to give the principal address on graduation day.

Now he had to decide what to do with himself. The decision was made for him. David Randolph, United States Marshal for

Virginia, was vacationing at Newport that summer and, impressed by the bright youngster who had finished college at eighteen, he invited Channing to return to Richmond with him as tutor for his children. The invitation was attractive: it provided an income, a new way of life and plenty of time for private study. Channing accepted. He agreed to stay with the Randolphs for three years.

He stayed only a year and a half. The heavy schedule of his private studies so absorbed him that he often went without meals and without sleep, a physical strain he could not endure without falling more frequently ill than before. Also, although he lived in luxury he also lived in an atmosphere so foreign to his Yankee upbringing that he was always uneasy. The Channing family had liberated its slaves immediately after the Revolutionary War and those who remained did so on small salaries out of love and loyalty. In Virginia, the Randolphs still had slaves, many of them, and when Channing visited their squalid quarters he was sickened and saddened, but his Yankee reserve prevented him from speaking out and so he suffered in silence. And there was the matter of politics. As a New Englander, Channing was a pro-British Federalist, and now he was living among pro-French Jeffersonian states-righters. As the occasion for American aid to the French revolutionists grew more imminent, Channing found he could not endure the Randolph family's approving table talk, so he missed more meals than usual, refusing even to ask to have his food brought to his room.

And there was the matter of religion. Through his studies, Channing gradually perceived that his concept of God was unitarian, that the orthodox idea of the trinity Godhead—of the Father, the Son and the Holy Ghost, consubstantial, coequal, co-existing through all time—was unacceptable to him intellectually. In the writings of British philosophers he found support for his convictions; what he needed now was a happier atmosphere in which to make his own definite conclusions.

Actually, the controversy over the trinitarianism of God was very old. In the fourth century, Arius, a Libyan theologian, put forth the idea that the Father had created the Son as a being apart and subordinate to Him and assigned the Son to the messianic mission. Another idea prevalent at the same time was Adoptionism, which claimed that Jesus Christ was a human creature, born of a virgin, who upon baptism was adopted by the Father and endowed with divine graces for the messianic purpose. In either case, the Father—the Creator—was a being unto Himself, separate from and above all others. The unitarianism of Channing's time differed considerably and was a modification of ideas proposed by Faustus Socinus (1539-1604), an Italian lawyer who had turned to religion.

Socinianism viewed Jesus Christ as a human being, born of Joseph and Mary, who became a demigod and was entrusted with government of the world as a reward for His crucifixion. The messianic purpose, according to Socinus, was not redemptive but restorative: Christ had been chosen to show the world the way back to God. To know God it was necessary to know Christ, and man got to know Christ through the Gospels. Socinus rejected Original Sin, thus the inherited guilt for it, and baptism became simply an overt act by which mature people declared their affiliation with Christianity. The Lord's Supper was considered only commemorative. The Holy Ghost was not a being but a divine power in the hearts of men. Socinus said that a good Christian demonstrated his faith by prayer, by thanksgiving and joy, by renouncing the world, by enduring hardships with patience and charity, by obeying the laws of the land, by not accumulating more wealth than he needed for basic comfort and by giving his surplus to the poor.

Socinus had been a Roman Catholic, but the Church denounced his new ideas as heretical and he left Italy. In Central Europe, he was persecuted by both Lutherans and Calvinists; it was in Poland and Transylvania that he received the protection of a few princes and was able to circulate his concepts freely. In the seventeenth century, Socinianism spread to England. It was banned by the Church of England by the Act of Conformity of 1662, then restored by the Act of Tolerance of 1689. Within fifty years, it crossed the Atlantic to the colonies where it won favor among many of the minister-professors at Harvard College. By the time of the American Revolution, a score of Harvard graduates in New England pulpits were preaching a unitarianism that was a blend of Socinianism and Arianism, depending on the individual's personal concept of Jesus Christ.

And in that was a vital factor: the individual's concept. In its hundred years of formulation, Anglo-American unitarianism appealed primarily to intellectuals who felt they had the ability to think for themselves, and companion to this was the conviction that others had the right to think for themselves. Perhaps more important, then, than unitarianism itself was the tolerance that grew out of it. Unitarians did not mind that trinitarians opposed them and they were not disturbed by the variance of opinions within unitarianism itself: it was important only that each man was doing his own thinking. There had not been much such tolerance in the history of Christianity in any of its forms; there had been none of it in the colonies. Thus although unitarianism was not making significant inroads into orthodoxy in the prerevolutionary period, the tolerance unitarians practiced and asked of others most certainly had a deep influence upon the national mind that was about to produce the Declaration of Independence and the United States Constitution, two documents that emphasized the rights of the individual more than any other in the world.

By breeding, education and conviction, Channing had practiced tolerance all his life. It was this that first attracted him to unitarianism; his own unitarian convictions were still to take shape.

He left Virginia in July, 1800, and returned to Newport. His Spartan months at Richmond had aged him; only twenty, he already looked old. His mother was worried about him. She stuffed him with food and forced him to rest and told him not to think about anything, but he was uneasy because now he was without an income and he had no idea what he was going to do with himself. Still in the back of his mind was the desire to enter the clergy, and yet he wanted to wait awhile before making a definite move. To occupy himself, he began to tutor. He also read a great deal, more than he had in Virginia, and he carried on a heavy correspondence on religious matters, sometimes with men he had not met but whose ideas, either like his or sternly opposed, intrigued him. The letters got him talked about in intellectual circles; men who had never set eyes on him agreed that he showed promise and should be helped. To his great surprise and joy, he received, in December, 1801, an appointment as regent at Harvard. The appointment offered a title, a small salary and the opportunity to study, and all he had to do in return was serve as a dormitory master a few hours a week. He was back at Harvard in January, his mind made up: he would prepare for the ministry.

He was already considerably prepared: having read so much, there was not much left for him to learn. Also, he was known. Boston and Cambridge ministers were soon inviting him to speak in their churches. He spoke mostly about tolerance and benevolence, his two pet ideas for effective living, and when he touched on doctrinal matters he proposed that Jesus Christ was an eternally existent being, subordinate to the Creator, sent to earth to establish that "God is love, for the Gospel is an exhibition of love, and its end is to transform men into love." Thus he proffered a blend of Arianism, Socinianism and Unitarianism. In time, his sermons and writings were to take on more of an Adoptionist tone, as Unitarianism generally did, but he never privately put aside the belief that Jesus Christ was an eternal being.

He was successful from the start. His mastery over words and ideas, the clarity of his presentations and his carefully modulated voice attracted large audiences. Late in 1802, the Cambridge Ministerial Association made him a licensed preacher. Two important churches immediately invited him to take over their pulpits. Uncertain whether he had the physical stamina for the demands of a pastorate, he refused both at first, then accepted the smaller church, the Federal Street Society. The position paid twenty-five dollars a week, plus a house and firewood, which Channing considered a satisfactory circumstance for a man his age. In June, 1803, he was ordained a Congregational minister and thus took his first solid step toward becoming one of the best-known men of his time.

3

He had an agreement with his older brother, Francis. After their father's death they had pledged that neither of them would marry for ten years in order to remain breadwinners for the rest of the family. Now Channing had a good salary and a house. He invited his mother and the younger children to move in with him, he freed Francis from the agreement, and then introduced him to a friend's daughter, whom Francis promptly proceeded to marry.

Channing himself had no time to think of marriage. His pastorate kept him busy, and in addition to that he was a much-sought-after writer and critic for various Boston reviews. Being pro-British, Channing was anti-French, but instead of displaying this attitude by ignoring France he became an expert in French affairs, particularly the life of Napoleon Bonaparte, and was probably the Emperor's most eloquent critic outside France. Channing also wrote extensively on religious subjects, and one aspect of this—unitarianism—was to occupy him most of his life.

New England Congregationalism had been an outgrowth of the liberal wing of austere Calvinism, and it was natural that in Congregationalism there should evolve a conservative and liberal wing. The liberal wing of Congregationalism provided the seeds of New England Unitarianism. Harvard College, educating most of the New England clergy, figured strongly in the evolution: the more liberal the professors the more liberal the students. But what was considered liberal by one generation was sometimes considered outright radical by a preceding generation, so there was often the complaint among older ministers that Harvard was going too far. The unitarian sympathies of many Harvard professors while Channing was there were already being widely criticized by conservative Congregationalists. By the time Channing settled at the Federal Street church, the conservatives were openly accusing that Harvard was turning out a pack of heretics. Controversy was inevitable.

Channing loathed controversy. But as he became an increasingly convinced unitarian, he realized he could not avoid it. He fought on his own battlefields—in the pulpit and in his writings. In both, however, he was his usual benign self, brilliant, precise, persuasive, but always with his punches pulled. Nobody could present the unitarian cause better than he, but his personal distaste for the group-action involved in causes prevented him from spearheading it. A natural debater he did not try to win his point by destroying his opponent but rather by presenting the positive side of his own position. When the issue became a matter of pulpit combat among the Boston clergy on either side of it, Channing concentrated instead on what he defined as the human attributes of Jesus Christ that he felt people could and should emulate. Other unitarian ministers, on the other hand, openly added to the controversy by rebutting the conservatives. The time came when the conservatives announced that, if there was no other solution, the unitarians would be excommunicated from the church. The implied violence saddened Channing. He wrote a friend:

> Error of opinion is an evil too trifling to be named in comparison with this proud, censorious, overbearing temper which says to a large body of Christians, "Stand off, we are holier than you."

An important victory for unitarianism, both in essence and in fact, occurred in 1805 when the liberals at Harvard succeeded in electing to the influential Hollis Professorship of Divinity an aggressive unitarian, Henry Ware, Sr. Provoked by their defeat, the conservatives decided to resort to excommunications, but in doing so they failed to reckon with the possibility that the liberal trend among the laity might be even stronger than among the young clergy. A test case was arranged, and because of the congregational structure of the church it backfired. The morning one conservative minister announced to his flock that those holding unitarian views must leave the building and never return, he discovered he was evicting the majority of his people. They reminded him that Congregationalism put supervision of the church in their hands, not his, and that they had no intentions of being barred from a house of worship they had paid to have built. The case went to court. The minister argued that since the unitarians had discarded a basic Christian tenet, they had actually excommunicated themselves and all that remained for them was to depart. The unitarians replied that Congregationalism did not restrict its members to any specific creed, and that since it was the trinitarians who were insisting on a separation of the two groups they should be the ones to go. The court upheld the unitarians; the minister was dismissed from his post; the conservative laymen had a choice of adopting unitarianism or surrendering all claim to the church building. Thereby an important precedent was set. In time, twelve of the fourteen Congregational Churches in Boston were to turn to unitarianism, spiritually and actually. Before the conflict ended, ninety-six Massachusetts churches were thus separated from the Congregational organization. But before this could come about, unitarianism needed a leader.

He was Channing, certainly, but Channing was not certain he wanted to be the leader. He continued to deplore the conflict, the rising bitterness, the spreading unrest. "There is," he once observed, "no moral worth in being swept away by a crowd, even towards the best objects." He could not understand why unitarians and trinitarians refused to worship side by side. If, as Christianity required, they were all trying to emulate Jesus Christ, why should they be so un-Christian toward each other on a matter that had nothing to do with personal virtue and piety? But he refused to become involved.

Despite his elusiveness, Channing's popularity increased. In 1809, it was necessary to build a larger church on Federal Street to accommodate the growing congregation. His pamphlets and his published sermons were widely purchased, bringing him additional stature and income. He took on further national importance as spokesman for the New England opposition to the War of 1812, which again put America on the side of France against England, but when the New England states met at Hartford to consider secession from the Union he was strong against it. As with the church conflict, he believed that the differences between men should be settled by compromise, not by separation.

In 1814, he married Ruth Gibbs, a cousin, whose personal income eased his own financial concerns. Ruth owned a house at Oakland, where Channing now went whenever he wanted to write or rest. Also, he was able now to take a cut in salary to hire an assistant at the Federal Street church, thus acquiring more free time to spend at Oakland. He wrote increasingly on unitarianism, not so much to support its doctrine as to encourage its tolerance, but the more he wrote the clearer the doctrine became to him. Friends who discussed it with him urged him to speak out for unitarianism once and for all, to spell out its premises so that everyone, unitarians themselves, would know what the doctrine proposed. Channing was reluctant for one reason: he was afraid that so specific a definition might change unitarianism into Unitarianism, that what was now considered unorthodox might spawn its own orthodoxy, that to those who upheld it doctrine might become dogma, that a conviction might evolve into a church with its own rules, restrictions and restraints, and he wanted no part of that.

In 1819, however, he felt that the time had come for a specific definition, and he chose to declare it in the speech he had been invited to give at the ordination of Jared Sparks, a Harvard graduate who had been offered the pulpit of a Baltimore church. The mere fact that Channing was willing to travel all the way to Baltimore indicated to other leading unitarians that he intended to say or do something important, so they all went to Baltimore ahead of him. Thus, on Sunday, April 25, when Channing rose to give his speech, he looked down on the faces of what might have been called the hierarchy of unitarianism, could there be such a thing. He called the speech "Unitarian Christianity," and it was the most forceful, forthright speech on the subject he had ever given. For some, it contained a bit too much Arianism, but Channing firmly explained that this was his conviction and no one else need accept it. "The ultimate reliance of a human being," he insisted, "is and must be on his own mind."

The Baltimore speech lasted an hour and a half, and when it was ended the Unitarian Church was begun. The decisive move to Unitarianism, initiated by the court case of 1805, now swept the country, particularly New England. Even Plymouth Church, founded by the Pilgrims in 1620, went Unitarian. Had Channing not resisted efforts to put him at the head of the movement, the church might have developed an orthodox structure similar to other churches, but he insisted on the congregational type of government: each church independent, with no minister, no member, nor bound by any creed. He defined the basis of Unitarianism this way:

> We believe in the moral perfection of God. We consider no part of theology so important as that which treats of God's moral character. We believe that His almighty power is entirely submitted to His perception of rectitude, and this is the ground of our piety. It is not because His will is irresistible but because His will is the perfection of virtue that we pay Him allegiance. . . .
>
> We believe that all [human] virtue has its foundation in the moral nature of man, that is, in conscience, or his sense of duty, and in the power of forming his temper and life according to conscience. We believe that these moral faculties are the grounds of responsibility and the highest distinction of human nature, and that no act is praiseworthy any farther than it springs from their exertion.

Years later, Unitarianism was to express its purpose thus: "In the love of truth and in the spirit of Jesus Christ, we unite for the worship of God and the service of man."

4

There were repercussions, of course, but it was part of Channing's unique character that although he had opponents, he did not have enemies. His published speech was blasted by defenders of orthodoxy of all denominations, but Channing did not hesitate to invite such men to his home for dinner or ask them to serve with him on civic committees for social reforms in Boston. Certainly nobody could have been more opposed to Channing's ideas than Bishop John Cheverus, the Roman Catholic prelate of Boston, but the two men were good friends, they visited each other often and worked together on Boston committees, and when, in 1822, the Channings went to Europe, the bishop equipped them with letters of introduction to his friends there. Channing invariably measured men not by what they believed but by how much they were willing to do to help others, and because of this he was able to disarm with genuine friendship men he had riled with genuine convictions.

Despite his own full schedule in Unitarianism, Channing was always ready to work on any committee that advanced social reforms in the city. He recognized, for example, that the children of lower-class working families had rare chance for an education because most of them had to go to work early themselves. He opened his own parish school to them at any hours they could attend, and he urged other churches to do the same. He knew, too, that there were men who regretted their lack of learning, so he opened the school to them as well, thus providing the first adult-education classes in the country. He also knew that the Boston waterfront was crammed with alcoholic derelicts who would never rise from their pits without a helping hand. He therefore organized a group of his wealthy parishioners to raise funds to provide such men with food, medical care, housing and jobs. Concerned about young rural men who moved into Boston to find jobs and often fell victim to the city's vice, he led a movement to provide them with hostels with Christian atmospheres—forerunners of the YMCA that had its American beginnings in Boston twenty years later.

A tolerant man, he was keenly interested in the civil rights of all. Any denial of such rights was, he felt, a denial of the individual dignity of a man, and he was ready at all times to defend that dignity. This attitude led him inevitably into the growing controversy over slavery. His sentiments were, undoubtedly, with the Abolitionists, but once again his reluctance to join organized movements and causes kept him from developing his sentiments into a definite stand, and for awhile nobody was quite sure where he stood. There were strong feelings in New England on both sides of the question, and Channing seemed to fluctuate between them. Actually, he did not, but he puzzled both sides when he would write a pamphlet against slavery, then refuse to allow an Abolitionist group to conduct a meeting at his church. Again, he would write Secretary of State Daniel Webster that the admission of Texas as a slave-state must be regarded as dissolution of the Union; then, when secession talk began in the South, he would plead that nothing, even slavery, merited such extremes. And again, he would denounce the Abolitionists for inciting riots in Boston, then would enter his pulpit the following Sunday and condemn slavery as the moral outrage of all times. Because of all this, he was intermittently cheered and denounced by both sides, and if he seemed to waver it was simply because his own peaceful, tranquil nature prevented him from openly taking any side whenever there were crowds, clamor, controversy.

But the time came when he knew he had to take a side. In March, 1835, he went to the State House during a debate on a proposal to ban Abolitionist groups in Massachusetts. He said nothing; he merely sat with the delegation of the Massachusetts Antislavery Society. The presence alone of a man so respected and revered for his integrity and charity in other spheres was enough to be effective. Shortly thereafter, Channing attended an antislavery rally for the first time, but as an observer. A year later, he attended another, this time on the platform and as a speaker. "I feel," he said in his remarks, "my place is here." Only once before had convictions driven him to such public overtness, in Baltimore, but this time he put aside his lifelong belief that each man had a right to his own thinking. There was only one right way to think about slavery: it was wrong.

Unfortunately, the rally broke out into a riot. The shouting and the fighting were too much for Channing. From then on, he confined his abolitionist efforts to his writings. That they were effective writings could be measured positively in their popularity among the abolitionists and, negatively, in the withdrawal from the Federal Street church of proslavery members of the congregation. There was another measure of Channing's effective writings. They were still being read more than twenty years later, and the clear arguments, moral and social, they put forth against slavery so stirred men's minds that of the one hundred and fifty thousand Massachusetts soldiers who marched off to the Civil War, almost ninety percent were volunteer—a record in the North and a record of Channing's lasting influence.

In the summer of 1842, Channing took his family on a combined vacation and lecture tour. He was sixty-two years old. His health, always delicate, was now failing fast. In Pennsylvania, he contracted a cold that laid him up for a month. On August 1, he gave his last public address; it was entitled "Emancipation." Returning to Massachusetts, he visited friends at Lenox, then decided to detour through the Green Mountains on his way back to Boston. At Bennington, Vermont, he developed typhoid fever, and for almost a month battled for his life. On the evening of Sunday, October 2, he heard the sound of church bells in the village and he realized that the Sabbath was ending and he had not as yet prayed. He asked that the Sermon on the Mount be read to him; then he led those with him in the Lord's Prayer.

He said: "I take comfort, the greatest comfort, from these words."

It was fitting that his last thought should concern words, for through the words he himself had written and spoken he conveyed to the Americans of his time and of all times the important truth that free men using their free minds to communicate their convictions freely were the best assurance for freedom for themselves, their country and the world.

CHAPTER

SIX

The Harvest of Brotherhood

When Joseph Krauskopf was a student at the Hebrew Union College in Cincinnati, it was his custom to ask friends whose thoughts he respected to inscribe a word of personal guidance in an autograph book he always carried with him. Among those he approached with this request was Dr. Max Lilienthal, one of his professors, who wrote:

> Religion, and not mere theology, must be your motto in your future career as ministers! Religion is universal, theology is temporary. Religion is the way in which God and man are truly related; theology is the fleeting teaching of the various churches. "And the Lord shall be king over all the earth" is the great prophet's heavenly message and teaches the common Fatherhood of God and the common Brotherhood of man. The older you will grow, the more knowledge you will acquire; the more you will investigate and gather experience, the better you will understand these short sentences and the advice of
>
> Your friend and teacher
> DR. LILIENTHAL

Joseph Krauskopf grew older and acquired knowledge; he investigated and gathered experience, and he came to understand precisely what Doctor Lilienthal meant. The understanding developed him into one of the most remarkable men of his time.

2

Joseph Krauskopf was born in Ostrowo, in Prussia, January 21, 1858, and at the age of fourteen he traveled alone to America to join his brothers and sisters who had come here earlier. Arriving in New York City in July, 1872, he went directly to Fall River, Massachusetts, where he found employment as a clerk in a tea merchant's company which also employed an older brother. He dedicated himself to two aims: to learn English so that he could improve his status in his new homeland, and to save money for the higher education he considered essential to the improvement. For two years he made steady progress toward both goals, then tragedy struck. His brother had become a traveling salesman for the tea company, and one day at Princeton, New Jersey, he was attacked, robbed and beaten so brutally that he died.

The death took much of the life out of young Joseph. Puzzled, hurt, lost, he was unable to adjust to the tragedy. He could not even bring himself to continue at his job. For months he wandered around the city, too stunned to fret about whether or not he had anything to eat or a place to sleep. The person who was most concerned about him was Mrs. M. B. Slade, one of his former customers. One day while making a delivery to Mrs. Slade's house and waiting to be paid, he had noticed her library and openly admired it. She had invited him to browse in the library whenever he wished and to borrow any books he might like to read. When she perceived his natural literary abilities in the book reports he wrote as exercises in the English language, she asked him to join the group that met at her home each week to discuss books and writing. Thus they had become good friends.

Joseph's reaction to his brother's death distressed Mrs. Slade, and she was even more worried when she learned the young man had quit his job. Encountering him on the street one day, she insisted that he go home with her. "You look as if you could do with a good wash," she said, "and I imagine you could also do with a good meal."

He went with her obediently, meekly, too disinterested in himself to care much what was happening. He washed, he ate the meal she brought him on a tray in the library, then they sat together talking for a long time. Joseph had little to say, and there was slim indication that he listened to what Mrs. Slade was saying.

"What about the schooling you wanted for yourself?" she asked. "You used to be so impatient for it. Have you given that up, too?"

"I don't know," Joseph said. "I don't know what's going to happen to me."

She went on. "What about your relatives in New York? You haven't written them for months, have you? Don't you realize how worried about you they must be? Have you thought of going to New York to live with them?"

He shook his head.

She tried a new tack. "Joseph, why don't you go and talk with a rabbi?"

This surprised him. He glanced up at her, questions in his eyes.

"I'm a Christian," she said, "and I don't know much about your religion, but I've always believed that when a person needs a certain strength he can't find in himself or in others the place to look for it is with God. You need that strength now, Joseph. Perhaps if you talked to a rabbi . . ." She waited. He said nothing. She went on:

"When you came to the meetings here every week, I got the

impression from some of the things you said that you were fundamentally a religious person, Joseph. Do you come from a religious family?"

He nodded. "My parents are very religious."

"And have you been going to church here? To synagogue?"

He nodded again. "Sometimes. But it's different here. I did not feel at home."

"Different in what way?" Mrs. Slade asked.

"The people are mostly Reformed Jews," he said. "I was raised Orthodox."

"And is there a great difference?"

"In the services," Joseph said, "and in other ways, too. Reformed Jews don't have to obey the dietary laws."

"But the principles are the same?"

"Yes. Mostly."

"Well then, Joseph," said Mrs. Slade, "will you promise me that you'll go and talk to one of the rabbis? I'm sure he'll be able to help you overcome the shock of your brother's death. Will you do that for me?"

"All right," said Joseph.

"And will you promise to come and see me again—soon? I don't want to have to drag you in off the streets whenever I wish to talk to you."

He smiled for the first time. "I promise."

"We won't have to talk unless you feel like it. You can just sit here and read, if you prefer. I merely want to know that you're all right."

"I'll come back," he said.

Joseph Krauskopf never told Mrs. Slade whether he had gone to see a rabbi, but she noticed when he returned four days later that he was as clean and neat as he used to be and that he seemed more willing to talk. She asked if he had any money;

he explained that he had taken a few odd jobs that provided an income without imposing any routine he still felt unable to accept. He spent the afternoon reading in the library. When he came back the following week, he brought flowers.

Meanwhile, Mrs. Slade took steps to overcome her own ignorance of Joseph's religion. Jews, she learned, had come to America with Columbus; four members of his crew had been *marranos*—Jews converted to Christianity during the wars against the Moors. The first Jewish settlers—twenty-three of them—had arrived in New Amsterdam in September, 1654, from Brazil to elude persecution when that country was recaptured by Portugal from Holland. After the Dutch colony on Manhattan Island was taken over by the British and named New York, the first synagogue was established there in 1692. Although there had been outbursts of anti-Semitism in most of the American colonies, Judaism continued to grow, and soon there were congregations in Newport, Savannah, Richmond and Philadelphia. Jews had fought in the Revolutionary War, the War of 1812, and on both sides in the Civil War; they had entered many professions, they held public office, and they contributed greatly to the opening of the West by roaming the prairies as itinerant merchants.

Reformed Judaism, Mrs. Slade discovered in her reading, was much more distinctive than Joseph had indicated. Evolving in Germany in the eighteenth century and introduced into America during the heavy Jewish migration prior to the Civil War, it held, for example, that the only divinely inspired Bible passages were those regarding ethical behavior. In other matters, it put personal reason above faith, particularly in such areas as worship in the synagogue and the home, dietary laws, local customs, and the use of local languages. The Reformed leader in America at the time was Rabbi Isaac Mayer Wise, who had been born in Bohemia in 1816 and moved to America in 1846. He wrote a great deal on Reformed Judaism, translating many Hebrew works into English. At his synagogue in Cincinnati, he preached in English, he instituted the family pew, he told men they need not have their heads covered during services and he advocated a Sunday sabbath instead of a Saturday sabbath since Sunday worship was the national custom. It was also the custom of the time for rabbis to be educated in the old schools of Europe—preferably in the schools in Palestine—but Wise insisted that Judaism was adaptable to all countries and he urged an American-trained clergy for American Jews. With this in mind, he took steps in 1875 to establish the Hebrew Union College in Cincinnati for Reformed rabbinical students.

Mrs. Slade learned about the college from her reading. She learned, too, from her talks with him, that Joseph had occasionally thought about becoming a rabbi and that only his brother's death had removed the idea from his mind. He read her books and found Reformed Judaism increasingly acceptable and they discussed the subject often. One day she said to him, "Joseph, I'm so pleased with the change that's come over you these past months. You're almost your old self again. I've been wondering if you've given any further thought to going on with your education."

He sank back in his chair. "I'm not sure," he said. "I'm eighteen now, I haven't got a penny to my name, and by the time I saved enough to pay for a year at school I'd be too old to go."

"Nonsense," said Mrs. Slade. "You have friends. They'll be willing to help you."

Her hint stunned him, and for a moment he could not speak. Then: "I'm not sure what I want to study."

"Why not go out to Cincinnati? To Hebrew Union?"

"A rabbi?" He felt uncertain.

"You told me that you used to want to be a rabbi," Mrs. Slade said.

"Yes, but . . ."

"Give it a try. If you change your mind, you can always transfer to some other school."

He was worried about the money. "It will take years."

"You have the years," said Mrs. Slade, understanding. "And I have the money."

He was touched but bewildered. "Why," he asked, "should a Christian be so willing to help a Jew become a rabbi?"

She pretended to be annoyed with him. "Joseph, what a strange attitude for you to have," she said. "We worship the same God, don't we?"

3

In the autumn of 1875, twenty-three young men constituted the first class at Hebrew Union College. Eight years later, only four remained to kneel before Rabbi Wise to hear his prayers, to feel his hand upon their heads, to accept the kiss upon their brows that made them rabbis. Joseph Krauskopf was one of them.

The eight years had been extremely difficult, spent almost entirely at studies. Mornings were occupied with classes at the Hughes High School, filling the gaps in his preparatory education; in the afternoons he attended classes at the University of Cincinnati in subjects leading to his degree; evenings he studied religious subjects at Hebrew Union. Despite this strenuous routine, he found time to tutor in Cincinnati homes, to write for Hebrew journals and to publish translations of Hebrew literature, thereby lightening the financial burden of himself on Mrs. Slade. During vacations, he assisted at synagogues in

Peoria and Kalamazoo, gaining practical experience in the ministry and gaining, too, an early reputation as an effective speaker and leader.

An appointment was awaiting him even before he was graduated—at the Congregation B'nai Jehuda in Kansas City, Missouri. He was just twenty-five years old—a child compared to most rabbis in the country. American-trained in Reformed Judaism, he was also, compared to most rabbis, liberal almost to the point of being radical. The changes he introduced at Kansas City dazzled his followers, who had expected reforms but were not prepared for revolutions. He preached on evolution, showing that it was not in conflict with religion; he preached on Jesus Christ, pointing out His traits which Jews should emulate. Aware that many Jews employed by Christians could not honor the Saturday sabbath, he began holding Sunday services, and after the initial shock wore off, the congregation was gratified both by the increase in attendance and in activity.

He was, most significantly, American. He told his people: "You are not merely American Jews; you are Jewish Americans. You must be of this country, of these times."

He was his own best example. He knew that, out of centuries of persecution, Jews were inclined toward a kind of social inbreeding that often resulted in the erection of invisible ghetto walls. This, he felt, should not happen in America: in a country that was already proving itself to be the world's melting pot, Jews ought not be insoluble. Krauskopf worked at this. He observed that in bustling Kansas City there was a floating population that was only periodically employed. Some of them were Jews; most were not. He organized what he called the Free Labor Bureau and virtually drafted members of his congregation to it to canvas the city to find jobs for these people.

He also saw to it that children were kept from work that overtaxed their physical endurance, and he arranged for low-cost housing for the impoverished families. For his efforts, the governor of Missouri appointed Joseph Krauskopf a life member of the Board of National Charities and Corrections, but the personal honor meant less to him than the fact that his efforts had made Jews active social factors in their community.

In November, 1885, a nucleus of Reformed leaders called a conference in Pittsburgh for the purpose of preparing a credo of their convictions. Joseph Krauskopf attended; because of his work in Kansas City he was well known. He was elected vice-president of the conference and chairman of the Committee of the Whole on Platform—remarkable recognitions of the young man who was half the age of his confreres. He was extremely active, darting from one meeting to the next, debating, arguing, coddling, cajoling.

By its nature, Reformed Judaism was not Zionist, and this was a sensitive point among older rabbis who still clung to both the hope and the triumphant significance of a Jewish homeland. Others were uncertain of the trend toward a Sunday sabbath, having sensed resentment to it among their congregations. And there were others who did not favor so complete a break with orthodoxy as the extremists advocated. Out of such varied attitudes had to come a coherent declaration of principles acceptable to all, and that this was done was due greatly to Joseph Krauskopf's talent for compromise. The declaration was clearly a liberal one, stating in part:

> We recognize in the Mosaic legislation a system of training the Jewish people for its mission during the national life in Palestine, and today we accept as binding only the moral laws and maintain only such ceremonies as elevate and sanctify our lives, but reject all such as are not adapted to the views and

> habits of modern civilization. . . . In full accordance with the spirit of the Mosaic legislation which strives to regulate the relation between rich and poor, we deem it our duty to participate in the great task of modern times, to solve on the basis of justice and righteousness the problems presented by the contrasts and evils of the present organization of society. . . .

Krauskopf's own influence upon the declaration was evident. Evident, too, was the advice of Doctor Lilienthal that religion was truly demonstrated only when it crossed theological boundaries in the cause of brotherhood. To the Reformed Jews, service was equal to prayer; service *was* prayer. It was true, however, that at this point Reformed Judaism was stressed mostly by a handful of ministers who had been disciples of Rabbi Wise, and it was their personal enthusiasm that swept along other ministers who were less convinced of the advisability of sudden change. The hesitant ministers knew that many of their people back home would resist portions of the Pittsburgh declaration. Thus no attempt was made to consider the declaration to be the new law; each rabbi would introduce the Pittsburgh precepts into his congregation at a speed he considered tolerable. Some of the rabbis felt it was a good idea to have the new tenets put to their congregations by someone who was openly identified with them, someone like Joseph Krauskopf. Invitations for this purpose soon flooded Krauskopf's Kansas City office. He accepted those he could; others he reached through his writings. In this way, each passing month brought him more popularity and influence.

In 1887, Hebrew Union College awarded Krauskopf its first doctorate. A few weeks later, a delegation of the Reform Congregation Keneseth Israel, of Philadelphia, went to Kansas City to ask Joseph Krauskopf to take over their synagogue. It was a great honor, a summons to the leadership of Reformed

Judaism: the synagogue was literally the cathedral of the movement and its rabbis had all been men of power and prominence. But Krauskopf was not anxious to leave Kansas City. He had been happy there; he had married and had a child; his congregation had become devoted, loyal and effective. It was only on the insistence of his fellow rabbis that he could do more for Reformism in Philadelphia than in Kansas City that Krauskopf agreed to make the move. He was aware of the honor and grateful for it. But if the members of the Congregation Keneseth Israel were proud of their previous rabbis, they had yet to encounter the likes of Joseph Krauskopf.

4

Although it labeled itself Reform, the Keneseth Israel Congregation was, like most American synagogues, a mixture of the liberal, the moderate and the orthodox. The situation prevented the congregation from presenting a solid front for Reformism, and it was this situation that many rabbis at the Pittsburgh conference had both confronted in their own congregations and dreaded. Krauskopf's predecessor at Keneseth Israel had promoted the synagogue's leadership in Reform primarily in his writings, but in the synagogue itself he tolerated individual preferences. He had introduced English sermons, organ accompaniment to singing, family pews and a lessening of dietary restrictions, but whether or not men had their heads covered during worship was a matter of personal choice, there were no Sunday services, no conformity in devotionals and no agreement regarding ceremonies in the home.

Krauskopf was installed in the synagogue on Sabbath, October 22, 1887. His inaugural sermon dealt with the nature of the ministry. Rabbis, he said, were not merely worship coordinators but messengers of God who should be listened to, obeyed and followed. This was his clue of what he expected of his people. He clarified his position by announcing that on October 30, he would hold his first Sunday service. The Orthodox resented the news; the moderates weren't sure how they felt; the liberals were hopeful for progress.

For the next few months there was considerable controversy over the new trend, but Krauskopf ignored it and went on with his plans. The synagogue had no devotional for Sunday services. Krauskopf wrote one. Also, he noticed that the ritual book used at the usual Sabbath services was a faulty translation of a German book that contained many throwbacks to the old ways. He wrote a new one. He also prescribed ceremonies for home worship, he systematized the dietary laws, and he told the men to take off their hats when they were indoors. Such frontal attacks were bitter experiences for the reserved. Some withdrew from the congregation; others said they would wait around and pick up the pieces after Rabbi Krauskopf finished his destruction. But there was no destruction. Second- and third-generation American-born Jews who had drifted from Orthodoxy were attracted by the young, energetic rabbi, and the congregation grew in three years to the point where a larger building was necessary.

It was Joseph Krauskopf's contention that a devout adherent to any religion was a better American because ineluctably he practiced greater tolerance, sympathy and charity. Krauskopf thus strove to stir in his people a curiosity about their religion, believing that from this would come a desire for a deeper and wider practice of it, outside the synagogue as well as in it. He organized what he called the Society of Knowledge Seekers, a group that met at the synagogue to discuss books, ideas and current events as they pertained to Jews and Jewish philosophy. When one man complained that Jews didn't have a sufficient active role in the Philadelphia civic affairs, Krauskopf asked: "Are you waiting to be invited? Why don't you volunteer?"

In a short time, there were many Jewish volunteers in civic affairs, all surprised to find themselves welcomed. The subject of another meeting was the shocking state of child labor in the city. Krauskopf said: "I wonder how many of you have child laborers on your own payrolls. If you paid the parents enough, the children wouldn't have to work and would be free to go to school. Start first with yourselves, and when you have cleaned up your own places of business, then you will be able to go to the factories and the mines and demand the same."

The start was made, and out of it grew a committee that pioneered against child labor throughout the state. It was the same with slum clearance, aid to the sick poor, racial prejudice, juvenile delinquency, assistance to immigrants. Always Krauskopf insinuated the problem through his choice of the meeting's topic, always he pointed out the initial corrective steps, always the group was ready to set up a new committee for action. The results were evidenced in city improvements, in a new brotherhood of effort between Jews and Gentiles, in the increased vitality of Keneseth Israel Congregation.

One night Krauskopf baited the Knowledge Seekers with: "Why is it when I walk the streets I see the Baptist Publishing Company, the Episcopalian Publishing Company, the Methodist Publishing Company, but not the Jewish Publishing Company? Are we illiterates? Have we no great literature to pass on to our children? Are there no outstanding minds among us today with ideas for us or the country?"

Once again the bait was snapped up. Once again a committee went out, this time to confer with printers, distributors, booksellers. At the group's suggestion, Krauskopf put the same questions to his entire congregation, adding: "It will cost a great deal to set up this publishing firm. I will call on each of you to give it birth and to keep it alive."

With that, an idea became a reality. The Jewish Publication Society of America was soon a flourishing concern, with Krauskopf as a board director and major contributor. Demands for Jewish literature seemed endless and it was quickly evident that the thriving publishing house should be put into the hands of professional men who would know more about the complicated affairs. For this reason, the company was moved to New York, a staff was hired, and thereafter the Society remained a leader in the religious publishing field.

The success of the publishing venture delighted Joseph Krauskopf. Loving books himself, he was pleased to see how widespread the love was among his people. He remembered the first Jewish books he had read, the writings of Rabbi Wise that Mrs. Slade, now dead, had loaned him in Fall River. What doors those books had opened, what roads they had led him down! He was happy that now those roads and doors were open to others. He had no idea, meanwhile, that he was about to open a new door that would lead him down a new road to a new prominence in a new area to which he had never given a serious thought in his life.

5

With the partition of the old Polish republic between 1772-95, Russia had acquired the largest Jewry in the world, and it was not a happy acquisition. Bitterly anti-Semitic, Russia transported large numbers of Jews to the eastern provinces of the empire into a Pale of Settlement that amounted to a gigantic ghetto. For almost a century the Jews had lived as slaves, deprived of citizenship, of the right to own land or a business, even denied promotion in the armies into which thousands were conscripted. The state-tolerated, even state-financed, mass massacres of Jews were undisguised savagery. By condoning such brutality on the old and false premise that all Jews shared an inherited responsibility for the crucifixion of Jesus Christ, the czars were able to distract attention from their own corrupt governments. There had been under Alexander II (1855-81) a brief spell of leniency during which the serfs were liberated—liberated but left to starve. The next czar, Alexander III, revived the persecutions, putting the Jews to work as forced-laborers on farms.

Joseph Krauskopf knew all about this and his heart ached because of it. Early in 1894, he invited several wealthy friends, both Jewish and Gentile, to his home, and he put an unusual proposition to them. "From what I hear," he said, "the Pale of Settlement is so overcrowded that Jews who aren't being murdered are dying of disease and starvation. And yet just a few miles away is a vast, vacant, unused area. I've been wondering: suppose it were possible to buy some of that empty land and arrange to move some of the Jews there. Wouldn't that help things a bit? With more room, wouldn't the people have more of a chance to survive? Isn't that simply humane?"

The wealthy friends perceived that they would be asked to put up the money to buy the land when the time came, and they agreed to do so. Krauskopf went to Russia to negotiate with government officials. To his surprise, his idea was sympathetically received and discussions were begun to work it out. However, it soon became clear that the basic Russian interest was in the payment of American dollars. The available land was little better than tundra; it would be almost impossible to grow anything on it. Even so, Krauskopf was willing to go ahead; he would happily have bought a desert if it meant that the thousands of Jews, crammed into so small an area, had a bit more room to move, to breathe.

There were delays. Again and again, Czar Alexander's representatives balked at the last moment. Months dragged by. Then, in November, Alexander died, and his son, Nicholas II, took the throne. Nicholas promptly announced that since the Jews were responsible for all the troubles in the world he saw no reason why anything should be done to ameliorate their plight at the settlement. The deal was off.

Before leaving Russia, Krauskopf called on Count Leo Tolstoy, whose novels he had read and whose new religious philosophy intrigued him. A few years previous, Tolstoy turned from the Russian Church in which he had been raised and arrived at his own religious precepts which, without being Mosaic, resembled a sort of pacifist Reformed Judaism. Tolstoyism, as the new philosophy was called, never actually flourished, but those who accepted it were sincerely demonstrative. One aspect of it involved assistance to Jews—not because they were Jews but because they had suffered from the accident of being born Jews. Tolstoy himself divided his enormous properties into small farms and invited Jews to operate them as their own.

"You know," Tolstoy said to Joseph Krauskopf, "Jews were an agrarian people for centuries before the Diaspora. Farming is in their blood."

Krauskopf nodded. "I also know," he said, "that they haven't been given many opportunities for over a thousand years to remain in one place long enough to harvest whatever they might plant."

"True and sad," Tolstoy granted. "When we began our work here, we discovered that their generations away from farming had made the Jews forget all they ever knew about it. We had to open a school where young Jews could learn the skills of their ancestors. Do you have many Jewish farmers in America?"

"Very few, I would imagine," said Krauskopf.

Tolstoy suggested, "If I lived in a country with as much freedom as yours, I would urge Jews to return to the soil. That would be their best assurance of security and stability."

The suggestion haunted Joseph Krauskopf. When he visited the farm school, he was struck by the open enthusiasm of the young Jews for the noble occupation of making things grow. All the way back to Philadelphia he pondered Tolstoy's idea. Reaching home, he talked about it to his friends. Forming in his mind was a plan for a similar agricultural school, and the plan followed the pattern of brotherhood that was so much a part of Joseph Krauskopf.

"The school," he said, "should be for young Jews living in cities who feel they would be happier and more effective on farms, but its doors should also be open to young people of all religions. I'm going to ask Jews to build the school, but I want them to demonstrate the American ideal by welcoming all people to it."

To Krauskopf's astonishment, his plan was rejected by practically everybody. In the entire country, he was told, there were not two hundred Jews in agriculture. Farming simply did not attract the modern Jew, whatever the history of his people, and to open a school for the purpose of producing Jewish farmers was a waste of time, money and effort. Krauskopf could not bring himself to believe this. Jewry's retreat from the soil had merely been an exigency of the wanderings enforced upon Jews by persecution. Given freedom, peace and the opportunity, there would be in Jews a revival of the desire to own and farm land that was natural in all peoples.

Furthermore, Krauskopf argued, there was a moral factor

involved. Cities could be dangerous places for the young, especially the poor: the ratios of juvenile delinquency in the cities and in the country showed that. Why not salvage the city youngsters—Jew, Gentile, boy, girl—by stirring in them a desire for the more wholesome country life? Why not provide the proper training for those who wanted it?

It seemed hopeless, but Joseph Krauskopf refused to be dissuaded. For two years he battled the cynical opposition that surrounded him, slowly winning converts more by persuasion than by principle. At last, in 1896, he had raised enough money to buy a hundred and sixty acres in Bucks County, Pennsylvania, and to erect a one-building school and dormitory, and with that the National Farm School came into being. Its students were a dozen boys taken from the Philadelphia streets; its professors were four farmers who lived near the school. Scoffers laughed at the meager beginnings and predicted an early failure, but Krauskopf was determined that this, if anything in his career, must succeed.

It did. Within twenty-five years, the school's property expanded to more than fifteen hundred acres, with thriving orchards and fields, herds of cattle and horses, gigantic flocks of poultry and enormous greenhouses for experimental work. In that time, the school graduated over five hundred boys, youngsters who came from every major city in the East to receive not only a free three-year course in agriculture but also to be provided with free housing, food, and clothing. On the school's twenty-fifth anniversary, personal commendations came from President Calvin Coolidge, Secretary of Agriculture William M. Jardine, and the leaders of farm organizations across the land. In this same period, significantly, the number of Jews engaged in farming rose to over two hundred thousand. Those who had challenged Krauskopf's conviction that Jews could be and wanted to be effective in the most stable occupation in the country had cause to reconsider their doubts.

More came out of the school than Krauskopf anticipated. From the start, its success marked him as a skilled organizer and leader. Thus in 1898, during the Spanish-American War, he was appointed Special Field Commissioner of the National Relief Commission to investigate relief conditions in U. S. Army camps. In 1900, the Secretary of Agriculture sent him to Europe to report on agricultural education and the general condition of agriculture there. At the outbreak of World War I, he was appointed director of the Food Conservation Program for the Jewish factor in the interfaith project. After the war, he was a consultant to Herbert Hoover's Inter-Allied Food Council. While continuing his pioneering efforts in slum clearance, child welfare and social services, he specifically served his church as well. In 1901, he organized the Board of Jewish Ministers of Philadelphia. Two years later, the directors of Hebrew Union College decided to raise five hundred thousand dollars as an Isaac M. Wise Memorial Fund. Krauskopf was made chairman of the fund and, traveling across the country, personally raised over three hundred and twenty-five thousand dollars. That same year, he was elected president of the Central Conference of American Rabbis. Thus in serving his church, his community and his country did he exemplify the admonition his college professor had written in his autograph book—that the universality of the ministry had to expand beyond denominational horizons if it was truly to be in the service of God.

Evidence of this conviction in Joseph Krauskopf was found among his personal papers after his death. In 1923, at the age of sixty-five, he heeded the warnings of his doctors that he needed a long rest if he expected to overcome the ill health that had plagued him over the past few years. He went to Atlantic City. It was there, on June 12, that he died. In the process of disposing of his effects, his family came upon a paper in his desk, on which was written:

One God over All
One Brotherhood of All
Peace and Good Will Among All.

CHAPTER SEVEN

The Preacher's Son

"I WAS thirty," Henry Ward Beecher once said, "before I learned that Christmas could be a joyous time. As a child, I never had any toys. I must have been fourteen or fifteen before I heard a Christmas carol for the first time, and then accidentally because I was on an errand for my father and happened to pass an Episcopal Church. I was not brought up to believe that being religious was any reason to be happy."

Henry was born on June 24, 1813, in Litchfield, Connecticut, the seventh of eight children born to Lyman and Roxana Foote Beecher. Lyman Beecher was a Congregational minister, sternly Calvinistic. To him, any unnecessary merriment in the house bordered on sin. The effect of this upon Henry was deep and lasting. By nature, Henry was affectionate and outgoing, and reconciling this to the loveless atmosphere in which he grew up was an agony for him for years.

In Lyman Beecher's austere household there was little room for family affection. Poor as he was, Beecher was an important man in the New England movement to retain the stricter aspects of religion. He thought that Unitarianism was pagan and that Catholicism was the work of the devil. In his battle against any emotion that might weaken resistance against evil, Lyman Beecher squelched all affectionate displays in his home. He looked upon his children as burdens God had given him to test his moral sturdiness and he loved them in proportion to their own severities. His first child, Catherine, was a born martinet, so she ranked first with him. Henry, on the other hand, struck his father as a weak, elusive dreamer. Worthless.

Lyman Beecher once wrote to friends in Boston a letter full of family news and Henry was not even mentioned in it. The rest of the family felt the same towards him. Years later, when the family was temporarily broken up among relatives, Henry went to Hartford to visit his sisters, Catherine and Harriet, and when they came down the stairs in answer to his summons they did not recognize him. He was, the family felt, too much like his mother, and Roxana Beecher, they said, had cared too much for things of the world.

Henry's mother died when he was three. He never really knew her, but he had come to seek protection from loneliness in a world of daydreams, and from this he developed the lifelong habit of telling others what a tremendous influence his mother had been in imbuing him with an appreciation for music, poetry and art. True, Roxana Beecher had loved these things, but Henry learned about it only from his questions as he grew up— Who had painted this picture? Who had played the piano now idle in the parlor? Who had pressed the flowers in the books of poetry? Mother. So Henry painted his own portrait of his mother and put himself in her arms and remained there all his life.

Lyman Beecher married again within the year. He had gone up to Boston to preach a vituperative sermon against Unitarianism, then drawing liberal Congregationalists into its fold. Among his listeners was Harriet Porter, a well-connected spinster. They were married in a week. Harriet Porter Beecher met all the specifications of a New England Congregationalist stepmother; there was no more affection in the house than there had ever been.

The parsonage was a busy place, made so not only by its population but mostly by Lyman Beecher's prominent role in church affairs. There were always three or four other preachers staying at the house, planning under Lyman Beecher's vitriolic leadership their war against sin, Unitarianism and Catholicism. Also, each day a score of parishioners came to Lyman for help in avoiding Hell. Lyman Beecher was obsessed with a fear of Hell. Writing to an older son in the seminary, he said: "My only thought for you is that you don't go to hell. You must not go to hell."

Lyman Beecher expected all his sons to become ministers, including Henry. The ministry was, he felt, the only sure road to heaven. Henry's education began when he was four. His sister Harriet, one year older, led him to the day school operated by Catherine Beecher. Henry was the only boy there. After a year he was put into a boys' school, but he was so indifferent about his studies that his father decided it was a waste of money and he was transferred to another girls' school, this one run by two women who boarded at the parsonage and who were willing to take him in free for a decrease in their rent.

Henry shared his room with Charles Smith, a Negro servant who was a few years older, and each night Charles would read his Bible aloud, discussing it with Henry as they fell asleep. Unlike the Beechers, Charles viewed God as merciful and loving, which Henry could not reconcile with the stern, vengeful God his father always talked about. Charles would say to him: "Boy, Jesus was born for sinners, not for saints." Henry, at the age of eight, was convinced his sins had already shut him away from Jesus and he would fall asleep trembling at the thought of the hell that awaited him.

In 1826, when Henry was thirteen, his father accepted a call to Hanover Church in Boston, and when the family was settled there Henry and younger brother Charles were entered into Boston Latin School. Henry continued to be a poor student, disinterested in his subjects, unable to learn. Lyman Beecher believed that boys should work, so Henry found a job delivering packages for a men's clothing store during his free hours. His deliveries frequently took him in the vicinity of the harbor and the place soon enchanted him. The ships that had been to the far corners of the earth filled him with a desire to travel; the sailors, so boisterous, so zestful, so jaunty together, made him want to be one of them. He dallied along the docks as much as he could. "I went to school in Boston Harbor," he later said.

He decided to run away to sea. He made his plans carefully, and as his chosen day neared he grew so excited that his family asked him what was wrong with him. But when the hour came he could not do it. He was terrified by the thought of how his father would react. There was only one thing he could do.

He went to his father and admitted, "I ought to tell you that I'm planning on running away to sea."

"Oh, you are, are you?" Lyman Beecher bellowed. "Why?"

"I think I'd like it," Henry said meekly. "I don't want to go into the ministry and I'd hate working in the store all my life."

"So you'd rather spend your life hauling cargo and mopping decks and throwing garbage over the side," said Lyman.

"I suppose I'd have to do that for awhile," said Henry, "but not always. I could work my way up."

"Well, you won't do it at all," Lyman assured gruffly.

The boy had never been able to talk with his father. He swallowed. "Yes, sir."

"No son of mine will handle garbage," Lyman Beecher said.

"If you want to go to sea, you shall have the proper training for it and start your career with some dignity."

"Yes, sir."

"I will think about it."

"Yes, sir."

Lyman Beecher thought about it this way: whatever the young fool had in mind for himself, he was going into the ministry, no doubt about that. But he had been a failure at every school he attended and was of no use around the house. His job paid him next to nothing. He could do with some discipline. What he needed was a school where he could get it. That year, the Mount Pleasant Classical Institution had been opened at Amherst, with courses for boys planning careers at sea. Already the school had a reputation for its discipline. Lyman Beecher wrote the school and discovered the tuition was two hundred and fifty dollars a year. He suggested that because of his prominence in the religious field, the school would well benefit from a testimonial he was willing to write for its brochure—provided Henry would be accepted at a hundred dollars a year. The school agreed.

Getting away from his family while he was still flexible enough to develop his own personality was an important opportunity for Henry. Mount Pleasant provided this freedom; it also provided friends of a type Henry would never have met within the circumference of his home. Mount Pleasant made a point of attracting foreign students, which meant that Henry was surrounded by young men whose backgrounds, religions and attitudes were entirely different from his. At first Henry feared he would be corrupted, but when his new friends failed to sprout horns he was both relieved and happy. He made a hero out of each one. An instructor who was also Henry's roommate had been thrown out of West Point for drunkenness, an extreme of worldliness Henry had never encountered before. Henry expected the worst debaucheries, but he found that his roommate wore his *savoir-vivre* as casually as old shoes, and Henry began to wonder if sampling the pleasantries of life was the road to damnation that his father had warned. Thereafter, Henry was always intrigued by men who lived a little dangerously.

Henry's closest friend at Mount Pleasant was a Greek boy, three years older than himself, named Constantine Fondolaik, an orphan whose parents had died in the Turkish invasion of his homeland. Fondolaik made his way alone to Boston, where he was adopted by a wealthy woman who sent him to Mount Pleasant. His hope was to become a naval officer with the Greek fleet. Fondolaik was the star of Mount Pleasant, the best athlete, the best scholar. Dark, muscular, handsome, he was the direct contrast to the small, skinny, moon-faced Henry, yet perhaps it was their opposites that brought them together. They were inseparable. Other students also liked Fondolaik and invited him to their homes on vacations, knowing that the invitation must necessarily include Henry. On these trips, Henry met his friends' sisters, who seemed so attractive, so bright, so openhearted, so responsive to his efforts to be entertaining—none of which he had experienced with girls he had met through his family—that he fell in love with them all. Back at school, he took up correspondence with his classmates' sisters, spending hours at it, spending more hours debating with himself which one he would eventually marry. With most teen-agers, this would have been normal stuff, but with a boy who until now had no adventures in reciprocated affections it became a dangerous obsession that would one day break his heart.

2

Away from home, Henry no longer felt the need to run away to sea, and so his interest in it gradually faded. He had no mind for his studies; his professors warned him that unless his grades improved he would have to leave. The dread of being ousted from the Mount Pleasant world where he was so happy drove Henry to apply himself more, but with barely passable results. And there was something else. After fifteen years in the rigorously somber atmosphere of his father's house, Henry could not shake the influence entirely. By nature, he was a religious youngster; by inheritance, his religiosity was dour. Other students drank and smoked and gambled and occasionally sneaked off the campus to visit women. As much as he liked them, Henry felt compelled to warn his friends of the burning reception awaiting them in the next world. Because he amused them, they heard him out, then laughed and told him: "On your way, Preacher." Aware that he was uninspired by his naval studies, Henry began to wonder if indeed he was destined for the ministry.

His wondering deepened when he realized that his lone scholastic success at Mount Pleasant was in the elecution class. He took up the subject in his second year and was immediately effective at it. Shy though he was, he had a flair for public speaking, and the self-confidence he gained from his new friendships soon enabled him to stand before a roomful of people and, complete with practiced gestures, blast forth with all the fire of his father. More of his friends began to call him "Preacher," but now with a touch of admiration in it. In his third—and last—year at Mount Pleasant, he attended a revival meeting, his first intense religious experience since leaving home, and he was so stirred by the fervor of the congregation that he wrote his father that he now believed he was meant for the ministry. Could he continue his studies at nearby Amherst College? Satisfied that he had been right about the boy all along, Lyman Beecher said he could.

Constantine Fondolaik also entered Amherst, and the two young men planned to room together, but Lyman Beecher felt that dormitory life was too distracting for Henry and ordered him to move into a private home. On their first vacation, the boys were invited to visit the home of Ebenezer Bullard, a classmate, at West Sutton, fifty miles away, and because Henry lacked the coach fare the three of them walked it. By the time they returned to school, Henry was in love with Bullard's sister Eunice. In his first letter to her, Henry asked Eunice to marry him. She said she would but she didn't think she should right away. Seven years passed before she did.

They were years that took Henry into new worlds. At Amherst, he made no impression except for his brief presidency of the debating society. At his commencement exercises in 1835, twenty-six of the thirty-nine graduates took individual parts in the ceremonies, but Henry was not one of them. His grades had been too low to warrant him a distinction of any kind. But Henry didn't care. Constantine was the star of the ceremonies, and this was joy enough for Henry.

The Beecher family had moved from Boston to Cincinnati, from Congregationalism to Presbyterianism, both moves based on Lyman Beecher's dread that Catholicism was about to turn Ohio into a papal state. He was convinced that large sums had been brought into the country to buy Ohio for the Pope, and he went west to Cincinnati to fight it. Since Congregationalism was almost strictly a New England sect, he affiliated himself with Ohio Presbyterianism, and in addition to holding a pastorate, fighting the Catholics and editing a newspaper, Lyman

Beecher also founded Lane Theological Seminary, now ready to accept young Henry as a student.

Henry found the seminary almost empty when he arrived, emptied by controversy over the slavery question. As New Englanders, the Beechers were opposed to slavery, but they were also opposed to any Congressional act that would free the slaves overnight. This, they felt, would produce too great a strain on southern economy. They favored instead the process of the American Colonization Society, which stood ready to ship to Liberia any slaves who cared to go. They also approved of the plan by which the children of slaves would be born free, thus decreasing slavery gradually. The trouble with the colonization project was that, in fifteen years, it had sent only fifteen hundred slaves to Liberia. Three million of them remained in the country, mostly in the South. Radical abolitionists rejected the colonization plan because it made so small a dent in the slave population and also because most of the slaves had been born in America, some of them second or third generation, and they had no links with Africa except their race. The radicals also rejected the freedom-by-birth plan because, although Negroes were being born at a rate of a hundred and fifty thousand a year, it would take almost a century to eradicate the slavery they wanted to get rid of now.

In America, Presbyterianism had developed as a southern denomination, but it also flourished in the North, especially in the Central States, and the Church soon found itself divided on the slavery question. The South, of course, was proslavery. The negotiable value of southern slaves was almost four billion dollars and any act of sudden abolition would certainly be a severe economic danger. The northern Presbyterians were, for the most part, antislavery and favored immediate abolition at any cost. As a Yankee, Lyman Beecher stood partially on the side of the northern Presbyterians—the New School; but because he preferred a gradual solution to the problem he was more with the southerners—the Old School. Both schools were represented in Ohio and Beecher found himself unofficially leading the Old School. The Seminary was similarly divided. Sometimes debates on the subject were fierce. For the sake of peace, Lyman Beecher ordered that slavery would no longer be discussed. With that, the majority of students quit and most of the faculty walked out. Upon his arrival, Henry found only five or six students and three or four professors awaiting him.

Henry shared his father's views, both by family breeding and Amherst training, views that were the sole gulf between him and Constantine Fondolaik. But Constantine was gone now; they would write each other and Henry would later name one of his children after his friend, but they would never see each other again. Returning to Greece in 1842, Constantine contracted cholera in a few months and died. Eunice Bullard, however, held Henry's views and she could write him sympathetically when he told her of the Ohio controversy, but more on her mind was the subject of marriage and she wondered when Henry would get around to it. Once she wrote him that an offer of marriage was as binding as marriage itself. Henry assured her that he knew that and would send for her as soon as his studies ended.

As before, Henry did not enjoy studies. He shared rooms with one of his professors, Colonel Calvin Stowe, who subsequently married his sister, Harriet Beecher. An older man, Stowe was quiet and reserved, with the annoying habit of reminding Henry that he should be studying when he preferred to write letters. Also, Henry was once again under his father's stern, unloving influence, and this annoyed him too. Henry was sure now that he wanted to be a minister, but he knew he could not bring himself to be the kind of minister his father was. Lyman Beecher's sermons were full of fear of the Lord and the dread of Hell; Henry felt more inclined to preach about the love of the Lord and the fraternity of Christians. He realized, however, that as long as he remained with his father the man would try to mold him into a copy of himself, as he had done with other sons already in the ministry. Henry knew he would have to get away. He considered becoming a missionary. He wrote to Eunice: "It will be a difficult life, but will you go West with me?" Eunice replied that she was ready at any time. A year older than Henry, the passing spinster years worried her.

By coincidence, the reverse occurred: Lyman Beecher went away from Henry. The New School had gained control of the synod and declared that anyone holding Old School ideas was a heretic. Lyman Beecher was summoned for trial. This left his newspaper, the Cincinnati *Journal,* without an editor. He gave the job to Henry.

Thus at twenty-three, Henry was editing one of the most important religious publications in the Midwest. He had had some editorial experience on school papers at Amherst; he could handle the job. He could handle the *Journal's* editorial policy as well. By sentiment an Old Schooler, he could write editorials along this line with effective verve. The paper also attacked Catholicism; raised in an anti-Catholic atmosphere, Henry could deal with this subject, too. But he felt uneasy about it. At Amherst, he had met Catholics and liked them. Were they all the devils his father accused them of being? Constantine had been Greek Orthodox, which, while not Catholic, certainly wasn't Protestant, and there was no one finer than Constantine. And what about Charles Smith, the young slave who always talked about a God who loved everybody whatever they were? If God loved the Catholics, shouldn't the Beechers?

In this frame of mind and as temporary editor of the *Journal*, Henry attended, in January, 1837, a series of debates between Bishop John B. Purcell, Catholic prelate of Cincinnati, and Reverend Alexander Campbell, founder of the Disciples of Christ. Campbell was alert, incisive, penetrating; Purcell was knowledgeable, patient, historic. Whenever Campbell had a question, Purcell had a fact; whenever Purcell had a question, Campbell had an opinion. Whenever Purcell conceded that the Catholic Church had erred in some of its temporal relations, Campbell extended the error into the spiritual realm. Purcell would smile. It was probably the smile more than anything that affected Henry; he was not seeing many of them around the *Journal*. The debate stirred a great deal of publicity without any particular victory for either side. However, Henry later wrote in his diary:

> I made up my mind distinctly that, with the help of God, I would never engage in any religious contention. I remember promising Christ that if He would strengthen me and teach me how to work I would all my life preach for His kingdom and endeavor to love everybody who was doing that work. Not that I would accept others' beliefs, not that I would embrace their theology, not that I would endorse their ecclesiastical organization; but, whatever the instruments be, if they were sincerely working for the kingdom of Christ I would never put a straw in their way and never strike a blow to their harm.

A bit of this new conviction began to creep into the columns of the *Journal*. Lyman Beecher, whose heresy trial ended as unresolved as the debate, returned quickly to Cincinnati and relieved his son of the editorship. Henry gave the next six months to the completion of his seminary course.

Now he was ready for a pulpit, and he wanted one as far from his father's as he could get. He remembered his earlier intention of entering the missions in the West. He began to cast about for an assignment. The assignment he got was just seventy miles away, in Lawrenceburgh, across the border in Indiana. The Lawrenceburgh Presbyterians were sternly Calvinistic Old School, and even a Beecher's conservative attitude toward slavery seemed radical to them. However, there was no other choice and Henry was taken on at five hundred dollars a year. He borrowed three hundred against his salary and hurried to West Sutton to marry Eunice Bullard.

3

Eunice hated Lawrenceburgh. It was a small, dirty town with about two thousand people and far more than its proportionate number of saloons and gambling houses. The people were unfriendly. Despite the reticence usually attributed to New Englanders, Eunice, compared to her tight-mouthed neighbors, was almost maddeningly garrulous. The newlyweds obtained a two-room apartment above a warehouse, which meant mice and roaches. Furthermore, Eunice was immediately pregnant and seemed to remain so for years, losing most of her babies but nevertheless presenting Henry with a platoon of sons and daughters. She aged quickly; she lost whatever appeal she had; she felt and looked perpetually petulant.

Henry was not fond of Lawrenceburgh either. His church was small, with perhaps twenty members. In two years he added two new members, one of them his wife. Slavery, pro or con, was a popular pulpit topic, with the view of the preacher reflecting the view of the congregation, but since Henry's was not the proslavery view of his congregation he felt he could not touch the subject. Instead, he preached mostly against drinking and gambling, and although most of his congregation were against these things, most of them also were deriving their income from them, however indirectly. What disturbed Henry most was that he did not like preaching *against* things; he preferred to preach positively. The idea was revolutionary and he could not figure a way to go about it. As a result, preparing his weekly sermon was invariably a discouraging, frustrating chore.

He tried. With the best of intentions, he made a list of plans for Lawrenceburgh. He would make men more active in the Church, he would visit homes to attract converts, he and Eunice would both strive to increase the congregation through friendship. Indicatively, he added: "Get the young to love me." But he did not succeed at any of these things. He thought seriously of resigning his position and buying a farm.

There was a custom at this time among those who advocated the program to hold ceremonies each Fourth of July to stimulate support of the American Colonization Society and, because of his father's influence, the site of the 1838 services was Henry's church. Crowds came from all over. Henry, as host, was one of the principal speakers. Out of his own convictions, he was able to produce a stirring speech. Although it was not successful with his own Old School congregation, it went particularly well with the delegation from Indianapolis. When the delegation returned home, it formed a group of about thirty Presbyterians and voted to start a New School church and to invite Henry to be its preacher. There were two handicaps: in terms of immediate abolition, Henry was not entirely New School; and he was not as yet ordained. To overcome both shortcomings, he presented himself for ordination to the New School synod but was rejected. Despite this, the Indianapolis group was willing to accept an Old School ordination, which Lyman Beecher arranged. Happily, the young Beechers left Lawrenceburgh.

In a short time, however, familiar problems arose. Eunice complained that Indianapolis, then not much bigger than Lawrenceburgh, was nothing but a mudflat. Malaria was rampant; the children were frequently ill. The small and dark and damp house provided for the family looked out on an alley. The optimistic congregation had overlooked its poverty; Henry's salary was often late and sometimes did not appear at all. To pay bills, Eunice had to take in boarders.

Henry was also uneasy. In Lawrenceburgh, he had been unable to say a word for abolition; in Indianapolis, he was expected to say more than he actually believed. He found it necessary to resort again to sermons against drinking and gambling. And yet his most constant companion was Elijah Alvord, the town's leading gambler whose casual worldliness reminded Henry of the West Pointer at Mount Pleasant. Henry got Alvord to join the Church without obliging him to change any of his habits. This raised brows among the rest of the congregation but did not disturb Henry at all. The congregation also raised its brows over Henry's growing tendency to spend his time with the young men of the town, playing soccer, broad jumping, Indian wrestling. He had not been hired, the congregation pointed out, to be an athletic director.

Yet these friendships produced a factor that proved a turning point in Henry's career. Although their conduct with him was proper enough, Henry deduced from their jokes that, away from him, the young men were given to more fundamental sports. Out of this, Henry wrote what he called "Seven Lectures to Young Men on Various Important Subjects." The title was suggestive enough to pack his church when Henry gave the lectures. They were, actually, mild in their scope, and though they touched on sex, they did so by presenting book reviews of current novels Henry said the young men should not read. Whether the subject was liquor, gambling or women, Henry's summation was always the same: when tempted, run away. It was sound advice. The popularity of the lectures encouraged Henry to publish them, and their immediate success across the country soon relieved Henry of the worry of whether or not his congregation paid him.

Meanwhile, the same women who criticized Henry for his hours with the young were all too happy to have him address their garden clubs on horticulture, a hobby he had taken up as part of his campaign to make himself popular with prospective church members. When the Indiana Association of Garden Clubs held an annual convention, the Indianapolis clubs chose Henry as their delegate, and here, too, the charm he could effuse when he wanted to be liked made him a success. He was invited to write for horticulture magazines. It was natural, then, that when the publishers of the *Indiana State Journal* decided to bring out the *Western Farmer and Gardener,* they should give Henry the post of editor. In addition to horticulture, Henry wrote editorials on current affairs. The magazine's religious tone, its guarded liberalism and its grasp of Midwestern problems soon made it one of the most quoted publications in the country. Also, it gained added stature from the literary fame of Henry's two sisters, Catherine and Harriet, who let him print some of their novels and short stories.

Thus through a series of coincidence, Henry Ward Beecher graduated into national prominence, and at each level he felt freer from the restraints society usually put on ministers. He could be more himself, and he was both a simple and complex person. He was convinced that his sudden success had evolved from friendship. Out of friendship he had written the lectures for the young men; out of friendship he had written the horticultural articles for the women. As indirect as the routes had been, Henry believed they had led both groups of people closer to the church, closer to God. He therefore needed no further assurance that it was easier and more effective to attract people to God with love than with his father's hellfire technique. He was determined to inject more of God's love into his sermons and he immediately saw the effects. People no longer left church frowning over their sins; they left smiling over the promise of richer lives they contained. This was the uncomplicated side of Henry Ward Beecher.

His complexities, on the other hand, stemmed mostly from his own uncertainties. He was the product of two worlds, his father's and his own, and the roots of the first were deep whereas the roots of the second were still shallow. For this reason both his writings and sermons were often criticized by men of more solid substance who were impatient with Henry's indecisiveness. He found it difficult to take a definite stand on public issues, perhaps because he was able to see both sides of a question, perhaps because he was reluctant to take one at the risk of offending the other. He never fully overcame this, but when his hour struck he overcame it enough to make himself one of the most effective men of his era.

4

Word began to spread about him. In a few months, his congregation soared from thirty to almost three hundred. When easterners came to Indianapolis on business with the state, it was Henry's church they attended on Sunday mornings. Unbeknownst to him, a group of Brooklyn men were planning to build a new church and were looking around for a minister to lead them along liberal lines. They were considering him. Summoned East to give the church board a sample of himself, Henry made a stirring impression and was offered the position.

He was thirty-four years old but had retained much of his boyishness. He was still small, compact, with a smooth moon-face and straight, unkempt brown hair. Although he had been born and raised an easterner, the Indiana mud had taken the polish off him. Arriving in Brooklyn in the summer of 1847, he saw that eastern men wore beards, top hats and tight-fitting, loudly checkered suits. Henry usually went hatless and his suits fitted him like tents. He had no concern for social graces because he had never been able to afford them. Among his new elegant friends, he should have been as out of place as a sparrow among swans, but he charmed them all. Years of prying love out of people had made him an old hand at charm. He also saw to it that he was soon even more elegant than they.

The Brooklyn group, headed by Henry C. Bowen, a wealthy dry goods merchant, acquired a building on Cranberry Street —in the swanky Brooklyn Heights section, overlooking Manhattan—and called it Plymouth Church. It was to be Congregationalist without being Calvinistic. Henry's starting salary was fifteen hundred a year, more than twice his Indianapolis salary, and now he would not have to worry about getting paid. Furthermore, he was to be raised to two thousand in two years. This was big money in an era without income tax and with steak selling at five cents a pound. Eunice was happy at last. She could live in a fine house, have servants and shop at exclusive stores. Now the mother of five, she had turned gray and looked more than her thirty-five years. Eager to please her, Henry took her shopping for fashionable clothes soon after arriving in New York. She proved as difficult to satisfy as though she had always been rich. Henry kept scurrying around the store to find something to her liking. At one point, the clerk said to her: "I know how trying this must be for you, ma'am. It's a good thing you have such an attentive son." Eunice was furious.

Plymouth Church began with a congregation of less than fifty, but Henry's sermon theme of love in all things went well with them, and the congregation grew slowly but steadily. They were also abolitionists, more so than Henry, but with time their attitudes became his. Henry opposed only the violence to which some abolitionists resorted to win their cause. No one, he said, should force his ideas on others; abolition could best come about by persuasion. Slavery, Henry preached, was a sin in itself because it bred further sin through the unwholesome atmosphere in which it forced slaves to live. For this reason alone, he claimed, it should be abolished, but it should be abolished peacefully out of the love for morality that God had put into the hearts of all men. The more Henry preached along these lines, the more determined he grew for abolition, and the more eager he was for a larger audience to convince.

One day Henry Bowen talked to Henry Ward Beecher about the success of the *Western Farmer and Gardener,* and he suggested that a weekly semireligious paper for Brooklyn, with Henry as its major contributor, would be a good idea. Henry fully agreed, and the *Independent* was founded. The apparent need for the *Independent* assured its success. A professional staff was brought over from Manhattan to handle most of the copy, but Henry's weekly contribution was the outstanding feature. Most often, his article was his sermon of the previous Sunday, but frequently he wrote additional articles as well on current affairs, signing them with an asterisk. By their flowery language and penetrating opinions, however, they were readily recognized as Henry's work. In a long article, he defended *Uncle Tom's Cabin,* written by his sister, Harriet Beecher Stowe, against the criticism that it exaggerated slavery conditions in the South. The book was violently debated in many circles and was considered by some to be a factor in sparking the Civil War. On meeting Harriet, Abraham Lincoln reportedly said: "So this is the little lady who started the war?" In a way, Henry was equally responsible.

Henry did not think much of the lanky Illinoisian when he first appeared on the national scene, believing, as many did, that Lincoln lacked the dynamism to persuade the South to abolition. Out of both Henry's complaints and his invitation, Lincoln went to New York in February, 1860, for his Cooper Union address at which he stated his conservative plan for abolition. Henry considered it too timid and he continued his demands for action during Lincoln's first months in office. When the South seceded and the war began, however, Henry gave full support to Lincoln and raised funds to pay Federal soldiers when the Government could not meet its bills, but he nevertheless complained strongly that the war was being badly commanded, which it was.

Reports from London indicated that England was sympathetic to the South and might give military support to its cause. Aware that this could not only preserve slavery in the South but also destroy the Union, Henry went to England and lectured to packed halls in several cities, defining the North's principles. When he returned home, Henry could announce that England would stay out of the combat. Honors flooded Henry: testimonial dinners were given for him; he was made a major general of a New York regiment, his fund-raising appearances drew both crowds and money. He was on the committee that went to Washington to urge Lincoln to declare the Emancipation Proclamation, which was issued several weeks later. The meeting changed Henry's feelings toward Lincoln and thereafter the two men maintained a cordial correspondence. When ceremonies were held at Fort Sumter to celebrate its recapture, Henry was invited to be the principal speaker.

Lincoln had once said that Henry caused him to lose more sleep than did southern generals, but there was a certain good in the gnawing criticism Henry flung at the White House for so long. Henry later conceded that at times he had been unreasonable in some of his complaints, but nevertheless it was true that he had goaded the Administration to decisions it reluctantly faced, and rallied to constructive actions many of his readers who otherwise would not have known what to do next.

What to do next was not a problem with Henry. He had written a novel on slavery that achieved popular success, and now he went to work on a life of Christ. During the war, he had taken over the editorship of the *Independent* for a year; now he resumed his role as its major contributor. Plymouth Church had to be enlarged to accommodate its two thousand members, and there were thousands more waiting to join. He compiled a successful hymnal, he wrote for other newspapers, he lectured, he campaigned for a low tariff and he crusaded for women's suffrage. He was busy, indeed. His income from his various enterprises was over forty thousand dollars a year. His success impressed even his family, at a time he no longer needed their approbation; his two sisters who once hadn't recognized him now visited him frequently; his father who once cared nothing for him now came to live with him. This was certainly a heady existence for a man who once sought the obscurity of the western missions, and it proved to be a bit too heady for Henry.

5

Henry Ward Beecher was not so much a theologian as a man with an idea. His idea: conduct inspired by love produces good. To profound theologians, this was featherweight religion, and they scoffed at Henry. And yet there was a lot to the idea. The results could be measured practically. In addition to his efforts with social causes, like suffrage and the low tariff, Henry was on the boards of many charities, and at fund rallies a five-minute talk by him on Christian love could stir more generosity than a house-to-house canvass. The results could also be measured emotionally. Even after the Civil War, much of America was still gripped by puritanical reservation: to display any emotion in public bordered on depravity. In this area, Henry was a radical. He had learned now that the best way to stir a congregation to anything was to aim at its emotions, and he could inspire a crowd to any emotion he wished—charity, courage, the women's vote, piety, or any politician he favored. Out of this, he became an extraordinarily effusive man for his day. He walked down the street arm-in-arm with his friends and swamped them with gifts and attentions; the women of his parish he boldly kissed on the cheek whenever they chanced to meet or separate. He left a wake of smiles wherever he went. All this was harmless in itself as long as nobody took it seriously, but there were some who did.

Elizabeth Tilton was the wife of Henry's closest friend. Theodore Tilton was a brilliant journalist who, at twenty, had turned down offers from the big New York newspapers in order to work on the *Independent,* whose religious atmosphere was more to his liking. Henry was then in his forties, approaching the peak of his career, the leader of liberal thought in the country. When he became aware of Tilton's blatant adulation of him, the two men became inseparable, and Henry was soon spending more time at the Tilton home than at his own. Elizabeth Tilton developed the same high regard for Henry that her husband had. When Henry went to Europe during the Civil War, Tilton replaced him as editor of the *Independent,* retaining the position after Henry's return. Following the war, Tilton, because of his job, became an important man in his own right and was often called to other parts of the country for conferences and lectures. Sometimes he was away for weeks on end. During this period, Henry was writing his biography of Christ. In the old days, he had read his sermons to Eunice to benefit from her reactions; he would have read his manuscript to her now, except for the fact that she was too busy with a houseful of children and relatives. So he read to Elizabeth Tilton.

One night in 1870, Elizabeth Tilton told her husband that for over two years Henry had been considerably more than a friend to her. Tilton was understandably furious, and yet he said nothing to Henry about it. Life in the Tilton home grew unbearable. After six months, both Tiltons turned to outsiders for help. Theodore told the story to Oliver Johnson, a Plymouth Church leader, who advised him to forgive everybody involved. Elizabeth told it to Susan B. Anthony, the suffragette, who was friendly with everyone on the *Independent* and who promptly proceeded to broadcast what she had been told in confidence.

By the time the story reached Henry Bowen, owner of the *Independent,* it had been distorted to the point where it seemed Tilton had been the one to be unfaithful. Bowen relayed it to Henry, who said, "I don't believe a word of it." Tilton heard this version of the story and, to save his job, told Bowen the story as he knew it. Bowen now gave this version to Henry, who said, "The man is crazy." Accompanied by Eunice, Henry went to Tilton's home and confronted Elizabeth with the charge. To Theodore's amazement, she admitted that she had grossly exaggerated the relationship, but the Beechers had no sooner left the house than Elizabeth told her husband she had lied to get Henry away; she could not stand the sight of him.

Months of torment passed. Tilton suffered because he didn't know whether or not his wife's charge was true. Henry suffered because he knew the gossip was spreading; he suffered more because he realized he had lost the affections of his devoted disciple. Perhaps time would have brought all the pains to an end and the gossip would have dissipated, but then a dreadful thing happened.

Victoria Woodhull, a prominent suffragette, had a personal grudge against Henry, whom she felt was getting far more credit in the movement than he deserved, and in December, 1872, she printed the gossip about Henry and Elizabeth in her own publication. For this, she was jailed for sending obscene material through the mails. Everybody expected Henry to sue her, but he did not. On the contrary, he did all he could to smother further public attention; but because he did not sue, other newspapers felt safe in reprinting the story clear across the country.

Theodore Tilton lost his job. Out of the old friendship, Henry wrote Tilton offering to set him up in a newspaper of his own, but he made the suggestion so incautiously that when the letter eventually became public it looked as though Henry were trying to bribe the Tiltons into making a public denial of the whole incident. Tilton rejected the offer and tried to earn a living as best he could from his writings. He tried, too, to salvage his marriage, but his own doubts were so great that his bursts of temper eventually drove Elizabeth home to her mother. Fresh gossip began: Elizabeth had gone mad, and it was Tilton's fault. Tilton's position was unbearable. On January 11, 1875, he filed suit in City Court, Brooklyn, charging Henry with the alienation of his wife's affections, specifying adultery. The trial lasted until July 2, and it was front-page news every day in every city of the land.

Throughout the trial, Henry steadfastly insisted he was innocent. The only evidence against him was a statement Elizabeth had written for Tilton during one of his angry outbursts and the incautious letters Henry himself had written. The jury could not agree on a verdict and finally the case was thrown out of court. Henry's thousands of loyal friends praised him for having won a victory, but he was not sure precisely what he had won.

He wished to retire, but the public demand would not permit it. He was, editorial writers said, too important to the liberal element of the country to lock himself away. As for the scandal, a jury had been divided in his favor; if the country was divided, it was in the same way. Also, the papers pointed out, the Plymouth Church congregation had asked him to stay on; that was verdict enough.

Slowly Henry returned to the life he had known. There were, he felt, other things more important than his pride. If the public image he once had was now somewhat damaged, then so be it. He began to write and to lecture again. Wherever he appeared, the crowds came. He told them that it was the right of women to have a voice in choosing the political leaders of the country. He told them that free trade was important because it opened the world to American manufacturers as well as opening America to the world. He told them that the carpetbaggers then rampaging in the South must be brought under control; the wounds of war, he said, would take long enough to heal without pouring salt in them. He told them not to let the suddenly popular Darwin theory destroy their faith, that whether men evolved from apes or descended from Adam and Eve they were nevertheless God's creatures, bound to love Him and each other.

On March 8, 1887, Henry was preparing to give a lecture on the plight of southern Negroes who had been freed from slavery only to be enslaved by second-class citizenship, but that afternoon he suffered a stroke and died. Among his notes was found the question: "If people say they love God, why is it they do not love each other?" He had spent his lifetime seeking the answer.

CHAPTER

EIGHT

The Rebel

WALTER RAUSCHENBUSCH said this:

> Socialism is coming, but it is still an open question how it shall come—as a freshening gale strikes a ship that has made itself ready for it or as a typhoon hits a junk of sleeping and gambling Chinese. If we are destined to pass into socialism, the more gradually we do it the better it will be for us.

That this prophecy should be uttered by a Baptist minister at the turn of the century when religion allied itself more with Victorian conservatism than with the budding influence of the working classes was revolutionary. Furthermore, that a clergyman should take so bluntly a political stand at a time when religion was insisting on the separation of church and state was virtually heresy.

And yet the remark was typical of Walter Rauschenbusch. In many ways, he was both a revolutionary and a heretic, but in many other ways he was no more revolutionary or heretical than Jesus Christ. It was, in fact, on an extension of Christ's social influences that Walter Rauschenbusch built his own social convictions. "I am," he said, "a Christian Socialist." Many Christian leaders doubted that such a contradiction of terms could be blended into a single philosophy, but there were thousands of Christian laymen who saw in Christian Socialism the only hope both for America and for Christianity itself.

2

The Rauschenbusches moved to America from Germany in 1854, settling in Rochester, New York. For six generations, the family had given its first sons to the church; Walter, born in Rochester on October 4, 1861, was to become the seventh. In Germany, the Rauschenbusches had been Lutheran; in America, they became Baptists. August Rauschenbusch had brought his family to America primarily to work among Germans then migrating here in great numbers, most of whom were Baptists. An author and educator as well as a minister, it was fitting that August Rauschenbusch should affiliate himself with the Baptist Theological Seminary at Rochester, which conducted a German department to meet the current needs. From the start, however, he insisted that the German aspect of the Church should be temporary, providing assistance to the immigrants in the language they best understood until they and their children could make the transition to English-speaking Americans. Like many European church leaders, he had seen his people in America drift away from religion because of the language difficulties. His aim, then, was to sustain religiosity while guiding the immigrants to the new way of life they had chosen.

Walter Rauschenbusch knew from his childhood that he would follow his father into the clergy. Although in his youth he showed a brief interest in law, the religious life was too deeply bred in his bones for him to take any other path. Once when he was a young boy he was asked what he wanted to be when he grew up, and he answered: "John the Baptist."

Two other childhood influences deeply affected Walter. He

discovered early that his father had married his mother on the rebound, having been rejected by the woman he preferred. This caused considerable tension and disaffection in the Rauschenbusch household. The second influence grew out of the first: in his discontentment, August Rauschenbusch was inclined to drink too much. In reaction to the first influence, Walter consciously became an ideal husband and father in his own marriage years later; in reaction to the second influence, he was a strong prohibitionist all his life.

Walter was four when, in 1865, his mother decided to take him and his two older sisters to Germany for a visit. The plan was for August to join them later to spend a year abroad, but he had been to Europe in 1860 and now, because of the Civil War, the seminary was too shorthanded to spare him. It was, therefore, 1868 before he could join his family, and thus four years before Walter returned to Rochester. During these years, Walter attended German schools, became proficient in the language and acquired an abiding affection for the country. He was, too, a bit out of place among the less inhibited youngsters who greeted him when he entered the Rochester schools. He was an amenable child, always eager to please, and his father once said the boy had so happy a disposition that apparently he would never have to be spanked. However, this did not turn out to be the case. Like many ministers' sons, he tried to escape the shadow of his father's reputation. In his teens, he was elected leader of his group of friends because of his originality in dreaming up new devilments for them and the scope of his profane vocabulary, for both of which his father rewarded him with beatings.

Even so, his religious nature was close to the surface. His two closest friends, Edward Hanna, a Catholic, and Munson Ford, a fellow Baptist, shared his intentions of entering the clergy, and it was this that held them together for years. During their school years together, the three friends competed for scholastic leadership, all of them always in a cluster at the head of their classes, and even when they separated to attend different colleges each was able to report to the others that he was winning top honors. Ford eventually abandoned his aspirations for the clergy and became a farmer, much to Walter's disappointment. Hanna eventually became the Catholic archbishop of San Francisco and was awarded a medal by the National Conference of Christians and Jews for his work in interfaith fellowship, the roots of which, surely, were in his boyhood friendships.

Walter was seventeen when he underwent a religious experience that definitely decided his future. In the process of finishing high school and considering his career, it was natural for him to wonder if he was attracted to the clergy merely because it was a family tradition. Also, he perceived that the daily religious practices of his family had become so habitual that they seemed to have lost their meaning for him. In his uncertainty, he did not know which way to turn, until at last he turned to prayer. The answer came with stunning clarity: the clergy. Walter later recorded: "Never before had I been so vividly aware of the presence of God in my life." Never again would he doubt it. Confidently, he presented himself to the church for baptism. Confidently, he planned his future studies.

It was decided that he would begin them at the Evangelical Gymnasium of Gutersloh, in Germany, where he arrived in 1879 and remained four years. On vacations he was able to tour Europe; in Rome, he visited with Edward Hanna, then completing his studies for the priesthood. In 1883, he entered the University of Berlin for six months, following this by attending a series of theological lectures at Leipzig. On his father's suggestion, he spent a few weeks in England before returning home. In Rochester, he carried the heavy scholastic load of his senior year at the university and his junior year in the seminary. The following summer, he worked as the supply preacher at the German Baptist Church, in Louisville, Kentucky, where he had his first rounds with parish life. He found the congregation in the throes of personality conflicts, with factions within factions, and he spent the summer trying to induce a little Christian charity by bringing together people at odds with each other and settling their differences with his own charm, wisdom and sense of justice. He was evidently successful, for the congregation asked him to return the following summer, which he did. He then spent one more year at the seminary, receiving ordination in the spring of 1886. He had hopes of going to the missions in India, but the mission board decided he should first obtain some pastoral experience. Two churches were interested in him, one in Springfield, Illinois, the other in New York City. He chose New York, and the choice put him on the road to importance in his church and in his country.

3

The Second German Baptist Church of New York was on West Forty-third Street, on the fringe of the tenement jungle known as Hell's Kitchen. The church had about a hundred members. Walter's salary was six hundred dollars a year, plus a three-hundred-dollar rent allowance. He lived in a small apartment on the top floor of the church. He was now twenty-five years old, but looked younger. He was tall, lean, with thick red hair; to give himself age he grew a beard.

Disillusionment awaited him. Like most young ministers, idealistic and zealous, he was to discover that pillars of the church usually stood in mud. In Louisville, he had his share of parish feuds and petty jealousies, but his two summers there had been happy because he realized he was actually a transient, doing his internship, soon to be on his way elsewhere, and he felt freer to make himself an aggressive peacemaker. In New York, however, he was a permanent fixture, not only involved in the feuds but sometimes the cause of them, and now there was no chance that he would soon be out of it all and away. He found that the people who had welcomed him most warmly were usually those least willing to do anything for the church. He found that people who seemed most disquieted by his unexpected house calls were usually the first to criticize if he called on anyone else too often. And he found that those who were most vocal regarding the social problems of the run-down neighborhood usually gave most resistance to his efforts to raise the necessary funds for improvements.

The neighborhood both depressed and appalled him. Although, as a church family, the Rauschenbusches had never been rich they also had never been poor. Walter grew up knowing nothing of extreme poverty or squalor. Now he was surrounded by them. He saw not only the sadness of them but the evil of them as well. At one point, he said he could not understand how a soul might possibly be saved in such circumstances. Every day he observed how being hungry, cold and miserable drove people to thievery, brutality and decadence. And he saw that little was being done about it.

Obviously something had to be done—but by whom? To be effective, it was apparent to Walter Rauschenbusch that something would have to be done by everybody. It was also apparent to him that the single agency through which everybody could act as a single group was the government, and so it was clear to him that it was up to governments to act. He felt, too, that it was the duty of churches to see to it that the governments acted. If, he said, churches did not put an end to the plights of the underprivileged, the plights of the underprivileged would put an end to churches, perhaps an end to America itself. The economic crises that produced the plights were not, he pointed out, any phenomenon of nature but rather the phenomenon of capitalism. If the plights were to be avoided, if the victims of them were to be protected and assisted, then governments would have to play a bigger role in the affairs of capitalism. He was, quite plainly, suggesting some degree of socialism, and even in the 1890's this was, to many, a dirty word. The writings of Karl Marx had been published forty years earlier. Walter Rauschenbusch had read them with favorable reactions, but for one vital reservation. Marx proposed an atheistic socialism. Rauschenbusch proposed a Christian socialism. It was, he felt, the duty of Christians to take care of each other, and even in his twenties he had learned enough about life to know that the rich would not take adequate care of the poor without a little coaxing from governments. "There is not," he once said, "a single great fortune in New York whose origin could bear scrutiny." The fortunes had been built on exploitation, and a sad by-product of the exploitation was a place like Hell's Kitchen. It was the responsibility of governments, Walter Rauschenbusch insisted, to prevent precisely that.

Even in his own small sphere, the young minister could see the results of proper church pressure on governments for the sake of the underprivileged. From the neighborhood police he learned that the major reason for the outbursts of teen-age vandalism was that the youngsters had no constructive outlet for their energies. Corraling the cooperation of local ministers, Rauschenbusch hounded City Hall for the construction of neighborhood playgrounds. He got them. The rate of teen-age vandalism plunged. Poverty and all its evils could be similarly overcome, Rauschenbusch argued, by similar action.

During his early years on New York's West Side, two personal events occurred that had profound effects upon Walter Rauschenbusch. In 1888, he suffered an attack of the grippe and he got up from his bed too soon. Physical strain damaged his eardrums and in less than a year he was almost totally deaf. Current hearing aids were too primitive and too cumbersome to provide much help, so he learned to read lips. During the period in which he was learning, Rauschenbusch decreased his social life in order to avoid embarrassments for others and himself. He read a great deal, mostly along the socio-political lines which life at Hell's Kitchen had sensitized in him, and it was now that many of the ideas that later made him famous were formulated. In his misfortune he nevertheless benefited.

The second event was much happier. On a trip to Milwaukee in 1889, he met Pauline Rother, a schoolteacher. He attended a party at her home and was quickly fond of her. But he also discovered that she was engaged to be married, so any serious thoughts he had of her he put out of his mind. Nevertheless, since she too was active in church work, he corresponded with her. In 1892, he returned to Milwaukee to give a series of lectures. Because of his deafness, he knew he would need someone at his side whose lips he could read in the process of having audience questions transmitted to him. He asked Pauline Rother to help him. On this visit, he learned she was no longer engaged. During a free moment, he asked Pauline if a woman might find a man's deafness too serious an obstacle to marriage, to which she assured him that no woman would if she truly loved the man. From New York he wrote her that he knew he was in love with her. Did she think she might be in love with him? She did.

They were married in Milwaukee on April 12, 1893. Pauline Rauschenbusch proved to be much more than a wife, much more than a minister's wife: she was virtually her husband's curate. She helped him greatly with his paper work, she accompanied him on his house calls, at group meetings she transmitted the remarks of someone too far across the room or drew his attention to others who wished to speak to him, and at lectures and conferences Pauline, by the soundless use of her lips, could relate to Walter everything that was going on without distracting others. Over the years, she presented him with five children, two girls and three boys, all of whom she raised to live with their father's deafness as normally as though he did not have it at all.

Pauline was of enormous value to Walter during their New York years. He had started what he called the Brotherhood of the Kingdom, a group of clergymen who shared his desires for better government and better men in government, and soon there were similar groups under his direction in Philadelphia, Detroit and other cities. Not all the members were as wholeheartedly socialist as he was, but they all agreed that governments at all levels must do more for the poor, the sick, the aged and the unemployed. The work involved much travel, many conferences and considerable writing, none of which Walter Rauschenbusch could have done without Pauline's help. The nature of the Brotherhood was this:

Jesus Christ, in teaching men to pray, had addressed the Father: "Thy kingdom come, Thy will be done on earth as it is in heaven." After much prayer, meditation and study, Walter Rauschenbusch inferred from these words that the Kingdom of God had indeed come to earth, through the act of God made man in Jesus, and now it was up to men to do God's will on earth as it was done in heaven. Christianity, Rauschenbusch believed, was intended to be a social factor, encompassing all. His study of church history showed that the first Christian communities were truly communal: all properties were held by the community and everyone worked for the common good. This, he felt, was the basis of the Kingdom of God on earth. The subsequent Christian emphasis on individual salvation was, he said, a drift away from the Kingdom. The Brotherhood of the Kingdom was intended to spearhead a return to Christianity as it originally was.

Rauschenbusch was realistic enough to know that the return would not occur overnight. High obstacles stood in the way, and the highest of these was selfishness. To Rauschenbusch, selfishness was a major sin, its roots in pride, profit, pleasure, prejudice and privilege, and in his opinion capitalism contributed to selfishness because of the opportunities it afforded the "haves" to exploit the "have-nots." He also believed that the stress on personal salvation nurtured selfishness: a Christian should care so much about others that he would not let them suffer any deprivations that would threaten their salvation. The current battles between management and labor assured Rauschenbusch that this idea was not very widespread, and he was convinced that it would never spread until a government upholding the idea took steps to enforce it.

The Brotherhood started small, a half-dozen men in New York, the same number in Philadelphia, and during the twenty years it existed it never totaled more than two hundred adherents, but they were men of influence and so the Brotherhood's influence was great. Once or twice a month, each group met in a quiet place for a day of prayer, meditation and discussion, then each man was supposed to go back to his own area of influence and practice the Brotherhood's principles. The Brotherhood was comprised only of Baptist ministers at first, friends of Rauschenbusch's, but it gradually expanded to the clergy of kindred denominations and to the laity.

There were two especially important occasions when the Brotherhood acted as a unit. One was the 1897 coal strike which put out fires in homes, factories and trains across the country. The Brotherhood issued a statement, written by Rauschenbusch, which said in part:

> . . . We hold this to be self-evident—that men are entitled to a fair living wage, and it seems to be conceded by all that the miners have been pressed down beyond the level of decency and humanity. When such things happen they concern us all, and we add our voice to the universal protest. We protest especially against the tendency to give capital a first lien on the proceeds of industry; we hold that on the contrary a fair wage to the workers should come first and interest and dividends second, for life is more than property.

Similarly, the Brotherhood supported the strike against the privately owned New York City transportation companies which required their employees to put in as much as eighteen hours a day. Men did not live to work, the Brotherhood statement pointed out, but rather worked to live, and an eight-hour day should be sufficient to provide a livelihood.

In both instances, the weight of the Brotherhood's opinion was instrumental in swaying public feelings to the workers and to their victory. In New York, the Brotherhood went further, urging municipal ownership of the city transportation system in order to take the prerogatives of public travel out of private hands. This gradually became common practice in major cities across the land.

Invariably, the Brotherhood took the side of workers who, the Brotherhood said, were helpless unless they were especially skilled. In a 1903 statement endorsing the growth of labor unions, Rauschenbusch wrote: "He [the worker] is subject to unhampered competition. The labor market fills up as western lands are settled and immigration comes in. Large employers have purposely increased the competition for the laborer, while diminishing it for themselves [through] tariffs and trusts." At the same time, the Brotherhood opposed alliances of big business. In the same statement, Rauschenbusch said:

> The present movement to organize employers is an effort to disarm the unions and make them harmless. If successful, the ultimate result would not be to bring back individualism in the laboring world but to transfer the conflict to the political field, intensify the class struggle and finally to make socialism the only practicable organization of industry.

The importance of the Brotherhood of the Kingdom, then, was not so much in what it did as it was in what it suggested. It gave people food for thought. It reminded people of their rights in a republic and in a Christianity. And its major contribution to the development of America was still to come.

4

Despite its many frustrations, Walter Rauschenbusch enjoyed his pastoral work. He once said that he would never give it up unless he was convinced that God wanted him to do something else. To him, the Brotherhood of the Kingdom was part of his pastoral work; in his sermons, he passed on the various ideas that the Brotherhood promoted. On his house calls, he gave first attention to any spiritual concerns his parishioner might have and then, because most of his people were in the labor class, he subtly did his Brotherhood missionary work. Pastoral work also allowed time for the writing he did for a publication called *For The Right,* which he had started with some friends. He had a simple, direct style that was bright and easy to read, and usually he wrote humorous fables in which he effectively caricatured struggling workers, unprincipled bosses and muddling politicians. By making people laugh at themselves, he could show them their weakness and their weapon; then he expected them to take up the battle from there.

In 1897, an important change took place in Walter Rauschenbusch's life. A plea arrived from the German Department of the Rochester seminary, then suffering a faculty shortage. Would Rauschenbusch return to his alma mater to teach? The decision was difficult. It meant, surely, the end of pastoral work. It meant a restricted life in a distant city, far from New York where the Brotherhood of the Kingdom was busiest. It meant, too, a kind of work Rauschenbusch was not sure he could do. There was only one way to decide: he prayed. He went.

He arrived at Rochester under the impression that he was going to teach New Testament interpretation, but he found there were other jobs awaiting him as well. He was also to teach civil government and the natural sciences. And would he mind teaching church history, English and zozology? He did not mind. Anything else? Well, there might be. There was.

He was, in effect, the entire faculty of the German Department, and yet he was happy at it. German immigrants were still arriving in great numbers; they would need a clergy that spoke their own language. Teaching, then, was important, especially since the teaching produced new ministers who would help mold the immigrants into good Americans.

He was a fine teacher. Although he distributed his lecture notes beforehand, his personal enthusiasm frequently sent him off on fascinating tangents that kept his classes exciting and full. Often other professors would attend Rauschenbusch's lectures for the sheer enjoyment of watching him at work. He was soon a popular and highly admired figure in Rochester. Even strangers knew of his deafness and when, deep in thought, he passed them on the street without acknowledging their greetings, they merely smiled patiently, aware that his thoughts probably concerned their welfare, about which he had already spoken and written so much. He usually traveled between his house and the Seminary on a bicycle, and again deep in thought he would often drift to the middle of the street. Drivers approaching from the rear invariably slowed down until he turned off rather than risk startling the deaf man by trying to pass.

In 1902, the seminary's German Department faculty shortage was relieved and Walter Rauschenbusch was asked to join the staff of the larger and more important English Department as a professor of church history. He now had more time to himself, and he was grateful for it because there was a particular piece of writing he wanted to do. It had been on his mind for some time: a full and detailed evaluation of Christian Socialism. Now he was able to start work on it, a task that would take him four years. When he finished it, he added the title: *Christianity and the Social Crisis,* and sent it off to his publisher. Weary, he took his family to Europe for six months, and when he returned he discovered he was a celebrity.

Christianity and the Social Crisis summed up the social influence of religion from the earliest Judean days, traced it through the first Christian centuries up to the present time, then predicted its future. The predictions were actually Rauschenbusch's personal hopes, but in presenting them he said the only alternative was social and moral chaos. What he foresaw in the year 1907 turned out to be remarkably accurate. The day would come, he said, when the Government would provide low-cost housing for the poor in a pleasant and healthy environment. There would be pensions for the aged and insurance for the unemployed and medical care for all. There would be graduated income and inheritance taxes. Cities would operate local transportation systems, plus the gas and electricity facilities. The work week would be decreased to fifty hours, perhaps less, and there would be laws to assure safe, clean and humane conditions where women and children worked. Local governments would provide recreational facilities. The Federal Government would own and regulate mines and all natural resources to prevent monopolies. Giant corporations would pass under sufficient government control to provide for a fair distribution of the national wealth. Free education at all levels would be available, and students in specialized fields that required long studies would receive subsidies for living expenses. The rights of small businesses would be protected against the behemoths of big business, and big business would find itself working more and more for the Government.

In 1907, these predictions were unthinkable, and yet within fifty years most of them were accomplished facts and others were on the horizon. But Rauschenbusch did not proffer them merely as predictions; he laughed aside remarks that he was a prophet. Rather, he presented his ideas as a blueprint and he said it would be up to men of good will to build a country on it. What evolved would depend entirely on such men. Rauschenbusch's attitude toward mankind was somewhere between the Millenarian concept of wholesale doom and the Pollyanna certainty that God planned one day to turn everybody into millionaire saints. Rauschenbusch said: "Ethically, man sags downward by nature. It is ever easy to follow temptation and hard to resist it. The way that leads to destruction is always broad and its asphalt pavement is kept in perfect order, with toboggan slides at either side for those who prefer a steeper grade."

But he also said: "There are two great entities in human life—the human soul and the human race—and religion is to save both. The soul is to seek righteousness and eternal life; the race is to seek righteousness and the Kingdom of God."

There was, Rauschenbusch said, a way by which the downhill tendencies of men could be reverted heavenward: religion. "The mischief begins," he said, "when the Church makes herself the end. She does not exist for her own sake; she is simply a working organization to create the Christian life in individuals and the Kingdom of God in human society. Religion must become less an institution and more a diffused force."

So there it was: the Kingdom of God existed on earth, erected by Jesus Christ, but it was like a village of model homes from which society had moved out. There could be no peace and happiness on earth until society moved back.

5

Quite certainly, there were many people who frowned over Walter Rauschenbusch's book, people who stood to lose the most if—or when—his predictions were fulfilled. But vocally at least these people were in the minority. Returning from Europe, Rauschenbusch was met at the dock by reporters, he was interviewed at his hotel by magazine writers, and awaiting him at Rochester were thousands of letters from readers who wanted to know what they could do to help bring about the world he had described. To answer them, Rauschenbusch went on a lecture tour that kept him traveling for almost two years. And he continued to write more books—*Prayers for the Social Awakening, Christianizing the Social Order, A Theology for the Social Order.* In each he said what he repeatedly said in his lectures: if the American people really wanted the world he had described, they already possessed the most effective weapon for getting it—the vote. Let their wants be known to the politically ambitious, who would then enact the appropriate laws if they wanted to stay in politics. Furthermore, he said, it was not necessary for clergymen to bring politics into their pulpits. Let them use their pulpits to put religion solidly into their people, and religious ideals of charity, justice and equality would irresistibly penetrate the political world. Always religion should be the incentive for all personal and public conduct, he insisted, or otherwise socialism would decay into what he foresaw for Marxism—a Godless dictatorship of savagely selfish men determined to rule the world on their own brutal terms.

The five or six years following the publication of *Christianity and the Social Crisis* were the zenith of Rauschenbusch's popularity and influence. He did not expect any great rush to convert America to socialism, and there was none, but he was being read, he was being listened to, and like rain upon dry soil his philosophy was slowly being absorbed. He was content to know that someday when others planted the actual seeds of his ideas there would be a fertile place for them to grow. This was the unique thing about him. Instead of a social leader, he was more a social conscience. He let people know what ought to be done, then left it to them to do it. He was, in many ways, an Old Testament prophet, crying down from his mountaintop. More accurately, he was a prophet of the Kingdom of God. As with prophets, the people who should have most listened to him thought he was a dangerous radical, a threat to the social order. But again as with prophets, he merely saw what was coming and sought to prepare people for the right path. The socialist label he bore would have worked against him fifty years later as it did in his own time, but this was because few people properly understood it. To him, it simply meant government protection of the weak and the small. In an era when the weak and the small were having trouble enough protecting themselves, the government assistance was vital if the government was to remain of, for and by the weak and the small. The strong and the big denounced Rauschenbusch for what they considered his similarity to Karl Marx, but Rauschenbusch pointed out the sharp difference between him and Marx when he said: "Religion is the only power which can make socialism succeed if it is to be established. It cannot work in an irreligious country." Here again he was a prophet, for what developed in Russia was not socialism at all. By Marxist measures, Rauschenbusch was a mild man. For example, one thing he fought for was a government parcel post system so that people would not be forced to pay the exorbitant shipping fees demanded by railroads. He also wanted a government money-order system so that people could pay their bills without also having to pay heavy bank charges. The day came when Americans take these services so much for granted that it seemed incredible they were once so seriously needed that they were subjects for lecture platforms.

Walter Rauschenbusch was a prophet in another way, a sad way. He was eventually without honor in his own country. The change of the public heart came on suddenly and grew out of World War I. Rauschenbusch had always been a pacifist at heart. His study of history convinced him that wars were fought, whatever the battle cry, for economic reasons, out of selfishness. In the Kingdom of God on earth there would be no wars because there would be no selfishness; selfishness was a sin, so was war. The only exception Rauschenbusch made with this axiom was the Spanish-American War. From what he could learn, Spain was truly exploiting its Caribbean holdings, and on the basis of the Monroe Doctrine, he felt it was the moral duty of the United States to put an end to the exploitation.

But he felt differently about World War I. To him, it was clearly a battle for power and money, and as such it was sinful. When the war erupted in Europe, he wrote and spoke against both sides, and when it became apparent that America was being drawn into it he warned that a war on such a basis could only be the first of many such wars. As an antidote, he proposed what he called the League to Enforce Peace, which would be a conference of all nations to settle their differences by consultation and negotiation, punishing aggressors by boycotts and resorting to the use of an international police force only as a last resort. Again a prophet. But he was both too late and too early.

Americans wanted to get into the war. Rauschenbusch's own son hurried to France to join a volunteer ambulance corps. And the great numbers of people who once listened to Rauschenbusch as though he were the rereincarnated Christ now turned on him. When he urged them to cool their war fever, they responded with threatening questions. Hadn't he spent his boyhood in Germany? Hadn't he studied there as a young man? Hadn't he gone back on visits numerous times? Hadn't he spent most of his life working among German immigrants? Hadn't he taught in a German school in Rochester? Hadn't he written most of his books in German before translating them into English? Well, what sort of a man was this Walter Rauschenbusch? Was he the pacifist he claimed to be? Or was he really a German lover? Was that really it? Well, let him go back there, then.

So American ships continued to transport war supplies into Allied ports and inevitably some of them were sunk by the German fleet. On April 6, 1917, the United States declared war on Germany, and with that thousands of young Americans rushed off to what they thought would be a glorious adventure but which turned out to be an enormous hell.

Walter Rauschenbusch was heartsick. America's entry into

the war was, to him, a sad mistake because it ended America's chance to act as a peacemaker, which he considered the proper role for the Kingdom of God on earth. He announced: "I will mourn for my country as long as I live." Thereafter he always wore black suits, and attached to his lapel was a piece of crepe.

He had not long to mourn, for he had not long to live. Known only to a few was the fact that he was suffering from cancer. On July 25, 1918, he died.

Writers of his obituaries who knew nothing of his illness said he had died of a broken heart, brought on by the war, and there was a certain truth in it. For several years he had watched a sense of moral purpose develop in America and upon this he built his hopes that the country would mature into the spiritual protector of the small and weak of the world. Suddenly he saw his hopes blasted by a burst of patriotism in a war which he felt did not involve patriotism at all but merely the age-old battle for power. By participating in such a war, Rauschenbusch believed, America would lose even if she won. Surely this attitude, coupled with the knowledge that he was fighting a losing battle against cancer, weakened him physically and hastened his death.

In his sorrow, Rauschenbusch forgot his own dictum that social progress was slow, that the things he wanted for America would be a long time in coming, that ideas in religion, science and politics that were considered heresy today would become orthodoxy tomorrow because of the simple fact that, however slowly he discerned it, man would gradually learn that his own salvation in this world and the next depended entirely on how much he was willing to do for the similar salvation of all men. Because of the life and work of Walter Rauschenbusch, America traveled a long way upon this road in a remarkably short time.

CHAPTER NINE

The King of Baltimore

IN 1916, when James Cardinal Gibbons was eighty-two years old, former President Theodore Roosevelt publicly said to him: "Taking your life as a whole, I think you now occupy the position of being the most respected and venerated and useful citizen of our country." This was an impressive statement for a President to make about anybody, and to address it to a man whose church had been widely denounced as incompatible to the American way of life was even more remarkable. But James Gibbons had spent his own life proving that the accusations against Roman Catholicism were wrong. In doing so, he occasionally found himself opposed by fellow members of the American hierarchy who lacked his vision and dedication, but by adhering to his principles and convictions he was able to build a bridge of brotherhood and tolerance that made Roosevelt's comment about him representative of the general feeling of the country.

James Gibbons was the Catholic leader of America during a period when both his church and his country were undergoing important changes. This was a factor he always kept in mind and he based his judgments on it. In both instances, the changes would be for the good, although there were men both in the country and in the Church who could not foresee this and thus did not believe it. Also, in both instances, the changes had been brought about by wars.

In America, the Civil War, which had so painfully divided the country, eventually served to unite it into a stronger, richer, more powerful Union. Carpetbaggers who had done so much damage were slowly eradicated. Northern industry increased; southern harvests improved. Regional problems persisted, naturally, and it was in solving the problems that the country ennobled itself.

The circumstances of change in Gibbons' church were more complex. Around the fourth century, it became the custom of the rich to bequeath property to the Church, until, over the years, the Church acquired large holdings in Italy that stretched across the country. The income from these Papal States, as they were called, was used to support works of charity among the sick, the poor and the aged throughout the world as Christianity spread. Sadly but understandably, the Papal States became the prized goal of ambitious kings who wanted both to capture the Church's property and to control the Church itself. It therefore grew necessary for the Popes to enter into alliances with friendly kings against the unfriendly and even to contribute to the armies of friendly kings against a common enemy. The dangers in this were evidenced in the political turmoil that rampaged in Europe for centuries, the reigns of a few ill-equipped Popes and the justified discontent voiced by men before and after Martin Luther. Now, in the years following the American Civil War, a growing desire arose among the people to rid Italy of its cluster of kingdoms and unify it into one nation. An important obstacle stood in the way: the Papal States. Although the proponents of unification were Catholics and therefore reluctant to act against the Church, they were nevertheless determined to succeed in their cause. Revolutionary armies swept across the Papal States, claiming them now to be the property of the people, and the temporal holdings of the Catholic Church were reduced to a hundred and eight acres in the city of Rome.

This tiny parcel of land bothered a lot of people. It was, however, necessary that it should exist. As leaders of an international religion that operated churches, schools, hospitals, orphanages and other institutions in many countries, which required negotiations with many governments, the Popes themselves could not be subject to any government because of the tremendous legal technicalities involved. The Popes had to have a country of their own, however small, in order to be free to conduct church affairs. What bothered people was this: did Catholics, by their faith, owe temporal allegiance to the small country called Vatican City? And if Vatican City found itself at odds with, say, America, which side would American Catholics take? Could, therefore, a good Catholic be a good American?

James Gibbons devoted his life to the answers.

2

He was born in Baltimore on July 23, 1834, the fourth of five children born to Thomas and Bridget Gibbons, Irish immigrants who had arrived in America in 1829. On August 4, he was baptized at the Cathedral of the Assumption by Father Charles I. White. In years to come, James Gibbons would reign in the cathedral as archbishop of Baltimore and he would preach at the funeral of the man who had baptized him. But a great deal was to happen to him meantime.

In 1837, Thomas Gibbons fell ill. Doctors contributed part of his condition to the hot, humid Maryland weather and suggested he seek cooler climate, at least for awhile. Gibbons decided to take his family back to Ireland for a visit; the visit turned out to be a sixteen-year stay. So James Gibbons grew up in Ireland. This was another of the strained periods in Anglo-Irish relations and Catholic schools were again closed. James was therefore educated in the private home of a Catholic tutor, along with six other boys. During vacations, he worked in the grocery store his father had opened.

Thomas Gibbons died in 1847; two years later, James's sister Catherine died. Bridget Gibbons tried to continue the grocery store, but her sorrow was too great and her experience too limited. In 1853 she sold the store and prepared to take her family back to America. Baltimore held too many memories for her, so she chose New Orleans. James was then nineteen. He found a job as a clerk in a department store.

These were bad times in New Orleans. A yellow fever epidemic broke out; James caught it and was seriously ill for three months. Also, the Know-Nothing political party was then at its height of influence. The party had evolved from complaints that immigrants, particularly Catholic immigrants, were too clannish socially and politically and that, functioning as a unit, they were a threat to the established, nativistic political machines. Membership in the party was held secret; the party took its name from the habit of its members to say they knew nothing when questioned by the police regarding riots the party incited against Catholic immigrants. The Know-Nothings were against the naturalization of Catholic immigrants, the holding of public office by them and aid to parochial schools, which was common practice in areas where states could not afford adequate public schools. At its height, the party controlled six states and many cities during the decade of the 1850's. Although James Gibbons was born in America, he was, in the eyes of Know-Nothings active in New Orleans, fresh off the boat, and there seemed little chance that he would amount to anything in an era where his future was doomed because of his past.

He had always been a religious boy. In Ireland, he had learned to serve Mass and frequently did. In New Orleans, he attended Mass daily and led the family Rosary every evening. In February, 1854, he heard a sermon on the priesthood, and before it was over he decided that the priesthood was for him. He discussed his decision with the priest who had given the sermon, and the man agreed James had decided correctly. New Orleans had a seminary, but the priest suggested it would be wiser for James to attend the older and better-staffed seminary near Baltimore. Bridget Gibbons was both saddened and pleased by her son's decision, saddened because she knew he would now spend most of his life away from her, pleased because she felt he was entering the finest service to God available to a Catholic man.

In church terms, Baltimore was a premier see. Maryland had been awarded to George Calvert, the first Lord Baltimore, by King Charles I in 1632 and was named after Queen Henrietta Maria. Calvert was Catholic; Maryland was to be a haven for British Catholics, then persecuted in England, and it was the first of the English provinces in the New World to offer religious tolerance to all. Later Catholics immigrating considered Baltimore a natural place for them. For awhile, Baltimore was the largest American city, and Catholic missionaries arriving on the East Coast entered at Baltimore. When, in 1789, the Vatican decided America was ready for its first diocese, Baltimore was chosen, and the first American bishop was also the first American to become a bishop—John Carroll, born in Maryland, whose family produced signers of the Declaration of Independence and members of the first Congress. For the next century, the bishops of Baltimore were the liaison between the

Vatican and the American hierarchy, holding precedence over all the other American sees, the word "see" being derived from the Latin *sedilia,* meaning chair, in this case a bishop's throne.

In September, 1855, at the age of twenty-one, James Gibbons entered St. Charles College at Ellicott City, a few miles outside Baltimore, to begin his two years of pre-seminary training. He studied Greek, French, Latin, Hebrew, English, church history and elocution; his hunger for knowledge and his gift for learning kept him at the head of his class. He then advanced to St. Mary's Seminary, on North Paca Street in Baltimore, for four years of philosophy and theology. The Seminary had been founded by Bishop Carroll in 1791; its professors were Sulpician Fathers, brilliant French teachers who had been evicted from France during the antireligious persecutions of the French Revolution. Bishop Carroll invited them to take over his seminary, and for the next hundred years they operated most of the seminaries in the East. Again, James Gibbons was at the head of his class.

Ordained on June 30, 1861, by Archbishop Francis Patrick Kenrick, Gibbons was assigned as a curate at St. Patrick's Church, near Fell's Point on Chesapeake Bay. He was there only six weeks when he was made pastor of St. Bridget's Church, in the Canton section, and also given charge of St. Lawrence O'Toole Church, a mile away and on the opposite shore of the Patapsco River, and to serve both churches he had to commute by rowboat.

The Civil War had already begun. Maryland had sided with the South, but Union troops quickly moved in and established military law. An election was held and representatives were sent to Congress, thereby holding the state in the Union. At heart, James Gibbons was a southerner—his younger brother was a Confederate officer, but by conviction James was a Yankee, and so he took on assignments as Catholic chaplain at Fort Marshall and Fort McHenry. As chaplain, he felt free to give spiritual and material comfort to both Union soldiers and Confederate prisoners. The Fort McHenry commander, however, ordered Gibbons to leave the Confederates alone, and when Gibbons refused, the commander revoked his pass to enter the camp.

"Unless I get my pass back," Gibbons told the commander, "I'm going to write President Lincoln." He got it back.

One day a Confederate soldier on furlough was captured while visiting his Maryland family, and the Fort McHenry commander sentenced him to hanging. Gibbons argued that the soldier had not been a combatant at the time of his arrest and did not warrant such a severe sentence, but the commander would not listen. This time Gibbons did write President Lincoln. Not receiving an answer by the day of the execution, Gibbons presumed that the soldier was hanged on schedule. A few days later, he learned that Lincoln had commuted the sentence to life imprisonment. After the war, the soldier was released and he went to call on Gibbons.

"You saved me from a noose once," the soldier said. "Now I'm asking you to tie one around my neck. I'm getting married. Will you perform the ceremony?"

"Maybe I ought to write the President again," Gibbons said.

At approximately this same time, Gibbons was invited to participate in another ceremony. Archbishop Kenricks had died and was succeeded by Archbishop John Lancaster Spalding, formerly prelate of Louisville. Gibbons had visited Spalding on a vacation journey to New Orleans and was the only priest in Baltimore the archbishop knew; thus when he needed a secretary, he appointed Gibbons. In his new job, young Gibbons was in daily correspondence with other bishops in America and with the cardinals who headed the various ecclesiastical departments in Rome. He became a well-known man. In 1866, Spalding decided to hold a conference of bishops—a plenary council—for the purpose of discussing with them various problems facing the church in America. Gibbons was put in charge of all arrangements, and the skill and ease with which he organized them brought him even more popularity.

One problem discussed at the council was the need for more American bishops. As required, the council drew up a *terna,* a list of three candidates, for each area in need of a bishop, and to his surprise James Gibbons found himself on the lists both for Erie, Pennsylvania, and the state of North Carolina. He was depressed. He did not want to leave Baltimore; furthermore, he was only thirty-two years old, too young, he felt, for the responsibilities of a bishop. He asked that his name be removed from the lists. It wasn't. The lists were sent to Rome for the final selections to be made; two years later Gibbons learned that he had been appointed to North Carolina. He was, at thirty-four, the youngest Catholic bishop in the world.

Gibbons was consecrated in Baltimore by Spalding, who then accompanied him to the small Church of St. Thomas, in Wilmington, which was to be his headquarters. After enthroning him, Spalding returned to Baltimore, where he wrote Gibbons: "I was truly affected when I left you Monday morning. I thought you looked like an orphan."

"I felt like one," Gibbons replied, and he had cause to. After the busy church life in Baltimore, he was now practically alone. In the entire state of North Carolina, there were only three priests and three churches. Out of a population of over a million, there were seven hundred Catholics, but no schools, hospitals or other institutions. He was starting from much less than scratch.

Part of his duty in building the Church in North Carolina was to seek converts, but Gibbons was less concerned about this than he was in bringing back to the Church Catholics who had fallen away because of the lack of facilities; some families had been out of the Church for two and three generations. Gibbons began to seek them out. Travel was primitive. To reach the people he sought, Gibbons had to make thousand-mile trips across the state, mostly on horseback. Protestant clergymen were extremely helpful. They invited him to sleep at their homes; they let him use their churches for his speeches; they led him to families who had Catholic backgrounds. This co-operation profoundly impressed Gibbons and was the seed of the interfaith fellowship he practiced all his life despite some criticism from Rome.

Gibbons was summoned to Rome in October, 1869, to attend the ecumenical council called by Pope Pius IX. He expected to be away three or four months, but was out of North Carolina a year. The main item at the council was the doctrine of papal infallibility, and it was highly controversial. By tradition, when writing or speaking about matters of morals or the practice of the faith the Popes had always been accepted as infallible, but Pope Pius IX wanted tradition to become established doctrine by a majority vote of the world's bishops.

As the youngest bishop present, Gibbons considered it wisest for him to say little and listen much. Like others, he had the right to express his opinion in writing on any matter, and he did so only when he suggested that the word "Roman" be dropped from the identification of the Church. The word "catholic" meant universal, and that was a far better label, Gibbons thought. The council's reaction was cool. Several bishops pointed out that there were others who called themselves Catholics—the English, a few sects in the Middle East and even some American schisms—and that furthermore the Roman label was important because of its allusion to apostolic succession from St. Peter, the first Bishop of Rome on which the Vatican hung its claim to being the church Christ had started. Very well, Gibbons countered, why not identify the Church for what it was: holy, catholic, apostolic and Roman? This was approved.

The infallibility controversy was more difficult to resolve. All the bishops agreed that the doctrine existed in essence, but many of them were reluctant to approve it as fact because of the possible public reaction. In countries where Catholicism was the state religion, government leaders usually thought they also ran the Church, and so, many bishops felt, there might be severe political repercussions if an official pronouncement were made that the Popes ran it. Other bishops feared that stating the doctrine would separate Catholics even further from their Protestant brethren. Although the nature of Protestantism granted infallibility to each of its adherents through the prerogative of personal interpretation of the Bible, the idea that a man officially became infallible in this same sphere for all Catholics upon his election to the papacy might, the bishops said, look like spiritual despotism.

In spirit, Gibbons was for the doctrine. Also, he had learned in North Carolina how well Catholics and Protestants could get along, but he realized this was not true everywhere and he felt it might be wiser to postpone the doctrinal announcement until interfaith fellowship had deeper roots. However, he knew what he would do when the matter was put to a vote. On July 11, 1870, the question was put: Was it true that the Popes, as vicars of Christ on earth, received such guidance from the Holy Ghost that they could not err in their proclamations on matters pertaining to faith and morals? The answer was overwhelmingly yes. Next question: Shall we bishops, as apostolic heirs of St. Peter, now proclaim this as Catholic doctrine? The bishops who feared political repercussions went home without answering. Of the five hundred and thirty-five who remained, all but two answered yes. The negative answers came from a bishop of the Kingdom of Naples, whose ruler was against the doctrine, and from the bishop of Little Rock, Arkansas, who felt the announcement would hamper his work. The majority ruled; the doctrine was established.

Returning home, Gibbons resumed his work and travels. By 1872, he had more than doubled North Carolina's Catholic population, mostly by attracting those who had fallen away. He also doubled the number of his priests by accepting seminarians who wanted to work with him. He built a dozen chapels across the state and opened grammar schools in Wilmington and New Bern. He gave personal guidance and encouragement to Thomas F. Price, the first North Carolinian to become a priest; Price went on to become co-founder of the Maryknoll Fathers, the American missionary society.

Then came news that the bishop of Richmond, Virginia, had died. Spalding wired Gibbons, asking if he would accept the Richmond diocese, retaining North Carolina as well until a successor could be found. Gibbons accepted. He was just settling in his new diocese when Spalding died, being succeeded by Bishop James Roosevelt Bayley, of Newark, New Jersey. Bayley was not known in Baltimore, and in his search for friends he turned more and more to James Gibbons, personally and professionally. In 1877, Bayley wrote Gibbons that he considered himself too old and too ill to conduct the important work of the Baltimore see alone, and he asked if Gibbons would be willing to transfer to Baltimore as coadjutor with the right of succession. It was like asking somebody to become Vice-President of the country. Gibbons replied that he would be willing, provided the other archbishops of America indicate their approval of him in writing to Rome. This was done; Rome consented to the transfer, but before Gibbons could make the move Bayley died. Thus, just as he had left Baltimore eleven years before as the youngest bishop in the Church, he now returned, at forty-three, as the youngest archbishop.

The swift events caught Rome unprepared. Months passed before Gibbons received from Rome the pallium, the white woolen pendant that was both a symbol of the archbishopric and its badge of authority. Donning it, Gibbons became the Catholic leader of the country. Although Archbishop John McCloskey, of New York, had been made America's first cardinal in 1875, Gibbons held the premier see of Baltimore and thus ranked first.

Because of his illness, Bayley had left Baltimore affairs in considerable disarray, and Gibbons was busy for many months establishing order. Meantime, Pope Pius IX died and was succeeded by Pope Leo XIII, which meant a further slow-down in church progress. It was therefore 1884 before Gibbons felt things were sufficiently under control for him to call a plenary council, the first since 1866, at which he had made his deep impression upon the hierarchy. At this one, he would make a deep impression upon the world.

3

In twenty years, many new and difficult problems had arisen in America. The council would certainly be an important one. In approving the council, the Vatican suggested that a representative of the Pope should be present to give the official view on anything discussed. Most of the American hierarchy was opposed to this. There was already too much criticism in the country to the effect that Catholicism was a foreign religion that had no place in America; the presence of the Pope's delegate at the council would only stir further criticism. On behalf of the American hierarchy, Gibbons sent this opinion to Rome, and in reply he was told that since an apostolic delegate was absolutely essential at the council, the Pope had chosen him to be it. The appointment was unusual and gave Gibbons even more stature. It would be up to him now to present what he considered to be the Pope's opinions of the various matters facing the council.

The most pressing matter involved an organization called the Knights of Labor, which had developed simultaneously in Canada and the United States. It was a labor union struggling to survive in an era when many states had laws against unions and others offered unions no protection. It was also a secret organization, and this was what the Catholic Church disliked, having already had its woes with secret groups like the Know-Nothings, the Klu Klux Klan and Freemasonry. Secrecy, the Church felt, prevented the execution of justice should the organization or any of its members commit crimes. Secrecy also often developed the organization into a semireligious group with pledges and practices and oaths that might be contrary to doctrine and thus endanger the salvation of Catholics in it. For these reasons, Archbishop Elzear A. Taschereau, of Quebec, Canada, banned Catholics from belonging to the Knights of Labor. It was expected that the United States hierarchy would follow suit.

Because of Gibbons, it did not. Gibbons believed labor had a right to organize and he approved of strikes and boycotts as legitimate means to obtain wage increases in cases where negotiations failed or were prohibited. He disliked, however, the idea of a closed shop, preferring that each worker should have the right to his own decision regarding union membership and should not be denied the right to work if he chose to remain non-union.

Aware that the Knights would be a council topic, Gibbons did his homework well in advance. He invited Terence V. Powderly, a leader of the Knights, to confer with him in Baltimore, and when the two men sat together Gibbons asked, "Will you let me see a copy of your constitution?"

"Certainly," said Powderly, and he handed a copy to Gibbons.

Gibbons was happily surprised. He asked, "And is it possible to see your membership list?"

"Here," said Powderly, "is a list of our officers. We have over half a million members and a list of their names would make quite a package, but if you want it I will get it for you."

"I thought you were supposed to be a secret organization," Gibbons said.

"We're gradually losing the need for secrecy," Powderly explained. "At one time, any man suspected of being a Knight would be fired. Today our membership is such that if any man were fired for that reason, half the rest of the factory would walk out with him. An injury to one is the concern of all; that's our motto. Then, too, at one time we didn't want management to know our strength, which wasn't much for a long time, but now that we are powerful we feel it might be a good idea to let management know."

"About closed shops," said Gibbons, "do you think it's fair to refuse a qualified man a job because he won't join the union?"

"The union can only be as strong as its membership on any given job," Powderly stated.

Gibbons said, "Yes, but don't you think that the worthiness of a union should be a matter of individual evaluation?"

Powderly smiled. "We look forward to the day when all workers feel all unions are worthy."

Gibbons said, "So do I. But the challenge is to the unions, not the worker."

They talked on, then Gibbons asked: "If I find anything in your constitution contrary to Catholic doctrine, will you be willing to change it?"

"I'd be willing to discuss it with you," Powderly conceded. "But I don't think you'll find anything."

Gibbons didn't. When the subject reached the council, Gibbons sat silently as other bishops stated why the Knights of Labor should be banned: it was a secret organization, its strikes were often accompanied by violence, the ban precedent had been established in Canada and for the appearance of unity should be followed.

Then Gibbons spoke up. He told of his meeting with Powderly and its, to him, satisfactory results. "Knowing this," he said, "if we proceed to ban the Knights simply because they have been banned elsewhere we shall be acting against intellectual honesty, and I shall not be a party to that. Furthermore, it is common knowledge that most American laborers are Catholic immigrants and their children. If we ban the Knights, Catholics will be forced to quit it. That will seriously deplete the union's membership and make it ineffectual, and the exploitation that has made the union necessary will go on for years. We will be harming our own people and the cause of unions, perhaps for generations. I recommend that on this subject we take no action whatsoever."

The recommendation was approved, and when news of it became public there was wide delight in America, specific anger in Canada and deep consternation in Rome. And there was no doubt anywhere: Gibbons had given labor the impetus it needed to become a vital American factor.

Another matter confronting the council also involved immigrants, but it was more specifically a Catholic internal matter. Facing a language barrier, Italian, German and Polish immigrants were inclined to cluster in big cities, particularly in the Midwest, where they continued to speak their old languages and live their old customs. They thus became both social and economic factors. They wanted newspapers in their native languages, they shopped where they could easiest be understood, they hired each other, married each other and influenced each other. In church, it was necessary to preach sermons in the European language, and the immigrants wanted their children in parochial schools to be taught in the family language. Moreover, they not only asked for priests who knew their language, but they were insisting that bishops of their own national background be appointed to the dioceses where they lived. In Detroit, Pittsburgh, Chicago, Milwaukee, St. Louis, the twin cities, they were a powerful and vociferous factor, and they made their wants known not only to their clergy but through their compatriot clergymen to the entire American hierarchy, even to Rome.

Here, too, there were mixed feelings. Rome, which had only a slim grasp on American mentality, approved the idea. After all, there were a dozen languages spoken in Europe. Why shouldn't a dozen be used in America? The American clergy and hierarchy of recent European extraction were either entirely for the idea or at least sympathetic to it. Most of them faced the language problem in their own parishes and dioceses and felt the only solution was to retain the foreign influences. Gibbons was sternly against all of it. Although he was the son of immigrants himself and had spent sixteen of his years living in a foreign country, he was American by birth and conviction. America, he felt, was to be a melting pot, blending into a new nationalism the best of what Europe had to offer and enriching it with the unique spirit that made America what it was, and this, he believed, could never be accomplished as long as immigrant groups clung to the customs and languages of the old countries. He told the council:

"A parish which has a large number of foreign-born adults should have perhaps one or two Masses on Sunday at which the sermon is given in the language which these people best understand, thus assuring them the full benefits of their attendance. But at the same time, these people should be urged to learn English so that the practice of foreign-language sermons can be discontinued as early as possible. In no instance should a foreign tongue be the teaching language in an American school. The language of America is English, and children must be proficient in it if they are to become effective citizens. Their parents came to this country in order to benefit from American opportunities; the children should therefore be raised in the American way. Lastly, we would act in error if we recommended to the Holy See as candidates for a particular American diocese men whose primary qualification was that they shared the European background of the laity. The Catholic Church is truly catholic, universal, adaptable. In Spain, let the church be Spanish; in Germany, let it be German; in America, let it be American. Let it develop its own American character. To do otherwise would be a disservice to our church, our country, our people."

In all this, Gibbons had the support particularly of Cardinal McCloskey of New York, and Archbishop John Ireland of St. Paul, Minnesota. Others who shared their sentiments were not quite as outspoken, while those with the opposite view were too much so. But Gibbons' arguments made sense, and the only valid argument his opponents could put forth was that some consideration must be shown adults who did not speak English and most likely never would speak it well. Gibbons granted that consideration—in sermons. In the circumstances, there was little to be gained by long discussion on the problem. Gibbons had taken his stand, unpopular though it was, and that settled it. As holder of the Baltimore see, he was ultimately responsible for the lists of recommendations for new bishops that went to Rome, and since he would obviously seek advice from others who shared his views on the foreign-language question, there was small likelihood that any man would become a bishop who stood too blatantly on the opposite side of the fence. There was, too, another factor that had to be taken into account: most of the nuns teaching in Catholic elementary schools were foreigners who had come to America specifically to work among their own language groups, which meant another obstacle in the use of English. But this would be remedied as more and more American girls become teaching nuns. It would all be a matter of time, and Gibbons wanted everybody to know there was a time limit.

A third question before the council also dealt with schools: the government aid to them. From the start, American schools were affiliated with religions, from the lower grades attached to parishes to colleges supported by denominations. As early as 1657, the Massachusetts colonial legislature exercised government influence over schools by requiring attendance and setting standards. In towns of fifty families where there was no church school, the local council was obliged to hire a teacher who was paid out of taxes, thus initiating public schools. Thomas Jefferson took steps to turn all schools into public schools, but this was strongly resisted by Protestant groups that could not agree what type of religion should be taught. As the Civil War neared, most states authorized local communities to tax to support public schools. Catholics opposed the trend because they feared it meant the gradual demise of the denominational schools.

Protestants were amenable, as long as the religion taught was nonsectarian Protestantism. A growing number of educators, however, urged that the public schools exclude religion courses entirely, declaring that this was the only way the Constitutional specification of separation of church and state could be upheld. After the war, President U. S. Grant announced that there would be no federal aid to denominational schools in the territories or on Indian reservations. By tradition, school boards were mostly locally controlled, and so there was a great variety of opinion on how the Grant idea should be executed with local schools. As the population rapidly increased so did the number of churches, but most Protestant congregations were too small to support their own schools and thus there was steadily growing Protestant endorsement of public school systems, with or without religion courses. Even so, public support of denominational schools continued in many areas. In two Minnesota towns, for example, the school board leased denominational schools for a dollar a year, in return for which they maintained the schools entirely, including the salaries of the teachers. However, as the Protestant primary and secondary schools faded away, the opposition to the use of taxes to support religious schools increased and the battle cry went up that such practices were unconstitutional. Lutherans, Episcopalians and Catholics were for awhile united in their hope for continued public assistance to their schools, but by the time of the Baltimore council the Catholics stood alone.

Gibbons shared the hierarchal conviction that public support of religious schools was within constitutional prerogatives, but he was unwilling to encourage Catholic pressures for an adjustment in the First Amendment in this regard. Gibbons had both great respect and love for the United States Constitution and felt that it ought not be too quickly modified. Furthermore, he perceived that the school issue had passed beyond the realm of constitutionality into denominational controversy. This, to him, was a bad turn of events. A public school system with no religion at all would be detrimental to all religions, for these were a child's most impressionable years and if during them, by a lack of religious studies, he did not develop an intuitive religious judgment, he might never develop it. Thus there was a great deal at stake. The Catholic uneasiness was based on the accepted fact that the majority of Catholics in the country were immigrants who would not be able to afford the tuitions that would become necessary should schools be forced to support themselves. Canon law required parents to give their children Catholic educations, but if there was no money and thus no school the law obviously could not be upheld. Even so, if the Protestants had a change of heart and no longer wanted public funds to be used for denominational schools, Gibbons felt the Catholics must resign themselves to finding some way to manage on their own. It would be difficult, it would be tremendously expensive, but Gibbons preferred these burdens rather than take on a public battle that would divide Protestants and Catholics more than they already were.

In this, too, Gibbons had little support from other prelates. Some thought he was being weak. Others accused him of settling for second-class citizenship. Explaining himself, he pointed to the Declaration of Independence and the Constitution, both of which, he said, put the emphasis on individualism, and he hopefully prophesied that perhaps one day Americans would catch up with the advanced thinking of their founding fathers by granting educational aid to students on an individual basis, regardless of which school they chose to attend. Meanwhile, he urged, Catholics should push their own school program, paying for it as best they could. Other bishops, despite their objections to the popular trend, recognized that Gibbons was right, and in the end they went along with him.

An important contribution to education that came out of the council was the founding of the Catholic University of America in Washington, D. C. Gibbons rightly expected some Rome resistance to the university. Although eventually the university opened its doors to the laity, it was originally intended to use the school only for the clergy. Ordinarily, American priests went to the centuries-old Gregorian University in Rome for their higher degrees in philosophy and theology, but this was very expensive and thus limited the number who could go. The American plan was to cull a faculty from among the best minds in the country, put it into one school and make it available to the promising students of all dioceses and religious societies. More seminarians would get better educations in this way and the standard of the American clergy would ineluctably rise on a broader scale. Rome's objections to such institutions was based on its dread of chauvinism. In other countries, extreme nationalism had weakened the intellectual ties to Rome, the world center of Catholic thought, and there had even been evidence of an actual drift from Rome. Now the danger seemed to be arising in America.

It was inevitable, because of the unusual stands the Baltimore council took on union, foreign-language schools, public aid to education and the university, that Gibbons, the Pope's representative, should be summoned to Rome for the purpose of explaining just what on earth was going on.

4

He was in Rome several weeks, conferring with cardinals of the Roman Curia, the papal cabinet, and with Pope Leo XIII himself. The Pope, more than others, was content with Gibbons' explanations. Moreover, the discussion the Pope and Gibbons had on labor unions subsequently proved to be the basis of a papal encyclical, *Rerum novarum,* which dealt with the conditions of the working classes and the responsibilities of the Church, governments and unions for improvements. The Pope was far more liberal than many of the cardinals who surrounded him, men whose European backgrounds convinced them that any division between church and state meant the end of the Church. Gibbons expressed the opinion that where there was a union of church and state it was invariably the state that interfered with the church rather than the other way around.

To the surprise of many, Gibbons returned to Baltimore with the Pope's blessing. President Grover Cleveland and Gibbons were good friends. They had attended many public functions together, Gibbons was often a guest at the White House, and Cleveland had taken Gibbons' advice against outlawing the Knights of Labor when there was a chance that the Government might do so. Soon after Gibbons' return from Rome, the Pope celebrated his golden jubilee as a bishop, and Cleveland asked Gibbons what might be a fitting gift to send to Rome. Gibbons said, "Send a copy of the Constitution." Cleveland did.

Cardinal McCloskey died. America was now without a representative in the ecclesiastical body that was sometimes called the Senate of the Church. Rumors spread about McCloskey's successor; the general feeling was that it would be Gibbons. On May 18, 1886, the rumors were confirmed: Gibbons was on the list of new cardinals announced by the Vatican. On June

29, a papal representative arrived from Rome with the zucchetto, the red skullcap worn by cardinals. Next day, the red biretta was presented to him. The following year, on March 17, the consistory was held in Rome at which Gibbons and the other cardinals-elect went through the ceremonies that officially made them members of the cardinalate. Traditionally, each cardinal was put in charge of a Rome church as evidence of his nearness to the Pope, also the Bishop of Rome. Gibbons was given the Church of Santa Maria, in the Trastevere section. Aware of his new importance in the Church in America and also aware of the confused conceptions many foreigners had of the American Church, he used the occasion of taking over Santa Maria for a remarkable speech. He began with a brief history of the development of the Church in the United States, and then he said:

> "For myself, as a citizen of the United States, without closing my eyes to our defects as a nation, I proclaim, with a deep sense of pride and gratitude and in this great capital of Christendom, that I belong to a country where the Civil Government holds over us the aegis of its protection without interfering in the legitimate exercise of our sublime mission as ministers of the Gospel of Jesus Christ. Our country has liberty without license, authority without despotism. Hers is no spirit of exclusiveness. She has no frowning fortifications to repel the invader, for we are at peace with all the world. In the consciousness of her strength and of her good will to all nations she rests secure. Her harbors are open in the Atlantic and Pacific to welcome the honest immigrant who comes to advance his temporal interest and to find a peaceful home. But while we are acknowledged to have a free government, we do not perhaps receive due credit for possessing also a strong government. Yes, our nation is strong, and her strength lies, under Providence, in the majesty and supremacy of the law, in the loyalty of her citizens to that law and in the affection of our people for their free institutions.

> There are, indeed, grave social problems which are engaging the citizens of the United States. But I have no doubt that, with God's blessings, these problems will be solved without violence or revolution or injury to the individual right."

These were strong words for Gibbons to utter at a time when in several countries the Church was struggling to retain her favored position. The world knew, of course, that America practiced a separation of church and state and that on this basis the American Church was being cut off from public support of its schools. Now for the country's leading Catholic clergyman to say he still felt the Church in America was in healthy circumstances staggered many of his European counterparts. The European Catholic press criticized Gibbons, whereas European anticlerics, then rising particularly in France, said he had spoken like a sage. In America, reactions were unanimous. Daily papers and both the Protestant and Catholic publications agreed that he had put the American position clearly and magnificently. Pope Leo said nothing, but he expressed his attitude later in an encyclical he addressed to the French royalists who had stubbornly refused to give support to the republic government France had adopted in hopes that, without them, it would collapse. As the principal contributors to the Church, the royalists expected the Pope to take their side. On the contrary, the Pope assured them that the era of kingdoms was coming to a close, that Catholics both could and should take an active part in republican governments, that if they didn't they would have no excuse if anticlerics gained control and instituted persecutions. The royalists were appalled by the encyclical and complained that they had been double-crossed, but American Catholics saw in it further church approval of the relationship that existed here between religion and government.

But that was not the end of the matter. Just as there were

men in the French clergy who admired the American position, so there were men in the American clergy who sympathized with the French royalists. However, as long as Gibbons spoke for the American Church its attitude would be as he had defined it in Rome, with which most American Catholics agreed. Then three unrelated events occurred which completely distorted the picture. In 1888 when President Cleveland issued his Thanksgiving Day proclamation, Gibbons issued a supplementary statement, urging Catholics to attend church on that day and instructing priests to say special prayers for divine guidance for public officials. Other bishops quickly complained, criticizing Gibbons for attaching Catholic significance to what was described as "that damnably Puritanical substitute for Christmas." Gibbons ignored the criticism.

The second event involved a biography of Isaac Hecker, a convert who became a priest and subsequently founded the Paulist Fathers, whose mission was to explain Catholic doctrine to interested non-Catholics. The book was written by Father Walter Elliott, himself a Paulist, and in interpreting some of Hecker's methods Elliott was inclined to exaggerate Hecker's tolerance with converts. According to Elliott , Hecker, who had died in 1888, readily accepted as converts people who nevertheless rejected such Catholic doctrine as papal infallibility, the virgin birth, the True Presence, hierarchal prerogatives or anything else. This was not true, as Gibbons, from his friendship with Hecker, knew. Hecker had been patient and lenient, but not unorthodox. Chances were that nothing would have come out of the unfortunate portrait of Hecker had the book not been translated into French by a translator who exaggerated even more than Elliott had. It now appeared that Hecker not only minimized church tradition and law, but he also assured converts that whatever doctrine they couldn't accept at the time of their conversion would be clarified for them by the Holy Ghost later on.

The Preface to the French edition was written by a zealously pro-American Paris clergyman who said that Hecker had produced a method of conversion which the French would be wise to emulate. The name he gave to what he thought was Hecker's method was Americanism. Overnight the majority of the French clergy spoke out against Americanism. Rome blasted the idea. In the United States, where Americanism was defined as the love of country, bishops had no idea what was going on in France and wondered what all the fuss was about.

The third event again involved Gibbons directly. At the Chicago Columbian Exposition, a Parliament of the World's Religions was to be held in September, 1893, and Gibbons was invited to speak for Catholicism. He was going to be in Chicago at the time, to attend a lay congress, so he accepted the invitation. When the time came, however, he was not well, and although he was present on the platform of the Parliament his speech was read by another bishop. The title was "The Needs of Humanity Supplied by the Catholic Religion," and he discussed what the Church had done for workers, for the old and sick and poor, for the abolition of slavery and in encouraging people to lead holier lives. The speech ended with a reminder that it was the duty of all Christians to work for the betterment of life, and the words: "Though we differ in faith, thank God there is one platform on which we stand united—and that is the platform of charity and benevolence."

When news of the session and the speech reached France, the Americanists interpreted both as an interfaith religious ceremony at which Gibbons had implied that doctrinal differences were unimportant and all that really mattered was charity and benevolence. Rome took the French report to be accurate and wrote Gibbons, asking that since Catholic laymen were not permitted to attend interfaith religious services, just what was a cardinal doing at one?

So quite a storm developed, stirred by the winds of exaggeration, misunderstanding and suspicion. In America, the three events would soon have faded from public interest, but the furor in Europe forced the American hierarchy to re-evaluate the events, to take sides on them, then to start a little battle of their own. Gibbons discovered that Rome had cooled toward him. Doors were shut to his friends in the Vatican; answers to his letters came from lesser dignitaries; his recommendations for new American bishops were ignored. He realized how serious the situation had become and considered going to Rome for talks that might clear things up. And yet he knew that the trip would be blown entirely out of proportion by the press. He decided the best thing for him would be to wait and watch.

Certainly if the laxity attributed to Hecker had existed in the United States, it would have bordered on heresy. But it did not exist anywhere but in the minds of a few radical Frenchmen who, envying America's separation of church and state, had extended it to a separation of church from church. If such an idea caught fire, a great deal of damage could be done. True, American governments, federal and local, were in positions to take over what was ordinarily church work in the areas of education and the care of the sick and the poor, but few other governments were, and little would be done in these areas without the tandem efforts of both the governments and the Church.

In light of this and in light of the growing Americanism in France, it was inevitable that Pope Leo should, on January 6, 1895, address an encyclical to the American bishops on these topics. Ordinarily, the bishops would have been consulted on the contents of the encyclical before its release, but this time there was no consultation. The encyclical came as a surprise, as a relief and as a disappointment. In it, the Pope praised the Church in America for its work and the American Government for the philosophy of freedom of religion it encouraged. Then he went on to say that as admirable as this philosophy was, it would be inadvisable to suggest that this was "the most desirable status of the Church or that it would be universally lawful and expedient for state and church to be, as in America, dissevered and divorced." This made American bishops squirm—not because the Pope was wrong so far as other countries were concerned but because of the way American Protestants might interpret the statement. Continuing, the Pope firmly declared that there was no exigency that warranted modification of Catholic doctrine merely for the sake of harmony or easy conversions, and with this the American bishops fully agreed.

Two things irked the American bishops. First, if the Pope saw fit to condemn French Americanism as heretical, why did he address his encyclical to America? Second, since the Pope surely knew Americans were not responsible for French Americanism, why didn't he say so? Gibbons referred to these two questions in officially acknowledging the encyclical, and he was informed through private channels that although it had been addressed to America it was actually aimed at France where, because of the encyclical, French Americanism now faded almost overnight. Papal indirection of this sort was not uncommon. A few years earlier, the Pope wanted to instruct Catholics in England, Holland and France that they could not participate in the slave trade then carried on by their countries, and he did so by addressing his encyclical to Brazil. The indirection was effective because it made its point without thrusting embarrassing fingers directly at the guilty. Gibbons passed this information along to his American confreres, much to their consolation.

Still the matter was not closed. Neither in the press nor the pulpit did Protestantism make anything out of the Pope's encyclical statement that a closer church-state relationship might be desirable in certain countries, but 1896 was a Presidential election year and the American Protective Association, a quasi-political organization similar to the Know-Nothings, grabbed at it. Its president, W. H. J. Traynor, said: "The keystone of the A. P. A., in fact, is that a papist, no matter how liberal nominally, is not a consistent citizen of the United States." The two Presidential candidates were William Jennings Bryan for the Democrats and William McKinley for the Republicans. Because of Catholics being considered mostly Democrats, the A. P. A. threw its support to McKinley. Daily from its offices came concocted stories of Catholic attempts to establish itself as the American religion, all of them printed by newspapers that rarely bothered to track them down to their fictional origins.

Gibbons was furious. In May, he released a statement pointing out that Catholics belonged to both major parties and that if Catholics were ever of one mind on any given subject, they would be a dull and ineffectual crowd indeed. He added that it was necessary for both candidates to repudiate the A. P. A. in order to expose it as the un-American outfit it was, and he warned that unless this was done there might be a Catholic trend toward the party that promised civil and religious equality for all, if only implicitly by its disassociation with the A. P. A. Although McKinley personally repudiated the A. P. A., the Republican Party said nothing about it. The Democratic Party, on the other hand, made religious liberty a plank in its convention platform. Whether this was sincere or merely politics, it was expected to draw the Catholic vote. However, when the votes were counted, McKinley won by a majority of six hundred thousand out of thirteen million. One of the first congratulatory telegrams he received was from Gibbons, the last person he expected to hear from.

5

Gibbons never revealed his own political affiliation. He was a stickler on voting, and when on election days he learned that a member of his staff had not voted, Gibbons sent him scurrying off to a polling place. But even after the election, Gibbons would never reveal whether or not his choice had won. This attitude enabled him to be friends with all Presidents, regardless of their party; it also assured Presidents that they could rely on his unbiased opinions whenever they consulted him. McKinley consulted Gibbons often during the months preceding the war with Spain. Gibbons opposed the war because he felt it was unnecessary, but he realized that McKinley was the helpless pawn of warmongers and he assured the President that if combat became inevitable, the American Catholics would not be reluctant to fight Catholic Spain. And it seemed that war was inevitable. At one point, Pope Leo was able to convince Spain to settle differences by negotiations, and this information was passed to McKinley through Gibbons, but then the *Maine* was sunk in Havana harbor and negotiations were out of the question.

During the war, Gibbons raised large sums to provide medical care for the wounded. One reason for the war was the desire of certain factions to acquire Cuba and Puerto Rico as American holdings, and as the war progressed the desire also encompassed Guam and the Philippines. Gibbons disapproved of all this because he felt it was wrong for Americans to acquire foreign holdings by force. McKinley summoned Gibbons to the White House to ask him how the Catholic Church would feel if an American type of government were established in the Philippines, and Gibbons replied: "It would be the best thing in the world for the Church but the worst thing for the United States." When McKinley asked why, Gibbons pointed out that the Philippines had not been a factor in the war itself and that for America to take it as part of the spoils of war would be contrary to the American ideal of justice and would forever reflect against the United States in history. McKinley was about to go along with Gibbons, but then American businessmen, who saw in the Philippines an important toehold in Oriental commerce, put their own pressures on the President and the American flag went up in Manila. Much Philippine property was controlled by Spanish religious orders; now they would have to give it up. Proper U. S. remuneration was arranged through Gibbons, a task Gibbons disliked, not because it meant a decrease of Catholic influence in the Philippines but because circumstances forced him to take part in settlements of a war he believed was fought on dishonest premises to begin with. In the years that followed, the rest of the country came to agree with him . . . too late.

Because of his position as America's leading Catholic and also because of his friendships with Presidents, Gibbons was often approached by people who wanted him to use his influence to obtain political favors. He invariably refused. He considered his basic importance to Presidents to be his ability to obtain, through bishops, a quick sampling of public opinion on any questions facing the country, and he never went beyond that unless he was asked. Anything more, he felt, would reflect against his well-known convictions on the amount of influence a clergyman should have upon a public official.

At the turn of the century, when once again France was torn by political-religious strife, Gibbons was asked to restate his opinions on this sensitive problem, and he said, "I am unalterably attached to the separation of church and state in this country and have always expressed my belief and satisfaction in it. I so expressed myself in this favor thirty years ago, I did so later on in Rome itself, and I have no hesitation in expressing the same solemn belief today."

He did not, however, hesitate to express his belief when he thought the Government was in the wrong, and one area in which he was particularly vocal pertained to immigrants. It was again at the turn of the century that certain Congressmen tried to force through a law that would require immigrants to pass a literacy test. It seemed strange to Gibbons that a man whose family had been in America only two or three generations should turn against immigrants as undesirables and try to keep them out. Gibbons fought it, pointing out that most of the people who came over on the *Mayflower* were illiterate, which, he added, was probably also true of ancestors of the men who now wanted to screen immigrants in order to assure a higher type. Gibbons was successful in this crusade to the day of his death; only afterwards was the requirement made law.

If Gibbons' public life appeared to be full of conflict, his personal life was calm. He was a cardinal, thus a prince of the Church; as an American citizen, his influence was enormous; in his native city he was so popular and respected that he was called the King of Baltimore. Yet he was a simple, humble, uncomplicated man. His episcopal house in Baltimore was a mansion, but his own room was Spartan, containing only a cot, a bureau and two chairs, one of which held a typewriter.

He arose at six every morning, spent a half hour dressing and exercising, then went to his chapel for prayer and meditation before saying his daily Mass at seven. After Mass, he made his thanksgiving for fifteen minutes and then read the morning portion of his breviary before going to breakfast, at most coffee and bread, during which he read a newspaper. He was at his desk at nine, remaining there until noon, when he took the first of his two daily walks through the neighborhood. Lunch was his main meal, but even that was meager; the yellow fever attack of his youth had left him with a sensitive stomach and he ate little. As he advanced in years, somebody asked him what advice he had for people who wanted to live a long life, and he said, "Acquire an incurable disease in youth." He enjoyed lingering over lunch to discuss affairs of the day. Then he went back to his desk until five, when he took his second walk. Afterwards, he said his Rosary while strolling the first-floor corridor of his house, read more of his breviary, then had a light dinner. If he had no evening engagements, he would go to his room to read and write until ten, when he retired.

He had a few minor vices. He enjoyed playing cards, he liked a little straight bourbon before his meals and a cigar afterwards. The cigars were notorious for their pungent fragrance. One day an unexpected visitor arrived after lunch and asked if Gibbons was in. "Yes," said the housekeeper, "can't you smell him?" When travels made him a guest in the homes of others, he went to his room for his cigar and smoked it at an open window.

His reaction to the public fuss often made over him was sometimes a jolt. He was once invited to a Friday dinner at the home of a family that went to great trouble to obtain fresh crab for the entree. Because of his illness, he knew he could not eat them but rather than go through a lengthy explanation, he merely said, "They look delicious, but could I have an egg?" The puzzled hostess was stunned. Another time, he was the principal guest at a wedding reception banquet, and because of him the bride had set the table with her finest silver and china. Down the center of the table was a long line of monstrous gold centerpieces that blocked Gibbons' view. Because he enjoyed chatting with everybody around him at meals, he pointed to the centerpieces and said, "These are lovely wedding presents, my dear, but why don't you put them away now so we can see each other?" They were the family heirlooms. They were put away.

Gibbons spent at least one week a year visiting his family in New Orleans, rejecting invitations to be a guest at fine hotels or the archbishop's house, in order to stay in the small frame home his brother occupied. Gibbons' favorite holiday retreat was the private estate of friends at Union Mills, New Jersey, where he could stroll through the woods, fish, pitch horseshoes or just loaf. At night when the cards came out, he was the first to move to the table. There was some criticism of this friendship, because the father of the family was not Catholic: Gibbons' frequent visits, the critics said, gave the impression that he condoned mixed marriages. He laughed off the criticism, saying that if all mixed marriages worked out as well as this one had, he would encourage them. In the same way, he dismissed criticisms of his friendships with leading Protestant and Jewish clergymen and his co-efforts with them in matters of mutual public interest.

Even when he was past seventy, Gibbons continued his active life. He read the opening prayer at both the Republican and Democratic conventions, he retained his office as chancellor of the Catholic University, he carried on his heavy duties as the country's leading Catholic churchman. In his lifetime, he consecrated twenty-three bishops and ordained almost three thousand priests. He wrote a great deal; he was among the first to detect the early inroads of Communism into America and condemned it long before many people had any idea of its threats. He urged labor to remain alert against Communism's false promises and he warned Catholics against being duped by its empty humanitarianism. During World War I, Gibbons headed numerous committees to sell government bonds and send gift parcels to men overseas. In this same period, he was instrumental in organizing the National Catholic Welfare Conference, through which the American hierarchy planned to discuss and resolve any spiritual, social and welfare questions facing the country's Catholics. Rome, always wary of nationalistic movements, looked uneasily upon the N.C.W.C. at first, and there were rumors that the Vatican might disapprove the conference. As it turned out, the organization proved so successful that the Vatican urged other countries to form their own conferences.

On November 7, 1920, Gibbons was in Havre de Grace, Maryland, to administer confirmation. He was not feeling well; his throat was sore and he felt he might not be able to preach, but because of the crowd there to see him, he tried. In the middle of his sermon, he lost his balance and would have fallen had not several people reached out and held him up. Doctors who later examined him could find nothing wrong, but he was now eighty-six years old. The doctors suggested that he had better start slowing down. Gibbons said he would as soon as he completed his present commitments. In the next few weeks, he continued as he was, attending conferences in Washington to plan improvements in living standards for Indians and Negroes, traveling throughout Maryland on his episcopal assignments. In early December, he went to visit his friends in New

Jersey. On the morning of December 9, he said his Mass in the family chapel, but he was too weak to come down from the altar to give the family Communion and they had to go to him. That was the last Mass he ever said.

Taken back to Baltimore, he was put to bed. From time to time there were brief periods of recovery and he was able to go for drives, and then even this had to be stopped. He began to suffer short attacks of unconsciousness. On the night of Wednesday, March 23, he opened his eyes and saw a priest nearby. "I am going to die tomorrow," Gibbons said. "Will you hear my confession?" The priest did. Next morning, shortly before noon, Gibbons died. It was Holy Thursday, the day commemorating the Last Supper at which Jesus instituted the sacrament of Holy Communion, the day on which the Church felt Christianity was born.

In his long life, James Cardinal Gibbons had accomplished much good for his church and his country, but probably the most significant did not come to light until after his death. Among the condolences sent to Gibbons' family were messages from both Protestant and Jewish leaders across the country, men who had been his friends for many years, men who had shared platforms and conference tables with him at discussions of all kinds and who had learned the truth of his remark that despite the differences between them, they were united in charity and benevolence.

If, then, there were doubts when Gibbons was born that Catholics could be good Americans, there was none when he died. The vital brotherhood that was a product of the life James Gibbons lived was certainly the most important contribution that any man could make to the life of his country.

CHAPTER

TEN

Shepherd of the Black Sheep

THE five Negroes were late for church. Entering, they heard the white minister reciting the opening prayer. To avoid the clamor of their boots upon the wood floor, they knelt in the aisle and lowered their heads. A white usher came to them and touched one of them on the shoulder. "You can't stay here," he said. "You'll have to go up to the gallery."

They did not move. The minister prayed on.

"Upstairs with you," the usher said. "You're not permitted down here any longer."

Two of the Negroes nodded, but they did not get up. The usher gripped one of them firmly and lifted him to his feet. The man said, "Wait until the prayer is finished and I will get up and trouble you no more."

The minister finished his prayer. The five Negroes glanced at the bleachers along the wall where they usually sat during services and saw that they were empty. They got up from their knees and went out to the vestibule to the stairs that led up to the gallery.

One of them said, "So now we cannot even pray with them. Let us leave this place and never return."

So they walked out of the church—and they walked out to greatness.

2

That November Sunday in 1787 was a sad day for Richard Allen. He knew that most of the Negroes in the gallery of St. George's Methodist Church, Philadelphia, were there because of his urgings. A licensed Methodist preacher himself, he had discovered that many of his people gave up the habit of attending services when they moved into the city and he had argued with them that their place on Sunday mornings was in church. Now they were going, only to learn that the white people who ran the churches were shunting them to uncomfortable bleachers along the side walls or up into overcrowded galleries. It was humiliating. It was disgraceful. It was un-Christian.

It was surprising, too, that Richard Allen was not embittered; he was merely hurt. "If it is true that we are all the children of God," he once asked, "then why can we not act like brothers?"

The answer was in the tenor of the times. There had been signs earlier, particularly in Pennsylvania, that the plight of the American Negro slave might be improved. The Quakers in Pennsylvania were leaders in this trend, proclaiming at state conferences that it was immoral for anyone to regard another human being a personal chattel. Quakers were thus the first group to act for the freedom of slaves, an action that made Pennsylvania a haven for escaped slaves and for others who had managed to buy their freedom from their owners. If other churches were slower to move in this area, it was primarily because of a lack of discipline: church leaders could not oblige their followers to accept an antislavery declaration, and so rather than face divisions within the ranks the leaders did nothing. By 1787, most of the northern states had already abolished slavery, and it began to look as though slavery would gradually fade from the national scene. But still ahead was the industrial development in the North and in England that would require cheap labor in the American southern fields. Instead of fading, the slavery problem was to become more intense.

It was not until late in the eighteenth century that the word "Negro" was applied to the enslaved people. Before then, they were called Africans, which was what they were and what they called themselves. As Africans they had a national origin, like the English or French or Dutch or Spaniards who had come to America, but as Negroes they were merely being described as having black skin—as though this made them different from other men. In the minds of many, it did. And yet the difference could only be a thing of the mind. Richard Allen had said: "Given equal opportunities, colored people can be equally as important as whites to the progress of a community." But there were few opportunities. Africans had been in America since 1619, before the Pilgrims landed, and yet, at Allen's time, one of them had still to be graduated from a university.

It was difficult to explain why this should be so. The contention that Africans were naturally a primitive people was baseless. There were great nations at the African equator at the time Europeans were still living in caves. Aspersions that Africans were uneducable were also without foundation; no one had seriously tried to educate them. Most of those who could read and write had, like Richard Allen, taught themselves, which was far more difficult than being taught and was thus a greater credit to them. If the Africans were in any way inferior, it was in the way they defended themselves in their homeland. They were still fighting with lances when the men who came to enslave them had gunpowder. This simplicity weakened them before their captors and thereafter they were considered lower then the men who had devised the more effective way to kill. Overpowered, a price tag was put on an entire human race, and it followed naturally that those who were purchasable were not the equals of those who could purchase. Slaves were needed for cheap labor at a time when there were no machines to do the work. Had the mechanical genius of mankind flourished a century earlier, there would have been no need for slaves in America, a continent would not have been decimated, a human race would not have been downgraded. But human affairs had developed differently, and so by the time there were machines to replace the slaves there was also an indelible state of mind that devaluated the human worth of Africans into the adjective that described them, and although men now had machines that could change the face of their earth, they had invented nothing to change the state of their minds. At Allen's time, slaves were being freed by law, self-purchase or magnanimity, but they were still required to sit along the wall or in galleries, and nobody could tell how long this would last.

Richard Allen was a victim of this plight. He was born into a slave family in Philadelphia on February 14, 1760. The Allens were owned by Benjamin Chew, a prominent lawyer, and when, as a boy, Richard Allen served the Chew table he eavesdropped on a great deal of legal talk that both was to be of help to him in his future and to affect his own manner of self-expression. Allen was in his teens when Benjamin Chew fell upon hard times and was forced to sell some slaves. He sold the entire Allen family—mother, father and four children—to a plantation owner near Dover, Delaware. It was rare for an entire family to be sold; ordinarily slave families were broken up indiscriminately. The Allens were fortunate.

Richard Allen had learned to read in a most unusual way. His family was Methodist; in his boyhood he learned many rousing Methodist hymns by heart. When he grew old enough to be given a hymnal at services and told which page to turn to, he studied each printed word as he sang the lyrics from memory until he was able to recognize the word wherever else he saw it. Thus linking the sight and sound of words in his mind, he learned how to piece together new words by phonetics. He taught himself to write in the same way, first in block letters, then in script. It was a slow process but effective, and showed remarkable personal industry. His whole life was marked with similar persistent singlemindedness.

When he was seventeen, Allen underwent two vital experiences. The first was religious. While attending a revival, he was struck by the tremendous emotional surge identified with the Methodist conversion. With others, he had gone forward in answer to the altar call; he had knelt and openly made his declaration for Christ. But, as often happened, the great flood of faith was followed by an excruciating siege of doubt. He later recorded:

> I went rejoicing for several days and happy in the Lord, in conversing with many old experienced Christians; [then] I was brought under doubts and was tempted to believe I was deceived and was constrained to seek the Lord afresh. I went with my head bowed for many days. My sins were a heavy burden. I was tempted to believe there was no mercy for me. I cried to the Lord both night and day. One night I thought Hell would be my portion. I cried unto Him who delighted to hear the prayers of a sinner and all of a sudden my dungeon shook, my chains fell off, and "Glory to God," I cried. My soul was filled. I cried, "Enough for me—the Saviour died."

The change in him was profound. He became a living testimony of grace. His friends led him around to neighbors as though he were some prized exhibit, and at each house he told the story of his conversion. Laws of the time prohibited Negroes from conducting religious services without the presence of a white man, usually a minister, but often the minister lacked the verve the Negroes preferred, and so surreptitiously they went when they could into the woods or to a riverside on the pretext of having a picnic but actually to hold services in their own way. Richard Allen had often attended such services; now he was a celebrity at them. Not only did he retell the circumstances of his conversion, but he began to preach as well. The pattern of his future life was taking shape.

The second great event of his seventeenth year was the purchase of his freedom. He had been sold once as a slave; he dreaded that it might happen again. When Richard was fifteen, he and his brother went to their master and asked if he would consider letting them buy their freedom. The man put a price of two thousand dollars on each boy. To earn the money, the two youths had first to work for their master all day, then go to the woods in their free hours to chop wood which they sold throughout the area. It took them two years to earn the required payment. For Richard, then, it was Providential that he should find his new place in religion and in freedom at almost the same hour. He vowed to fill both roles with the fullest heart.

3

He did not know what to do with himself. Free, he was now his own responsibility. It was a strange sensation to know that his comings and goings were entirely his own concern, but it was also his own concern to see to it that he had a roof over his head, food to eat, money in his pocket. Casting off slavery, he had taken on responsibility for himself, and it was an uneasy luxury. He decided to remain at the work that had earned his freedom payments, but, especially in temperate Delaware, selling wood was profitable only for part of the year. It was necessary for him to take on a second job, this one in a brickyard. Later he found a third job—hauling bags of salt from the beds of Sussex County. He particularly liked this job. It allowed for some travel, on which he often stopped to preach in Negro settlements along the way. It also allowed for quiet hours on lonely roads, and he used the time for his meditations. The Revolutionary War was being fought during these years. By personal conviction, Allen was opposed to combat, but he served in the only way his conscience would permit: he acted as chaplain for Negroes in uniform that passed his way. Because of this, he was made a licensed Methodist preacher at twenty-two.

When, in 1783, the war ended, Allen decided to expand his horizons as an itinerant preacher. Most such itinerants of the time were Methodist circuit riders assigned and supervised by Francis Asbury, the leader of American Methodism and soon to become a Methodist bishop. Asbury was an outspoken critic of slavery, which had attracted many Negroes to Methodism, but even so there were no Negro circuit riders. There was nothing, however, to prevent Allen from being a volunteer itinerant, and with this in mind he left Delaware and headed north into Pennsylvania. He walked. In the next few months he walked hundreds of miles, preaching wherever he could attract a crowd. When winter came, some friends insisted on giving Allen a horse to ease his journey; he accepted it with the reservation that he would pay for it later. Years passed before he was able to do so, but he did.

Inevitably, his path crossed those of Methodist circuit riders. They were impressed by his sincerity and his selfless efforts, and when they went to hear him speak they were even more impressed by his ability. At each service, when he issued the altar call several people invariably came forth—evidence of his effectiveness. Various riders began inviting Allen to travel with them, serving as a helper by organizing the services, leading the hymns and giving the introductory talk. Occasionally Allen gave the principal sermon. Audiences at these revivals were preponderantly white, and if any of them were disturbed by being preached to by a Negro, they soon got over it once Allen began to talk. He was more subdued than most Methodist preachers, less eloquent because of his meager education, but he had warmth, insight and understanding, and what he lacked in dramatics he made up for in sincerity. His audiences were always won over. The circuit riders often expressed their regret to Allen that they could not pay him for his help, but he did not mind. Whenever he needed money, he could chop wood for a few days, then sell it. He was too happy spiritually to fret about his poverty.

Allen's travels took him through eastern Pennsylvania, into New Jersey, then southward again into Delaware and Maryland. He was in Baltimore at Christmas, 1784, when Francis Asbury was made a bishop by Bishop Thomas Coke, the English missionary. Although Asbury had been born in England, he had become an American, and Allen was happy to see an American Methodist rise so high in the Church. The split between English and American Methodism was already apparent; it was good, Allen felt, for American Methodism to have so strong-minded a leader as Asbury. On the other hand, Allen objected to the pomp that accompanied Asbury's consecration. All the robes, candles and incense were, in Allen's opinion, outside the scope of American Methodism as he knew it. Allen was among the first to complain when Asbury subsequently made appearances in episcopal robes. Even so, there was a warm feeling between Allen and Asbury. When Asbury planned an extended tour of the South, he asked Allen to accompany him.

"I won't be able to pay you anything," Asbury said, "but I'll pay all your expenses."

"How long will the trip be?" Allen asked.

"Three or four months. Maybe more. It's difficult to plan these things."

Allen squirmed. "I'm twenty-four years old," he said. "I've been thinking it's time I got married. I'm going to have to start earning some money."

But Asbury was a perceptive man. "What's the real reason you don't want to go?" he asked.

Allen sighed heavily. "You don't know what it's like for a Negro, even a free Negro, to travel in the South. We wouldn't be allowed to enter the same places; we wouldn't be allowed to sleep under the same roof. If I got sick, there would be no one to take care of me."

Asbury understood. "Very well. Maybe we can make a trip together some other time. I hope so."

"I hope so, too," Allen said.

There was some truth in Allen's remark that he wanted to settle down. He expected he would always do some traveling for the sake of religion, but he wanted a home base, he wanted a wife and children, and he knew that these required money. It was in February, 1786, that he went back to Philadelphia in search of roots. He was known there from his previous visits, and thus he had no trouble finding a place to stay, obtaining a job in a cobbler's shop and affiliating himself with the St. George Methodist Episcopal Church. The church had a mixed congregation. Already known as a preacher, Allen was able to obtain permission to hold services for Negroes in the church at five o'clock in the morning. At regular Sunday services, he joined other Negroes on the bleachers along the wall. Because of Allen's conviction that professed Christians ought to attend services on Sundays, there was an increase in the Negro membership of the church, with the inevitable result that the bleachers were soon too small and the Negroes were eventually shunted to the gallery. It was here at St. George's that Allen was dragged from his knees one Sunday morning after having arrived late. Ordered to the galleries, he walked out instead.

The attitude that Negroes ought to have their own church in which to worship was already growing in Allen at this time. He had always been annoyed and embarrassed by the custom in mixed congregations which required Negroes to wait to partake in the communion ceremony until after the whites had finished. Few things irked him more than to hear the announcement from the pulpit: "Now that the white brethren have finished, the colored people may come forward if they choose." Often Allen went forward full of resentment instead of full of the love which the ceremony indicated.

Among the men who had stalked out of St. George's with Allen was Absalom Jones. Like Allen, Jones had been born a slave, had educated himself, bought his freedom and eventually settled in Philadelphia. He worked hard, saved his money, bought some property and built two houses on it, from which he derived an income that made him moderately independent. Also like Allen, Jones was a devout man, well versed in religion, and he too led Negro worship services when the occasion arose. Twenty years older than Allen, Jones was a more conservative, subdued man, but he agreed with Allen that the racial inequalities in Philadelphia, especially in church, had grown intolerable and that something had to be done about it, particularly for those Negroes who had acquired their freedom and were thus supposed to be on a par with all other free men.

Together, Allen and Jones set out to do what they felt must be done.

4

Both Allen and Jones had undergone the bleak experience of finding themselves free men without jobs, without income. Every day, other Negro men faced the same predicament, many of them arriving in Philadelphia without a penny or friend to their name. Puzzled and afraid, they tried to lose themselves in the growing Philadelphia Negro ghetto, there to become social problems as desperation drove them to crime. Friendless in a big city, their fate was no surprise.

Allen had been a good example of what could happen to a man who not only had a few friends but also had drive. Having obtained his job in the cobbler's shop through friends, he worked hard to become skilled at the work. Then he went from house to house to find shoes to repair, and he did so well at this that he was subsequently able to buy the shop for himself. While canvassing, Allen also took orders for wood, then hired men to go out to the forests to cut it. It followed naturally that anybody who heated his home with the wood would have to have his chimney cleaned at regular periods: Allen made arrangements to send in the necessary crews of chimney sweeps. In the same way, he found jobs for domestics, thus developing his own employment agency. With his profits, Allen bought property and built houses and shops to rent. By the time he was thirty, he was a wealthy man, married, and with the first of his six children in his home.

It occurred to Allen that other freed slaves could do equally as well for themselves if they had the necessary friends and opportunities. With this in mind, Allen and Jones founded the Free African Society, probably the first cooperative in the history of America. Membership was open to all Negroes with the freedom to pursue their own ambitions. Dues were a shilling a month. A committee of six, including Allen and Jones, was set up to pass on applications for loans, repayable at a modest interest. Allen and Jones provided the initial capital for the Society, but the Society grew so rapidly that soon it was operating on its own funds. At Allen's suggestion, the Society also opened a day school for children and a night school for adults in one of the houses he owned. Furthermore, the Society loaned money to the sick and contributed to the support of widows and orphans. News of the Society spread and soon there were similar organizations up and down the East Coast, as well as in England. There was talk for awhile of uniting all the societies into one organization for greater effectiveness, and although the plan never materialized, each group in itself nevertheless achieved a great good in helping Negroes at the time they needed it most.

Because of the personal temperaments of Richard Allen and Absalom Jones, it was understandable that the Free African Society of Philadelphia should have strong religious undertones. Their influence resulted in the requirement that society members should be living lives of proper morality. Men were expected to be married to the women with whom they were living—or at least be willing to marry them at the first possible moment. Others with criminal records or suspected of criminal acts had to undergo a probationary period to prove their worthiness. The Society, then, was an important moral influence as well as a social and economic one.

In its by-laws, the Society described itself as nondenominational, and it was; but as the Society grew, so grew also the desire for a Negro church, which implied not only racialism but denominationalism, too. The incident at St. George's Church had weakened the loyalty of many Negro Methodists, and their attendance had dropped off. Although Allen and Jones, two direct victims of the incident, continued to resent it and to avoid the church, they still considered themselves Methodists and their hope was to establish a Methodist church in the Negro part of the city, with a Negro minister and in loose affiliation with St. George's. They put the idea to the elders of St. George's, but it was rejected. Already there was friction in American Methodism, based on the questions of slavery, ritual and the firm authority of Bishop Asbury, and the St. George elders did not want to contribute further to threats of schisms by endorsing a Negro Methodist church over which they would have slim control.

Each year the society expressed stronger hopes for a Negro church. In 1791, a committee was formed for the purpose of deciding by vote which denominational theology a Negro church should adopt, then to go ahead and build a house of worship with the hope that once the church was a going concern the leaders of the chosen denomination would ordain a Negro minister for it. Allen and Jones were on the committee; they were the only two to vote for Methodism. Most of the others voted for Protestant Episcopalianism. The vote was indicative.

It was true that Bishop Asbury had been the country's most outspoken churchman against slavery and that, on the whole, Methodism championed for the abolition of slavery, but at this time American Methodism was on the verge of being split in half—North and South—because of this stand. Although many Negroes had joined the Church, there had been too many incidents, in the North as well, like that at St. George's, and the Negro ardor had cooled. On the other hand, Protestant Episcopalianism, the daughter of Anglicanism in America, was virtually a new religion, and in its search for members it had adopted many liberal attitudes. Moreover, before the American Revolution, the Church of England had been the state church in most of the Southern colonies; many Negroes had been raised in it and were familiar with it. However, the Church, supervised by the Bishop of London, had been remiss in its duties to its American members. There had been no American Anglican bishop in a period of almost two hundred years; visits by British bishops to ordain ministers and confirm the faithful had grown so rare that most of the American parishes were in the hands of laymen and thus few Americans were either confirmed or able to receive the sacraments. It had been a situation similar to this in England that gave rise to English Methodism in the first place, and which had caused American Methodism to catch on so quickly among neglected Anglicans.

Ordination in the Church of England required an oath of allegiance to the British crown. Thus most of the Anglican ministers in America at the time of the Revolution were Tories, and those who did not escape to Canada or the British army lines were arrested. The Church collapsed. There were, however, a few American Anglican priests in the country, men whose sentiments were pro-Revolutionist, and they were allowed to continue their work. Among these was William White, of Philadelphia, whose brother-in-law, Robert Morris, had helped finance the Revolution. White was assistant pastor at both Christ Church and St. Peter's Church, and with his own money he was able to keep both churches open during the war.

When the war ended and anti-British feelings still ran high, White realized it was hopeless to expect Americans to belong to a church whose head wore the British crown. Nevertheless, White still adhered to Anglican theology, as he believed many other American Anglicans did, and he felt the only solution to the problem was to organize an American Anglican Church which, while recognizing the mother church in London, would have its own bishops and manage its own affairs. He proposed this to the Bishop of London and it was immediately rejected. Undaunted, White wrote letters to the handful of Anglican clergymen in America and pamphlets to leading laymen, putting his idea to them. Most of them went along with White, providing that the men who were to become American Anglican bishops would be, at least first to assure apostolic succession, consecrated by British bishops.

In Connecticut, Samuel Seabury was chosen as bishop for that area. A Tory, he had been exiled during the war, then allowed to return; now he was to go to England as a test case for the American Church. Anglican leaders in London refused to recognize him or the ecclesiastical group he represented. He went north to Scotland. Although the Church of Scotland was not in communion with the Church of England, it claimed for itself the same Anglican apostolic heritage and felt within its rights in consecrating Seabury, thereby giving quasiofficial standing to his church. Three years passed before the Bishop of London faced the fact that Seabury's consecration made the American branch of Anglicanism a *fait accompli* and therefore conferred the episcopal orders upon White and Samuel Provoost, rector of Trinity Church in New York City. White and Seabury then formed the House of Bishops; the score of Anglican ministers in America and a handful of laymen organized the House of Deputies. With that, the Protestant Episcopal Church of America came into being.

When the committee of the Free African Society was looking about for a church for its members, the Protestant Episcopalians were looking around for members for their church. Under

White, the young church was energetic, farseeing and liberal, including among its adherents men like George Washington, James Madison and Benjamin Franklin. In such an atmosphere —Washington had freed his own slaves—Negroes could hope for the acceptance they yearned for. In the process of choosing a church, committee members sounded out Bishop White on the possibility of a Negro branch of the Church under Negro ministers and without specific white domination. Bishop White assured them it would all be easy to arrange. Furthermore, he offered to contribute to the building of a church; so did Benjamin Franklin. White also wrote friends in England about the movement and urged financial support.

Their decision made, the committee asked Richard Allen to put himself forward as a candidate for the Protestant Episcopal ministry, but he refused. "I was born and awakened under Methodism," he said, "and it is a Methodist I wish to remain."

Absalom Jones reacted differently. Although a Methodist, he was willing to go along with the majority vote of the committee. The St. Thomas African Church was dedicated on July 17, 1794, with Jones as its deacon. A few years later, when he had finished his training, Jones was ordained the first Negro Episcopal priest in America.

Allen's refusal to follow this same path himself displeased the Free African Society and he was voted out of the organization that he had helped establish. However, the act was intended more to impress others with the society's discipline rather than to punish Allen for uncooperativeness. He continued to advise the Society and to remain a principal factor in stabilizing Negro life in the city.

He continued, too, to be active in Methodist affairs. Two or three times a year he went out into the country to conduct revivals for Negroes. But he was not satisfied. He was convinced that Methodism had not as yet granted Negroes their proper place in the white church, and in his letters to Bishop Asbury he repeatedly suggested that if this equality would never arise then there should be a Negro Methodist Church in which whites could be given equality. "We do not wish to be separated from our white brethren," he said, "but we do wish to share with them the leadership and responsibility of the Church, and if this cannot be done in the present circumstances it can be done in the circumstances I propose."

He proposed an African Methodist Church, recognized by the Church itself but separate from it, preaching the same doctrine and discipline. Its ministry, hierarchy and ruling laity would be Negro; its congregations could be as racially mixed as communities allowed. But it would be a Negro and African church, if only to assure that Negroes would be able to rise to prominence in it. This, Allen warned Asbury, was the only way that Methodism could expect to sustain its appeal to Negroes, an appeal that was fast losing out to Episcopalianism due to the influence of the Free African Society.

Asbury saw the wisdom in Allen's idea, but he also saw that Methodism, already divided on the slavery question, was not as yet prepared to recognize an independent Negro affiliate as equal, however separate. Asbury took matters into his own hands, a habit of his that frequently annoyed Methodists. He told Allen to go ahead and build a church, provided it could be served by white ministers until there were qualified Negroes ready for ordination. Asbury assured he would see to it that the Negroes were ordained. The church, being supervised by Negroes, would necessarily be apart from the Methodism Asbury headed, but his approval of the new church would provide its unifying link with the rest of Methodism. Allen was now satisfied.

The Negro Episcopalians were then raising money in Philadelphia to build their church. Rather than cause confusion with a second fund drive, Allen suggested to his followers that they contribute what they could out of their own pockets and that he would put up the rest. Approximately four thousand dollars was thus raised through public subscription; Allen donated over six thousand to meet the building cost. The Bethel Methodist Episcopal Church was dedicated on July 29, 1794, about a week after Bishop White had dedicated the African Protestant Episcopal Church of St. Thomas a few blocks away.

There was, as expected, opposition from white Methodists who, refusing to recognize the new church as Methodist, called its members Allenites. Nevertheless, Bishop Asbury kept his promise by appointing a white minister to serve the church. He himself returned to preach at Bethel the following year; Bishop Thomas Coke also preached there. Some whites took legal steps to prevent Bethel from calling itself a Methodist church; they not only lost the case, but the Pennsylvania assembly granted the church a charter to incorporate itself.

However, as Allen had anticipated, there were whites who both approved of Bethel and took an active part in nonsegregated parish affairs. Records showed that both whites and Negroes came forward together in response to altar calls; there were whites on church committees. This was as Allen had hoped Bethel would be. Also as he had hoped, Bethel soon had schools for both children and adults; many of the Free African Society projects were adopted. The church began to grow. No one could foresee how much it would grow.

5

The missionary factor of Methodism required itinerancy of its preachers, and so Richard Allen continued to make periodic trips into the country. But now he traveled as more than a preacher. Although he was not in fact in charge of Bethel, it was well known that he was the true power behind the flourishing church. He traveled now as something of a celebrity: he had given Negroes their own church. Negro Methodist leaders in rural Pennsylvania, in Maryland and Delaware, envied Allen, and in so doing some of them tried to emulate him by organizing small churches of their own. Each church remained independent, but that there should one day be a closer link between them was evident and inevitable. Bishop Asbury perceived the trend and recognized the importance of Richard Allen in it. In 1799, he ordained Allen to the Methodist ministry, the first Negro to achieve that honor. Now Allen was indeed in charge of Bethel and indeed the leader of Negro religious life. All that remained was the official acclaim.

It did not come for several years. During this time, the number of Negro-directed churches increased, and with it increased discussions for some kind of unity. Allen's success as a minister resulted in the ordination of more Negroes, among them Daniel Coker, of Baltimore. Negro Methodist unity was a subject close to Coker's heart and he spent a great deal of time in correspondence with other ministers, proposing that there should be a conference toward that end. As the prospect of the conference grew more certain, an unfortunate conflict arose.

By tradition, the primacy in an affiliation of churches would go to the church and the man who had pioneered, and in this case without question the church was Bethel and the man was Richard Allen. However, two or three men in Pennsylvania and Delaware declared that, although Allen had obtained the most notoriety, their churches predated his. Allen personally could not have cared less. He had been raised in rural areas where a group of Negroes, worshiping secretly in the woods or at a riverside, considered themselves to be a church, and if these were the grounds on which the others were claiming seniority, then the question was merely a matter of semantics and he had no intention of arguing it. The date of Bethel's dedication was public knowledge; Bishop Asbury had been there. Daniel Coker, on the other hand, was a stickler for accuracy. It was he who did the research to establish Bethel's priority and it was he who managed to bring together in Baltimore, in the spring of 1816, all the ministers involved.

Even before the first session of the conference, it was widely assumed that a unity of some kind would come out of the meeting. And it was also assumed that Richard Allen would be elected the first bishop of the African Methodist Episcopal Church. A small but vocal faction let it be known, however, that though there should be unity it ought not be under Allen. The reasons were basically personal: pride, envy, jealousy.

Richard Allen attended the sessions pertaining to unity, but when the matter of the bishopric arose he chose not to be present. Coker, too, announced that he preferred to let others resolve the problem. Coker was later astonished to learn that the conference resorted to compromise and elected two bishops—himself and Allen.

"At this early stage," Coker heatedly told the conference, "there is no need in the church for more than one bishop. I urge those who voted for me to give their support to the man who is directly responsible for our being here at all—Brother Allen."

His earnest plea moved the majority of the ministers and Allen was elected. Still a small faction held out and went away and a few years later organized the African Methodist Episcopal Church, Zion, and thereafter remained apart. On April 16, Richard Allen was made a bishop by the imposition of hands of five ordained ministers, among them his old friend Absalom Jones. Bishop Asbury was not present; he could not be in view of the fact that Allen's consecration denoted a schism within Methodism. His personal sentiments, however, were indicated in the continued friendship between the two men.

When Richard Allen had been ordained a minister, he announced that he would serve without salary. As a bishop he continued this practice. He was, he said, devoted to the improvement of Negro life in America, and to this end he would give whatever years he had left.

He had fifteen years. They were years spent at guiding Negroes to self-improvement through schools, apprenticeships and fraternities that carried on the aid programs of the Free African Society. Travels took him north to New England and west to Ohio, and everywhere he left behind him a trail of new churches. In his time, membership in the Church grew from less than five thousand to over twenty thousand. In Philadelphia, there were eventually more Negro Methodists than white. The Ohio churches subsequently served a most unusual purpose. As slavery conditions in the South worsened and the number of runaway slaves soared, those who traveled via the Underground Railway knew they could always find food and haven in Bishop Allen's churches. Once safely in the North, the runaways joined the Church. By the end of the War Between the States, there were over two hundred thousand members of the Church in the North, a number which doubled when, after the war, Negro itinerant preachers were allowed to travel through the South. A century later, there were more than a million members of the Church active in every state and at every social level, from tiny churches in the backwoods of the South to the campuses of great universities, like Wilberforce and Howard and Clark, started by the Church.

Throughout his episcopacy, Allen's primary concern was the abolition of slavery. As a Negro, there was not much he could do about it directly, but he spoke and wrote a great deal on the subject and gave both personal and financial support to the abolition societies that were forming in the North. His presence at abolitionist rallies gave dignity and importance to them. His urgings for patience, caution and Christian love did much to quell the Negro uprisings in the South which were achieving little and resulting mostly in lynchings. He was convinced that tolerance, brotherhood and the exemplary lives of freed slaves would be enough to bring about the end of slavery peacefully, and when early rumblings of a possible war to end slavery reached him, his eyes filled with tears; he bowed his head and prayed against it.

He did not live to see the war. In 1826, overwork forced him to ask a General Conference of the Church to elect a bishop to assist him. Elected was Morris Brown, of Philadelphia, a close friend who shared Allen's views and hopes. Thereafter it was Bishop Brown who carried Allen's message across the country. Each year, age and ill health took their toll upon Richard Allen. He was unable to attend the Baltimore conference of 1828; at the Philadelphia conference the following year he sat by while Bishop Brown presided; and the following year he told a few friends that they would never see him at another conference. On March 26, 1831, at the age of seventy-one, Richard Allen died quietly in his sleep.

For the next few days, both northern and southern newspapers published panegyrics of him, emphasizing all he had done to provide stability and dignity for those of his people who were free, and hope and faith for those who were not. One fact drew considerable attention: after bequeathing modest amounts to his wife and family, he left most of his forty-thousand-dollar personal fortune to his church. In the minds of those who knew Bishop Allen well, who loved him and knew his dreams, this bequest was not of the utmost importance, for they believed he had given much more than money to his church, his people, his country. He had given himself, and in light of what his church and his people subsequently achieved for their country in every profession, art and craft, in war and in peace, the gift of Richard Allen to America was God-sent.

CHAPTER
ELEVEN

The Quiet People

It seemed as though the people would never get what they wanted—the right to worship as they pleased. Repeatedly their prayer meetings were broken up by the police; repeatedly their leaders were arrested and put in the stocks. One day in 1650, George Fox, who had started the movement, was arrested in Derby, England, and taken before the justice of the peace and sentenced to six months in jail.

". . . and God have mercy on you," said the justice of the peace.

"Sire," said Fox, "thou should quake at the name of the Lord."

The justice laughed. "I quake? Well, you can do it for me. You are the quaker."

As the guards led Fox away, the people surrounded him, laughing and jeering, and they taunted: "Come on, Fox, let's see you quake. You're a quaker. Show us how you do it."

So the movement had a name.

The first time William Penn heard of the Quakers he was twelve years old and living in Ireland. His family was in exile. It had come about in this way:

The Penns were royalists at heart, loyal to King Charles II, but the King had been ousted by a Parliament under the control of Oliver Cromwell. William Penn's father, who had the same name, was a high-ranking naval officer, and in order to practice his career he had to take orders from Parliament in the fight to keep King Charles out of England. The elder Penn carried out his orders well, for which he was made a rear admiral, then a vice-admiral. His victories made him a national hero. Cromwell rewarded him by giving him estates in Ireland. Even so, Admiral Penn's heart was still with the King; in 1654, he led a short-lived effort to turn the fleet over to Charles. Penn was too popular for Cromwell to punish too severely. To occupy Penn elsewhere, Cromwell sent him to the West Indies to capture San Domingo. The attempt failed, mostly because the troops, under General Robert Venables, had not been properly trained. Rather than return home empty-handed, Penn and Venables went farther south and captured Jamaica. This did not satisfy Cromwell. Reaching London, both Penn and Venables were put in the Tower. Venables was beheaded, but Penn was allowed to move his family to Ireland.

Admiral Penn knew perfectly well that his life had been saved by his popularity, and he also knew he had been exiled because of the royalist threat he was to Cromwell's regime. Thus he was able to settle in Ireland with a certain peace of mind, content that his day would come.

Religious conflict was also a factor in troubled England. For almost a century, Anglicanism had been the state religion, with Low Church becoming increasingly Puritan and High Church retaining its Roman traditions. Baptists and Congregationalists were growing in numbers; in Scotland, Presbyterianism was the dominant sect. The English royal family, of course, favored High Church; Cromwell was a Puritan. Whatever the faction, there was little tolerance of one for the others. For years there had been a ban on Roman Catholicism in England, which brought on an unusual problem. Whenever the English royal heirs sought an effective marriage-of-alliance with European countries they found their choice limited mostly to Catholic women. Such marriages included the agreement that Catholics would have freedom of worship in England, which the majority of Englishmen didn't want. King Charles I had married a Catholic, which partially accounted for his downfall and eventual decapitation in 1649. Charles II had not only married a Catholic but was suspected of espousing Catholicism as well, which was partially responsible for keeping him off the throne for ten years after his father's death. Cromwell gave religious freedom to Baptists, Congregationalists and Presbyterians, but he was against High Anglicanism and Catholicism for both doctrinal and political reasons.

In the midst of all this confusion, the Quakers arose. From his personal religious experiences, George Fox acquired the conviction that what he called the Light of Christ—the divine knowledge and love—was given to every man. While still holding to the Bible, Fox put the Light above it, declaring that although the Bible was a valid documentation of God's relation to men of the past, the Light was God now, communicating with living men through their consciences. To receive the Light a man had only to sit quietly in meditation, attuning himself to God. The Light would come. Then whatever a man felt inspired to think, do or say would be correct, right, good, proper, moral, of God, because he would be acting in conscience.

Viewed thusly, each Quaker was his own priest, his own church, for whatever he believed was right for him, however it might differ from what other Quakers believed. The early gatherings of Quakers, then, were not religious services but merely the convening of people who agreed upon the freedom of conscience. There was no ritual, no preacher. The people merely gathered for silent meditation, and when any one of them was touched by the Light and was inspired to speak, he stood up and did so. Sometimes nobody spoke; sometimes several spoke. It was up to the senior member to decide when the meeting was over, which he demonstrated by shaking hands with the men on either side of him, then walking out.

Because they believed every human being had a conscience which was responsive to the Light of Christ, the Quakers put aside the Calvinistic ideas of predestination and the salvation of the elect. Also, women took a higher place in Quakerism because, after all, they too had consciences; women were as free to speak at prayer meetings as men. For that matter, every person who ever lived could be—and probably was—responsive to the Light of Christ even before there was a Christ on earth. To Quakers, the Holy Trinity was this: God Eternal was of one substance; Jesus Christ was God Eternal in human form in order to define clearly the Holy Will; the Holy Ghost was God Eternal communicating as the Light of Christ.

The Quaker stress on freedom of conscience implied, therefore, that no man was greater than any other man, that no church or state or institution was greater than any one man, that reverence and obeisance should be shown to no one and nothing but God. Acting in conscience, Quakers would always act with honesty, justice and love, so they had no need for laws, judges or any rulers except those they chose to coordinate the common good. Concerned only with the things of God, Quakers would, regardless of any wealth or station, be plain in their customs and clothes. Honoring only God, they would not remove their hats to any man or institution, nor would they resort to the excessive courtesy of the times by addressing a man of reputed importance with the second-person plural. These things they considered as within the Light of Christ for themselves and for all others as well.

2

Young William Penn learned about Quakers from Thomas Loe. Although Quakers did not advocate proselytizing, if the Light of Christ inspired a man to travel about, explaining the Quaker idea, he was correct in doing so, and Thomas Loe had received this inspiration. An Englishman, he had gone to Ireland, and in the course of his travels he came to the estates of Admiral Penn in County Cork. The Admiral learned that Loe had been speaking to the household staff and invited him to address the family. Young William, going on thirteen, was deeply impressed. Years were to pass before he had further contact with Quakers, but he never forgot Loe's talk. It changed his life.

Cromwell died in 1658. His successors were unable to retain his stronghold on the country and soon there was talk of restoring the monarchy by putting Charles II on the throne. Parliament was dissolved and a new one formed. From the town of Weymouth, in Dorsetshire, came an invitation from the people for Admiral Penn to represent them in the House of Commons. The Penns returned to England in 1660. A royal escort was formed to bring Charles back from Holland, and Penn was an honored member of it. When King Charles saw him, he knighted Penn immediately. Because of his loyalty, Sir William was given a high position in the Admiralty Office, the chief clerk of which was a young man named Samuel Pepys who kept a diary the whole world was eventually to read. Though Pepys never really liked the Penns, he cultivated their friendship and was occasionally consulted on family problems.

One family problem was young William. In Ireland, the

Penns had lived in quiet comfort, but now they were back in London, in the swing of things. In addition to his high Navy post, Sir William was a friend of the King and had easy access to the royal chambers, with additional importance and pressures. The family entertained frequently and was entertained as often. They dressed the part. Young William was obliged to wear satins and furs and plumes and jewelry, and he did not like it at all. He also did not like Oxford, where he had been sent to study. The atmosphere was too elegant, the students too rich and rowdy, and there were the High Anglican services William had to attend. On taking the throne, King Charles II had promised religious toleration, but the heavily Anglican Parliament that had enthroned him nevertheless distrusted his Catholic leanings, and soon there was little tolerance in the land. William resented the Anglican services that were Oxford law, and with several students of similar conviction he refused to attend them. This got him into serious trouble with school authorities, and complaints were forwarded to Sir William. Father told son that he must obey the rules, but son persistently refused and he was thrown out of Oxford. Father put son into Cambridge, where son quickly joined a small Quaker group.

"I am sure," Sir William said to Samuel Pepys one day, "I don't know what to do with that boy. He seems determined not to take any joy from life. It's embarrassing to me."

"I have observed," said Pepys, "that French women invariably know how to turn a boy into a man. Why don't you send William to France?"

"And that will be good for him?"

"Perhaps not good, Sir William," said Pepys, "but certainly ripening. The experiment has yet to fail. You know the French."

Thus at eighteen and in the company of several other young Englishmen either in search of adventure or in need of ripening, William Penn found himself in Paris. Sir William's importance in England opened important doors in France: young William was to be ripened at the top of the tree. King Louis XIV himself was only twenty-four years old. The parties to which he invited William were packed with Europe's finest young adults on the worst behavior. France dazzled William; he was soon proficient in both its language and its customs. The experiment was a staggering success.

After several such months, William was walking home one night, dressed in all his finery, and he passed a drunken French nobleman on the street. As per custom, the Frenchman stepped to one side, removed his plumed hat and executed an extravagant bow. William hadn't noticed the man until he heard: "You swine, I will teach you to reject a gentleman's courtesies," and he turned around to see the Frenchman, sword drawn, rushing at him. William drew his own sword—another French habit he had adopted—and the two men fenced briefly. The Frenchman was too drunk to fight well; in a few moments William sent the man's sword clattering to the cobblestones. The man waited to be killed.

William frowned at him, then asked: "Is the tipping of a hat so important to you that you will kill a man over it?" And he walked away.

The question was still in his mind when he awoke the next afternoon, but now he asked it of himself. The shallowness of the past months was suddenly clear to him. He recognized what a fool he had been. Well, he had had enough. He packed. He knew where he would go. That night he took the coach to Nantes, in western France, and the next day he was at Saumur, the Huguenot center, and matriculated in the Protestant Academy. Headmaster of the Academy was Moses Amyraut, the leading French Protestant theologian who had modified Calvinism into a gentler philosophy that enabled a man to save his soul through piety and charity rather than suffer the lifelong dread that he had been damned since birth by some divine whim. Amyraut accepted William as a private student and invited the young Englishman to live in his home. For the next eighteen months, William gave himself to serious study of God and himself and the relation of each to the other. When he returned to London in August, 1664, he was again a changed man. He possessed an inner calmness and a clarity of mind and purpose that gave him a maturity he lacked when he had left. But this was not what people saw. Instead, people saw a confidence they thought French high life had given him. He could now wear his fancy clothes with proper indifference; after two years in France, he could not immediately break the habit of speaking French and he broke into it inadvertently; he used his hands loosely when he spoke, he stood with his hips thrust forward and he walked with an indolent swagger. So French.

"Fine, fine," said Sir William. "Now, son, what do you want to do with yourself?"

"I have no plans," said William.

How like a Frenchman! "What did you study at that school you attended?"

"Philosophy. Theology. Greek and Latin and Hebrew. Rhetoric."

Sir William considered it. "That didn't prepare you for much, did it, except the Church. Are you thinking of the Church? I know a lot of important people in the Church."

"Oh, no."

"Then what? Government? Business? Any of the sciences? Law, perhaps?"

William knew perfectly well what he wanted: he wanted to be engaged somehow in religion, but not the Anglican religion. Where, he did not precisely know, but he knew he could not discuss it now, especially with his father. "Law, perhaps," he said.

"Fine, fine," said Sir William. "I'll make all the arrangements. At Lincoln's Inn, of course." It was one of the four Inns of Court where the sons of rich Londoners took the legal training that could place them high in government offices.

"Of course," said William, and to himself he added: "For the time being."

3

There were some new laws in England that were important to William Penn both as a student and a religious man. They were called the Clarendon Code, after the Earl of Clarendon, who was then lord chancellor. Actually, the earl had opposed the laws, but the preponderantly Anglican Parliament wanted them passed and passed them over his objection. In all, there were four laws.

The Corporation Act required all officers of incorporated municipalities to be Anglicans. The Act of Uniformity required all ministers in England and Wales to use the Anglican Book of Prayer; two thousand clergymen were forced out of their pulpits by this. The Conventicle Act forbade the assembling of five or more people for religious worship other than Anglican. The Five-Mile Act forbade any nonconforming preacher or teacher to come within five miles of any corporate town or the place where he had served as minister prior to the Act of Uniformity.

The Code was aimed directly at keeping the Catholics in Europe and indirectly at keeping the Presbyterians in Scotland, but it obviously had its detrimental effects on anybody who wasn't Anglican. King Charles II tried to overcome the Code with his Declaration of Indulgences, but Parliament quickly squelched it. Studying the Code, William Penn was heatedly against it. His limited association with Quakers had convinced him of the importance of freedom of conscience; his months with Moses Amyraut had assured him further of each man's right and responsibility to save his soul in the way he felt best.

But there was little William could do. Entering Lincoln's Inn in February, 1665, he was soon taken out to accompany his father on a sea battle against Holland. William had just about returned to school when London was struck by an epidemic of the plague that took almost seventy thousand lives in a few months. The epidemic was scarcely over when the great fire of 1666 leveled the city. Quarantined at school during the plague and removed from the city with his family by the fire, William was lucky to be alive. He was lucky, too, to make an observation in the midst of the panic. He saw that the Quakers, who now called themselves the Society of Friends and numbered about sixty thousand, were the only group that tried to be of some help. As outlawed by the Clarendon Code as the Catholics, they disregarded the dangers of disease and fire and further persecution by coming forth as a unit to bury the dead and remove the debris. This display of Quaker charity impressed William profoundly.

Sir William sensed the reaction in his son and, deducing its cause from remarks he made, decided it would be best to get the youth out of the country. When Charles II had become king, Irish landowners whose property had been confiscated by Cromwell asked to have it returned; Sir William's estate, given to him by Cromwell, had to be restored to its rightful owner. However, King Charles gave Sir William other land, better land, but he had not seen it as yet. He told his son: "I want you to go to Ireland to make a survey of the new estates and set up some procedure by which the tenants will pay their rents on time."

William went. His first weeks were crowded with work; each night he fell exhausted into his bed. Gradually, however, he was able to have a little time to himself, and he gave thought to an idea that had been budding in his mind for months. He remembered that when he was a boy there was a shop in town that was run by a Quaker woman. One day he went to her. In Ireland, now, Quakers had no more freedom than they had in England, so when William tried to get the woman to talk to him about her religion she was extremely elusive. William understood. He was prepared to do all the talking until he convinced the woman of his sincerity in wanting to attend a Quaker meeting.

At last the woman said obliquely, "Some friends will be gathering at my home tomorrow evening. I think they would like to meet thee."

William grasped the innuendo. "I shall be there," he said, "and I thank thee."

The Quaker meeting so spiritually fulfilled William that he no longer had any doubts about himself. He attended another meeting, another, and he held one in his house. He was very happy. Then a meeting he attended in September, 1667, was raided and William, with the other Quakers, was put in jail. He wrote a letter to the Lord President of Munster, explaining what had happened and saying, "Religion is at once my crime and mine innocence." He asked for the release of himself and his friends.

The Lord President had only to see the signature on the letter to release everybody immediately; then he wrote to Sir William, apologizing for arresting his son. "We did not know who he was," the Lord President said.

Sir William was astonished to learn that his son was fraternizing with Quakers and he wrote the young man to return home as fast as he could. William reached home in December, and he was no sooner in the house than his father flew at him.

"Have you lost your mind?" Sir William shouted. "Don't you know better than to associate with Quakers?"

"I am one of them," said William.

"You can't be! How dare you do anything so outrageous without consulting me?"

"I didn't think thou would be interested."

"Don't call me 'thou.' I'm your father."

"I mean no disrespect, Father, but that is the way I must address thee."

They got nowhere. Frustrated, Sir William ordered his son to his room, to remain there until permitted to leave, but William was now twenty-four years old, a grown man, and he could not be treated as a child for long. He knew that his refusal to give up the Quakers was disobedience to his father, but there was no other way. Despite Sir William's orders, William left his room and the house whenever he wished, and when he left the house he invariably went to the Quakers. Sometimes he was out of the house for days at a stretch, sometimes weeks. By late summer, Sir William could stand it no longer.

One day when William came home, his father said, "You are embarrassing the family and endangering my position in the government. Since you evidently intend to go on with this Quaker business, I must order you to pack your things and get out of the house. And I want you to know that unless you return to your senses, you will never get a penny out of me again."

William moved out.

He did not have to worry about a place to go. Although half of England's Quakers were women and most of the men were from the middle and lower classes, some members were considerably wealthy; all of them were ready to take William into their homes. This was to be his life: moving from one home to another—and moving from one jail to another. Actually, the Quakers were harmless, especially since their philosophy included nonviolence and they would not bear arms even in war, but the nature of the Clarendon Code affected them because they were nonconformists. For them to meet even to sit together in silent meditation was against the law. As happy as William was to share in that silence, it was in the field of law that he proved most important to the Quakers, to England, to the world.

From the start, William worked to dilute the Code, to eradicate it if possible. Courageously, he went directly to government and Anglican leaders in hopes of resolving the country's religious conflict through reason. He could understand England's political apprehension regarding Catholic worship in the country, but as for Quakers he said, "We are Protestants suffering in a Protestant country, which must necessarily bring the Protestant religion under scandal abroad." But he argued in vain. Convinced by his legal studies that he could win a court case against the Code, he urged Quakers to continue their meetings. But he was too confident. Arrested at a meeting in 1669, he spent nine months in the London Tower. He used the time writing tracts. In one tract, he warned the bishops of the Church of England that the Code threatened all religion in the country. In another, he answered criticisms of the Quaker view of Christ. In another he discussed the Quaker interpretation of freedom of conscience. Because of who he was and because of what he was willing to endure for his religion, the tracts were widely purchased, and when he left prison he had some funds to support himself. And he left prison even more determined to carry on his fight.

The following year he was involved in a fight that changed the course of legal history. Arriving at the Quaker meeting house, he found it locked by the police. Undaunted, he began to speak to the Quakers in the street, a blatant violation of the Clarendon Code. Several Quakers were arrested, William among them, and their cases were brought into court a few days later. It was a noisy trial, with shouting on all sides. There was no doubt about it: the judge was out for William's head. William was not given a chance to testify, and when he was asked how he pleaded to the indictment he insisted that he did not know what the indictment was. He didn't hear it until the judge gave his instructions to the jury: William had led a nonconformist religious meeting, with more than five people present, within the limits of an incorporated municipality. William argued that the gathering had not been a religious meeting because it did not follow Quaker procedures. "I was standing on a corner discussing religious matters with some friends," he said.

The jury went to consider a verdict, returning to declare William not guilty. The judge was furious. He cited the charges again and sent the jury out for a new verdict. This time the jury said William was guilty of speaking on a public street, but not of unlawful assembly. Again the judge rejected the verdict. Now William rose and argued. "If not guilty be no verdict, then you make the jury and the Magna Charta a mere nose of wax," he shouted at the judge. To the jury, he said: "You are Englishmen. Mind your privilege. Give not away your right."

Three times the jury was sent out, coming back each time with a modified statement of William's innocence. The judge could no longer hold William, but he fined the jury for rejecting his instructions. Eight men paid the fine, but four went to jail prepared to fight the sentence. William worked hard to raise funds for hearings in higher courts. There were many hearings, until at last the Lord Chief Justice Sir John Vaughan handed down the ultimate decision that a jury was a free agency and could not be punished for its verdict. This set of vital precedent in Anglo-Saxon jurisprudence, putting justice with the people, where it belonged. But for William Penn, this might not have come about for years, if at all.

4

Two important factors now influenced William Penn. One was a reconciliation with his father. As Sir William gradually realized that his son's devotion to Quakerism was no whim, he resigned himself to it. Also, Sir William had fallen ill and felt his end was near and he did not want to die at odds with his son. Although William did not move back with his family, he made regular visits. When Sir William died at the end of 1670, he named his son as executor of his estate. The second important factor was Gulielma Springett, the daughter of a Quaker family William had met at Amersham in Buckinhamshire. William knew on sight that he was going to marry Guli, which he did on April 4, 1672, in the simple Quaker ceremony of the clasping of hands and the announcement of the state of matrimony between them.

And there was something else. In 1672, there was a brief respite from religious persecution in England, due to edicts by King Charles, but Parliament put a quick end to them and the situation was worse than ever. William began to feel there would never be religious peace in England. The only hope for Quakers was in another land, their own land. There were already Quakers in America, but they were having no easier a time there than in England. Only in Rhode Island were they allowed to worship openly in their own way. Rhode Island became something of a dumping ground for Quakers. Whenever they were discovered in Massachusetts or New York, they were taken to the Rhode Island boundary and pushed over the line.

But America was big; nobody was certain how big it really was. And it was still sparsely settled. Much of the Atlantic coast was already directly under the British crown, but there were parts, like New Jersey and Maryland, that were still in private hands. Maryland was the property of Lord Baltimore. New Jersey, divided into east and west parts, was owned by two families, with the boundary going from Little Egg Harbor, about twenty miles north of the present Atlantic City, to the Delaware Water Gap. In 1672, a dispute arose over debts and property rights in West New Jersey, eventually involving two Quakers. Since Quakers were not to go to court against each other, William Penn was called in to arrange a settlement. In doing so, he discussed his idea for a free land for Quakers and both men quickly approved it. Thus in August, 1677, two hundred and fifty Quakers sailed up the Delaware River to a place that became known as Burlington, and here they established the first free Quaker community in the country.

William Penn wrote the constitution for the Quaker colony. First, there was to be religious freedom for all. Second, courts were to be comprised of three justices and a jury of twelve; the justices were to develop the evidence, but the jury alone would decide on it. There was to be no slavery. Every property owner would have the right to vote in electing an assembly of a hundred, an executive committee of twelve and a governor. While in session, the assembly members were to be paid a shilling a day from a treasury derived from taxes, thus being reminded that they were servants of the people. All dealings with Indians were to be fair and honest, all agreements kept. If an Indian and a European found it necessary to go to court to settle a dispute, the jury should be composed of six Indians and six Europeans. There was to be no capital punishment except for murder; instead of a debtor's prison, a man was to forfeit his estate and work off the balance; thievery was to be punished by restitution in value or in labor. No one was to be required to testify against himself and everyone had the right to interrogate his accusers. These were tremendous innovations in government and law. They became the basis of the future laws of the entire land.

William Penn had another idea. In a pamphlet, he suggested that the colonies forming in America should be joined in some sort of federation with common laws for government and commerce. In this, he was a hundred years ahead of his time. He suggested, too, that there might be less war in the world if all nations joined in a forum where they could discuss their differences and settle them by a majority vote. In this, he was three hundred years ahead of his time.

William Penn did not get to see America himself for another ten years. For one thing, his wife's illness held him back. A delicate woman, she gave birth to delicate children; only three of her six survived to maturity. Penn was also held back by the necessity of arguing in courts for the release of imprisoned Quakers, occasionally himself. Furthermore, the interest in Quakerism in Holland and Germany required his presence there. And there was something else.

As executor of his father's estate, William discovered that the man had made a sizable loan to King Charles II during early efforts to put a solid economic foundation under the royal throne. Such loans were common and nobody actually expected them to be repaid. Sooner or later, the King would display some generosity in the form of a land grant or a special favor to balance out the debt. William Penn wanted land. He was able to convince King Charles that the land should be in America, an area roughly three hundred miles by one hundred and sixty miles, lying across the Delaware from West New Jersey. The King was willing to award the grant, plus the lease of an area to the south which eventually became the state of Delaware. However, Lord Baltimore felt this area belonged to him and there was considerable debate over the question. In the end, the Delaware counties were put under William Penn's jurisdiction temporarily. William wanted to call the entire area Sylvania; it was the King who prefixed the family name in honor of Sir William. Thus: Pennsylvania.

Many Quakers preceded William Penn to Pennsylvania before he was free to go there himself late in 1682. The town of Chester had been founded and plans were ready to build the capital city of Philadelphia, which Penn named from the Greek words *philos* and *adelphos*—love and brother: the city of brotherly love.

William Penn crossed the Atlantic with a hundred other Quakers, a third of whom died in a smallpox epidemic aboard ship. Even so, the joy of his arrival overshadowed the catastrophe. Many of the settlers had never seen William, coming as they did from other American colonies and from Europe. To them, he was a savior, and they greeted him like one.

There was a great deal of work to be done. The constitution William had written for West New Jersey had been adopted almost as written for Pennsylvania. By this time, the Quakers had also purchased East New Jersey, expanding their territory enormously. A government had to be set up, which William proceeded to do. Although he was the proprietor of most of the Quaker area, he preferred that a governor be chosen as the executive. Meantime, William completed a treaty with the Indians, one which Voltaire described as being "never sworn to and never broken." The Indian wars that scarred great portions of the country did not occur here. William also chose a site, some twenty miles upriver from Philadelphia, where he hoped one day to settle with his family.

All went well. Land was allocated, farms and villages began to spring up. At this point, all expenses in getting Pennsylvania going as a self-supporting colony came from William's own pocket, but the understanding existed that he would be repaid in the future when Pennsylvania had an established economy. He was confident that day would come.

Two years passed. The Penn country house was built and William also had a small place in Philadelphia. He was ready now to send for his family. Then, in October, 1684, he learned that Lord Baltimore was in London, pushing his claim on the Delaware counties, and it looked as though he was about to win it. William hurried back to England. Aware of the enemies he had at court because of his religion, William had little hope of retaining the land the King had leased to him, but just as the battle over Delaware was beginning King Charles died and was succeeded by his brother, King James II.

Because King James was a Catholic, there were strong feelings against him in England and steps were taken to keep him off the throne. He ascended it, however, and one of his first acts was to nullify the Clarendon Code and repeal the Test Act which, passed in 1673, banned from municipal and military office everybody but Anglicans. There was great unrest. William, on the other hand, was happy. The pressure on Quakers was eased. Also, he had been friendly with the King in the past and now felt confident about his own claims on Delaware. While this matter was being decided, William preached in

England and Europe and devoted himself to extensive writings both on religious matters and progress in Pennsylvania. He was just about ready to return to America when King James was dethroned by the leaders of Parliament. Because of his attachment to the King and his fervent endorsement of religious toleration, William was accused of being a Jesuit who had been given the right to marry in order to disguise his efforts to turn England over to the Pope. Despite the danger to his life, William twice declared his affection for the King, at the same time, however, assuring that he was a loyal Englishman. Unimpressed, Parliament decreed that William was no longer the owner of Pennsylvania. He was thus deprived of his holdings for almost two years, regaining them at last because the King managed to recapture his throne. However, the King's return was brief: his wife gave birth to a child, which meant a continued threat of Catholic rule in England. James was again evicted and William of Orange was invited to assume the reign of the country. A resumption of religious persecution took place, and William was grateful that at least he had now official possession of Pennsylvania, New Jersey and Delaware where, whatever happened in England, religious freedom was assured.

He was anxious to get back to America. Then, in February, 1694, Guli Penn died. He could not go.

5

He did not go for another five years. When he did, it was not in happy circumstances.

During this period, William married again, becoming the father of children who were a generation away from those of his first marriage. His first son, William, he had sent to Pennsylvania to represent him, but the young man was too interested in parties and women to do a good job. Affairs in Pennsylvania were deteriorating.

While William Penn was fighting for religious freedom in England, through his writings and more months in courts, it was somehow fading in Pennsylvania. The policy there of religious freedom had opened doors to all seeking it, but it developed that those wanting religious freedom apparently wanted it only for themselves. Friction on a religious basis began to arise. There were other problems. A booming town, Philadelphia attracted many ships, thus many sailors, thus many prostitutes. Thievery broke out. Saloons were selling whiskey to the Indians, owners thus duping the Indians out of their furs they traded. Politics had taken a turn for the worse, with a growing number of people dissatisfied with William's position as their proprietor. Scarcely anybody paid taxes and William could find nobody with the ability to collect them. His own resources dwindled. Borrowing from Philip Ford, his business manager, William unknowingly signed away large areas of Pennsylvania, a situation that was to bring on a complicated court case in later years when he discovered what he had done.

And there was this: Pennsylvania was to be a peaceful colony, with no militia other than a few men necessary to preserve the peace. As Quakers, Pennsylvanians would not fight their neighbors, but now there were many more Pennsylvanians than Quakers. Disillusioned, Quakers withdrew more and more from the political scene, and this made room for an attitude that was arriving from England. Through wars, the English had removed the Dutch from the Atlantic shores of America, the Spanish were no trouble, but there were the French. The French had Canada; they also had the Mississippi delta. Their hope was to converge in the American Midwest, ally themselves with the Indians and thus attack the British areas from the weakly defended western fringes. To prevent this, England wanted settlers in its American interests to form militias and also to pay for the maintenance of British troops in the colonies. William Penn opposed this mainly because he did not want to have Pennsylvania involved in a war, but there were many in his colony who did not feel that way.

These were some of the problems facing William when he returned to Pennsylvania in 1699. He arrived with an order from London. Because Philadelphia was practically a private city, legally outside British law, pirates of various countries flocked there to sell their booty. The order: get rid of the pirates. William succeeded in doing so, but that was about all he achieved.

To overcome complaints about a disbalance of power between the Pennsylvania executive and legislative branches, he made modifications in the constitution, but there was not much else he could clear up. He was most distressed over the increased religious friction and spent more time working against it than at official affairs. Again and again he emphasized that the vital factor in religion was the individual's freedom of conscience. This more than anything else, he said, was the attitude he wanted for Pennsylvania.

Rising pressure against precisely this was what sent him back to England in 1701. He had already made up his mind that his American holdings were becoming unmanageable, so when the suggestion was offered that New Jersey be turned into a Crown colony he conceded to it. Relieved, he felt he would have more time now to devote to his lifelong battle against intolerance in England. But then Philip Ford produced a bomb of his own. He presented William with a bill for fourteen thousand pounds, which Ford said he had loaned William over a period of years, and Ford said that if William couldn't pay the debt he would settle for Pennsylvania. Only then did William learn that the notes he had signed with Ford included clauses of payment on demand or the surrender of the American property. Convinced that he had been swindled, William refused to pay or to surrender Pennsylvania. The trial that ensued ended against William and he was put into prison for nine months. Against his wishes, friends raised half the amount Ford demanded and now he settled for it. William left prison an impoverished man.

He was now sixty-six years old, an old man for his time, and he began to realize that he could not go on much longer at the pace he had maintained for years. He was certain he would not live to see Pennsylvania again. Saddened by this, he wrote a long letter to Philadelphia in which he evaluated all that had happened there, for good and for bad, and he took more blame upon himself than he had to. He should have given more time to Pennsylvania, he said, less time to the troubles of England, but religious persecution anywhere was such a battle cry to him that he had been forced to spread himself thin; he was sorry. The letter was read at the Pennsylvania assembly and promulgated throughout the province and it had a remarkable effect. Taxes were paid, differences were resolved, Philadelphia cleaned house, Quakers revived their interest in politics.

Overwhelmed by it all, William reached the conclusion that the people of Pennsylvania were ready to conduct their own affairs without his proprietarian control over them. He proposed to Queen Anne, then on the throne, that Pennsylvania become a Crown colony, but with the important provision that freedom of religion be maintained. Before the negotiations could be completed, William suffered a series of strokes in 1712 and 1713 and he was helpless until his death in 1718. Pennsylvania remained in the Penn family until 1760 when, at the end of the French and Indian War, it went into British hands, but pensions were paid to the Penns for another hundred years because of their legal holdings in the state.

The surge of public support William Penn received from Pennsylvania just before illness incapacitated him for the rest of his life was a great comfort in assuring him that he had not failed in his effort to establish a land for free men. Less than seventy-five years after William's death, a new nation would build itself on his ideas, a nation where people would be free to vote, free to pursue justice, above all free to pray.

CHAPTER
TWELVE

The Woman Who Had Everything—Plus

THE privilege was rare, indeed. Visiting Rome, the family had been invited to attend Mass in the Pope's private chapel. After it, Pope Leo XIII would receive them, but they were instructed to be brief. The Pope was a busy man and it would be inconsiderate of them to take too much of his time. It was therefore surprising, awkward and a little embarrassing when the young woman suddenly asked, "Holy Father, may I speak to you alone?"

The Pope's attendants fluttered, annoyed: one did not do such things. Even the Pope seemed taken aback, but he said, "Yes, my child. Come with me." They went to another room. The Pope turned to the young woman and asked in French, "What is it, my dear?"

"I want to become a nun," she said.

"That is good," said the Pope. "And?"

"Well," said the young woman, "I want to become a cloistered nun, a contemplative, and I know that if I do that I shall have to give up all my money. I don't mind that, of course, but I want to put the money to a special use. I have some friends back home who are missionaries to the Indians and I want to find some way to assure them of financial support. Can you suggest any religious society to which I can give my money for that purpose?"

The Pope seemed amused. "There is an easy answer to that, my child," he said. "Why don't you become a missionary yourself?" The question stunned the young woman and she had no reply. The Pope said: "Now I will give you my blessing for your life and your future works." He blessed her. "You must excuse me now," he said, and he left.

The young woman returned to her group and they began the long walk through the maze of chambers that led to the street. They were almost out of the building when the young woman leaned against a wall and let her tears flood her cheeks.

Her sister asked, "Kate, are you all right?"

"Yes," said Kate. "I'm all right. Now."

2

The Drexels were one of the richest families in America. Francis Martin Drexel, a painter, had moved from Austria to Philadelphia in 1818 and three years later married Catherine Hookey. Portrait painting in Philadelphia did not promise much security for a young man with a wife and, soon, a family, and Drexel found it necessary to travel a great deal, mostly in Latin America where there were still enough members of royalty who were sufficiently vain and rich to hire him. For twenty years, Drexel hopefully practiced his art. Then, to his wife's astonishment, he announced that he was giving it up and going into business—the brokerage business. He went alone to Louisville and spent a year there, learning the mysteries of stocks and bonds, then returned to Philadelphia and opened his own firm, Drexel and Company. His staff: his two teen-age sons. The firm was an immediate success and quickly expanded into banking. Within ten years the Drexels were millionaires, and each year thereafter they became increasingly so. Retaining their Philadelphia headquarters, they eventually opened a branch in New York, in partnership with the House of Morgan, and in Paris with the House of Harjes.

The oldest son, Francis Anthony, married Hannah Jane Langstroth, and they had three daughters: Elizabeth, Louise and Catherine. When the girls were still in their teens, their father set up a fifteen-million-dollar trust fund for them. They were to live off the interest, and on the death of each a third of the principal was to be divided evenly among her children. Should any die childless, her share went to her sisters, and if they all died childless the money was to go to specified religious and charitable institutions.

The day, therefore, that Catherine Drexel told Pope Leo XIII that she had some money she wanted to consign to missionaries working with American Indians, she was talking in terms of a fortune. As a nun, she knew, she would have to take a vow of poverty and could thereafter own nothing in her own name. She could give her share of the trust fund to the convent she joined, but the chances were that a cloistered convent would have no missionary affiliations. And Kate definitely wanted to do something for the Indian missions. Her interest in them had been stirred by Bishop James O'Connor, formerly pastor of St. Dominic's Church in Holmesburg, where the Drexels had a summer home, and now vicar apostolic of the Nebraska Territory. On visits to Philadelphia, the bishop had told the Drexels of the severe hardships suffered by Indians who had been corraled on desolate reservations. The family contributed generously to his work and had even traveled to the Territory to see for themselves the specific needs that had to be met.

Kate's interest was particular and personal. With unusual

precocity, Kate had chosen Bishop O'Connor to be her spiritual director even before she was in her teens. This meant she confided her innermost thoughts and problems to him, outside the confessional as well as in it, and he in turn guided her spiritual formation with an understanding insight that was rare in such circumstances. When he was transferred to Nebraska, Kate was heartbroken, fearing that the departure put an end to the vital friendship. But then she discovered that the friendship could be kept alive through letters, the family's trips to the West and the bishop's periodic returns to Philadelphia, and she was content. Despite her age, the bishop was not patronizing with Kate. He seemed to sense the scope of her spiritual future more clearly than she did, and he knew that when she had spiritual decisions to make she would turn to him. He was thus adult with her, sympathetic and patient.

From the bishop's letters and conversations, Kate developed both a knowledge and love of the West. His vicariate included not only Nebraska and the Dakotas, but parts of Missouri, Wyoming and Montana as well. Most of the major Indian tribes, like the Pawnees and the Sioux, had been consigned to reservations in this area, and they were the bishop's concern far more than the Catholics who had migrated there. A vanquished people, they were also a poor people, illiterate, diseased, most of them starving and many of them still resentful of the treatment they were receiving from their conquerors. The rest of the country had mixed feelings about the Indians. True, there had been bitter wars and horrible massacres, but viewed objectively these were to be expected from a people who watched invaders take over lands that had been theirs for centuries. True, too, even now, after the Civil War, migrants to the West lived in constant fear of Indian raids. But it was also true that regimenting the Indians on arid reservations that provided slim livelihood was no solution to the problem. The tendency to ignore them afterwards only made things worse. America's Founding Fathers had hoped that the Indians would be assimilated into the new country and that there would be no conflicts over race or properties, but things did not work out that way. For more than fifty years, then, the only specific good done for the Indians was done by missionaries.

President Ulysses S. Grant recognized this, and in an effort to support the work, he proposed in 1870 that the Federal Government appropriate funds for the education of Indian children in mission schools. This, he felt, would result in future Indian adults who would be good Christians and good Americans. There was only one thing wrong with the plan. To avoid denominational competition, President Grant stipulated that the reservations were to be subdivided on a denominational basis, and that the sect that could prove it was the first religious influence in the subdivision would be given the civil administration of it. Other denominations would have to withdraw. The error in this was that the individual Indian was thus denied the right to choose the church he wanted to attend. Protestant families found their children going to Catholic schools; the Sioux, almost entirely Catholic, were cut off from their church. Despite the need for federal aid, leaders of both denominations objected to the divisive policy, but seven years passed before they could have it corrected and at last the Indians were given the freedom of religious choice that belonged to all Americans.

The Government granted land for the building of the mission, plus $108 a year to educate, clothe and feed each child. As helpful as this was, it was still insufficient to meet the costs and it made no provision for adults, many of whom wanted to be educated, all of whom needed food and clothing and medical care. For added funds, therefore, the missionaries had to turn to friends. Bishop O'Connor turned to the Drexels.

The family trips to the West were intended to be vacations, but Francis Drexel used them to survey the Indian plight in order to find ways he could help. He helped a great deal; nobody ever knew exactly how much. He built a dozen missions from the ground up for Bishop O'Connor, and on his Western travels he was forever taking struggling missionaries aside and asking if there was anything he could do for them. His sincere charity had no bounds: he was equally generous with Protestant institutions. His will, which provided that if his daughters had no heirs his fortune should go to specified philanthropies, included a sizable contribution to a Lutheran hospital.

His daughters emulated him. Their return trips to Philadelphia invariably took them into Chicago where, using their own allowances, they bought clothes and toys for Indian children. When, at fifteen, Kate Drexel was given her own bank account, her first check was a hundred-dollar donation to a missionary she had met the previous summer out in Washington. The pattern was set, and it was to be lifelong.

Kate Drexel could not name the precise day she decided to become a nun. It was a gradual thing, growing out of many influences. She had been born on November 26, 1858, in her father's mansion at 433 Race Street. It had been a difficult birth; both mother and child were in danger of death. Aware of this, Francis Drexel went alone to the room where his new and frail daughter lay and baptized her conditionally. On December 29, Kate was taken to the Church of the Assumption for baptism by a priest. The next day, her mother died. About eighteen months later, Francis Drexel married Emma Bouvier, of the leading Philadelphia family, and they settled in a new home at 1502 Walnut Street. The house was big and there were many servants. The children were educated by private tutors who lived in. Part of each year was spent at St. Michel, the Drexel country estate, and part at travel, and when a tutor did not accompany the family the children were expected to mail back regular reports of what they had seen and learned. It was a comfortable life and a happy one.

It was also a life of spiritual atmosphere. St. Michel, for example, had been given its name because of the Gospel testimony that St. Michael, the Archangel, had been present at the birth, passion, resurrection and ascension of Jesus Christ, and the family wished both to honor him and seek his protection. The French version of the angel's name was used because everybody in the family knew French and enjoyed speaking it. A private oratory was built at St. Michel, and it was blessed by Archbishop James F. Wood, of Philadelphia, who granted the Drexels the usual privilege of having Mass celebrated there four times a year. This privilege, formerly reserved for European noblemen who lived too far from a church their families and staffs could attend regularly, was almost unheard of in America and indicated the high regard the clergy held for the Drexels. It was a regard earned by more than generosity—more by the steadfast spirituality of the family, by their frequent participation in the sacraments, their daily Rosary, their family-reading each evening of the Bible and the lives of the saints.

All this, surely, influenced Kate and kept her responsive to the thoughts she occasionally had about entering the religious life completely. She mentioned this once in a letter to Bishop O'Connor, and she was puzzled when, in reply, he wrote only of her happy home life and how much he missed his visits with the family. She mentioned it again in a letter from Lourdes while the family was touring Europe, but again the bishop expressed only mild interest. So she went on with the process of growing up. In 1879, she made her debut into society; the following summer she spent on the New Jersey coast, attending a nightly succession of parties at which she was invariably a great favorite of the young men. The family thought she would soon marry, but she enjoyed her popularity so much that she never paid special attention to any particular suitor and none of them felt confident enough to push his luck.

Then, in 1883, Emma Drexel died. Her three stepdaughters took the loss so painfully that Francis Drexel decided that a trip to Europe might help them. In Italy, Kate visited the shrine of St. Catherine of Siena, after whom she was named, and while there she reflected on the many times she had considered becoming a nun, as St. Catherine had been. But whereas St. Catherine had spent her life working among the poor and the sick and in goading Church rulers to bring about necessary reforms, Kate preferred to think of a nun's life as a cloistered life, hidden away in prayer and contemplation. Kneeling at the shrine, Kate became convinced that this should be the life for her. On returning home, she put her decision to Bishop O'Connor when he visited the Drexel home.

He said: "This is not the time for you to consider anything like that. Wait. Wait and pray."

She was twenty-five. She wondered when the bishop expected her to start doing something with her life, but she trusted him and agreed to wait. In 1884, she accompanied the rest of the family on another tour of the Western missions. Early in 1885, her father died. Once again came the long months of deep heartache. This time it was Anthony Drexel, Kate's uncle, who insisted that she and her two sisters take a trip. They went back to Europe, and it was on this trip that Kate shattered Vatican decorum by asking Pope Leo XIII if she could speak to him privately, and learned definitely what she must do with her life.

3

She told no one of her decision: Bishop O'Connor must be the first to hear it. Instead, she completed the European tour with her sisters, then returned to Philadelphia in April, 1887. During discussions with their father's lawyers, the Drexel daughters discovered that he had been practically the sole support of three Philadelphia orphanages; they continued the donations. They also bought two hundred acres of land and built an industrial school for older boys. They added a wing on St. Agnes Hospital, Philadelphia, and they gave fifty thousand dollars to the Catholic University in Washington, D. C., for the Francis A. Drexel Chair of Moral Theology. And, of course, they continued their support of the Indian missions.

Kate wrote Bishop O'Connor and asked when he thought he might be coming East; she had something she wanted to discuss with him. He replied that he had a fairly good idea what she wanted to talk about, but that certain complications were preventing him from travel at the present time. Why didn't she and her sisters come out to see him? They went.

The bishop's complications arose shortly after the inauguration of President Benjamin Harrison in 1888. The President had nominated as directors of the Bureau of Indian Affairs two men who were known to oppose the missionary schools on the reservations and who had indicated their intentions of promoting public schools for the Indians. If Congress approved the nominees, their plan would certainly be put into effect. Protestant missionaries did not react to the threat as strongly as the Catholics. For Catholics, the distinctly religious atmosphere of an elementary school was considered extremely vital to the spiritual formation of children, a formation that could be seriously endangered in the nonreligious atmosphere of public schools. Without the federal aid, however, the Catholics could not possibly keep their mission schools open. Letters from the Catholic laity and clergy flooded Harrison's office, pointing out that the federal aid was to the individual student, not the school, and if the student was about to be denied his freedom to choose the school he wanted to attend, his civil rights would certainly be violated. A committee of the hierarchy called on Harrison to emphasize the same aspect, and similar visits were made to congressmen. The President and the congressmen assured the Catholics that their argument would be taken into consideration, but it was not. Harrison persisted in his nominations, Congress approved them, the two men took office and the aid to mission schools was terminated. Public schools were built at costs tremendously exceeding the student-aid program, with the result that any other plans to help Indians were bankrupt before they could be tested.

"So," Bishop O'Connor said to the Drexel sisters when they were with him, "the mistreatment of the Indians continues to be America's special sin."

"What do you plan to do?" Elizabeth Drexel asked.

"I'm going to try to keep our schools open," said the bishop, "but I'll have to do a lot of begging to get the money for it."

"We'll help you, of course," Louise Drexel assured him.

"I knew you would," the bishop admitted, "but it may require even more than the Drexel millions."

Kate laughed. "We know a lot of millionaires in Philadelphia. We'll see to it that they help."

"I hope you know a few in New York and Boston, too," said the bishop, and he smiled, satisfied. At least there was hope.

Later when he was alone with Kate, he asked, "Now, what was it you wanted to discuss with me?"

"I'm going to become a nun," Kate said.

"I expected that," the bishop said. "Which cloister?"

"I'm going to become a missionary nun," Kate clarified, and she told him about her conversation with the Pope.

The bishop was ecstatic. "When I advised you to wait and pray, this was exactly what *I* was waiting and praying for."

Kate smiled and nodded. "I'm not surprised." Then: "I want to work with the Indians, of course."

"Of course."

"But I still don't know which congregation to join or what to do with my money."

Bishop O'Connor considered this. "There are several excellent congregations working out here; you could be happy in any of them, and you could give your money to the one you choose when you take your vows."

"Yes," said Kate, still unsure.

"There's something else," the bishop said. Kate waited. "You know about the vow of obedience, of course. When you take it, you'll have to go wherever your superiors send you and do whatever they assign."

"I know."

"And despite whatever you want, you may not be sent to the Indians."

"I've thought of that."

"There's a way to take care of it."

"How?"

"Start your own congregation."

Kate laughed. "I couldn't do that."

"Why not?" Bishop O'Connor asked. "Others have. In the

whole Church, there's not a single congregation of Sisters dedicated exclusively to the Indians. We could use one."

"Yes," Kate said, "but I'm sure I'm not the one to start it. I wouldn't know how."

"I would," the bishop said, leading her. "You have lots of friends who would. Why not Archibishop Ryan?" He was now the ruling prelate of Philadelphia. "Think about it."

She thought about it all the way home. One night at dinner she announced her plan to her sisters: she would do exactly what the bishop had suggested. Elizabeth and Louise were far from surprised and they were very happy. On the same occasion, Louise announced that she was going to marry Edward Morrell, a young lawyer. "We're both going to be very busy this year," Louise said.

Kate didn't expect to spend a year preparing to enter the convent, but it took that. There were many family business matters that had to be resolved in addition to matters pertaining to the religious congregation Kate planned to establish. The year passed quickly. During it, Kate's interests spread to the plights of another down-trodden people—the Negroes. For years, Louise had been sending help to southern missionaries. A request for donations from the Bishop of Nashville sent Kate to Tennessee, and when she saw the sad state in which Negroes there were living she gave not only the money but also the promise that her new congregation would include Negroes in its program. Later when she was discussing the congregation with Archbishop Ryan, he asked what she intended to call it.

"I have always derived my greatest spiritual consolation from Holy Communion," she said, "so I would like to call the congregation the Sisters of the Blessed Sacrament."

"Sisters of the Blessed Sacrament," said the archbishop, savoring the words. "Fine."

"For Indians and Negroes," Kate added.

"*And* Negroes?"

"Yes."

"That's an ambitious horizon," the archbishop observed.

"I shall try to reach it, with God's help," said Kate.

The reach first required Kate's own training as a nun. In May, 1889, a few weeks after acting as maid of honor at Louise's wedding, Kate entered the convent of the Sisters of Mercy in Pittsburgh. Her decision had already been front-page news across the country. To avoid further publicity, she traveled to Pittsburgh under her mother's maiden name, Langstroth. Even so, a Pittsburgh reporter tracked her down and went to the convent; he was told she could not receive guests.

Important changes now came into Kate's life. She was thirty-one years old, twice the age of most women beginning their training, she was set in her ways, she was independent by nature and by wealth, she was more used to giving orders than taking them. Now all that was over. The Sisters of Mercy knew, of course, that she was not going to enter their congregation, but as long as she was taking her training under their supervision she would be treated like all others. She received only two special privileges. First, she was allowed to receive and send more than the usual one letter a week, so long as the letters pertained to her congregation and missionary work. Even then the mail was censored. Second, she could receive as callers any missionaries who either sought contributions to their efforts or hoped to be included in her congregation's future plans. Otherwise, she was regarded as an ordinary postulant. Away went her beautiful clothes, replaced by a simple, black, full-length, long-sleeved dress and a veil. There was no mirror in the house for her to see how she looked; how she looked in God's eyes was all that mattered. She was up at five-thirty every morning, and from then until nine at night she was busy with prayers, meditation, study and work. Work included serving table, scrubbing floors, sewing and the day nursery where working mothers left their children. Kate was also called upon to teach catechism to some of the older children. She had to make her own bed, keep her room spotlessly clean and be ready to find the bed torn apart or her dresser emptied onto the floor if an inspecting nun found anything improperly done or out of place.

There was a reason for it all. In taking steps to become a nun, she proclaimed her intention of living only for God. Whatever she achieved as a nun was to be for His glory, not her own, and she was to be always aware of her uselessness without Him. Thus pride, the most insidious of vices, had to be replaced by true humility. One test of humility was obedience, obedience not only to the Will of God but to the will of one's superiors. A nun in charge of training aspirants would sometimes go to the most unreasonable extremes just to see how much needling they could take before pride stirred them to anger, resentment, sullenness or open disobedience. Those who broke too easily would be bad risks in the religious life: they had not put God before themselves. If they did not have enough self-control to endure harassment from a superior over some minor infraction of the rules without flaring up, how would they behave in the face of a serious temptation? Pride, then, had to be brought under rein; deep spirituality had to be nurtured. This was the test of the two-year training period, and anyone who survived it could just about survive anything.

For Kate, the test was a breeze. Although she had never done a moment's housework in her life, she went at each chore as if it were a new game. She accepted abrupt corrections gratefully, aware that she might not know how to do the menial tasks other women had grown up on. Aware, too, that she had not earned the great wealth she had and the luxurious life it had brought her, she did not consider herself any different or any better than anyone else. She was also aware that one day other nuns would be submissive to her in obedience. To be a good superior, she knew she could best exercise authority through her own obedience to her superiors.

After six months as a postulant, she donned the black habit and white veil of a novice, and after eighteen months in the novitiate, an even sterner training period, she was permitted to put on the black veil. During these two years, Kate suffered two severe heartaches that challenged her stability. The first, in May, 1890, was the death of Bishop O'Connor, who had so patiently guided Kate to the religious life and to whom she had hoped to turn during the early days of her congregation. Without him she felt utterly lost. Friends wondered if she would give up her plans; she wondered so herself. In her meditations, she had to decide if she was becoming a nun for the sake of the bishop or the sake of God. It was only when she managed to put God first that she was able to remain in the convent. The second heartache was worse. Shortly after she entered the convent, Elizabeth Drexel married. Several months later she wrote happily that she was pregnant. Just as Kate was finishing her training, Elizabeth's husband wrote that she had developed a liver disease the doctors seemed unable to cure. A few weeks later, Elizabeth delivered her baby prematurely; both mother and son died. Attending the funeral and then returning to the convent demanded all the love and faith in God that Kate Drexel possessed. In the years to come, Kate discovered that this love and faith were the only possessions worth having.

4

Now the Drexel fortune belonged to two. Because of this, the newly formed Sisters of the Blessed Sacrament for Indians and Negroes was in a unique position. In practically all other such congregations, a major problem at the start was finding funds for self-support until there were enough members to staff the hospitals and schools that could provide an income for expansion and the training of newcomers. With Kate's congregation, there was more than enough money. During her training period, thirteen women applied to the congregation. At the time she finished her own novitiate, eleven others were at various stages of theirs. In 1891, Kate moved her group to St. Michel, inviting a Sister of Mercy to come along as novice mistress for those still in training. Nearby, construction work was progressing on the convent that was to serve as the congregation's mother house. Requests were already coming in from bishops and missionaries for the new congregation to take over schools among the Indians. Everything was going smoothly, unusually so, and much too fast. No sooner were the first novices ready to take their vows than Kate was ready to send them out on their first assignments, and she was surprised when both Archbishop Ryan and the superiors of the Sisters of Mercy urged her not to.

"But they are needed," Kate pointed out.

"They are not ready," insisted the archbishop.

"What more must they do?" asked Kate.

"They have to grow up a little," the archbishop said.

"They're already grown women," said Kate.

"But they are not grown Sisters," Archbishop Ryan said. "Let them get used to that for awhile before you try to make missionaries out of them. If you send them out West without practical experience they'll scatter the first time they encounter serious trouble."

Kate knew the archbishop was right, but it was difficult for her to be patient. She recognized, however, that patience was not only wise but it was also the archbishop's order. In obedience, Kate had to practice it. To provide practical experience for the Sisters, Kate opened a boarding school for Philadelphia Negro children where the qualified Sisters taught. She was due for some practical experience of her own. Nightly the Sisters returned home in tears and in anger because the children, being children, were unmanageable. Kate comforted and advised them, and gradually she grew aware that good teachers were not merely the products of good intentions but rather the results of skillful combat on the classroom battlefields. She shuddered at the thought of what might have happened had she sent the untried Sisters out West on their own. So she waited three years before she responded to the many pleas for teachers that came to her. Then she chose nine of her most able veterans and assigned them to a school among the Pueblos near Santa Fe, New Mexico. She made the trip West with them and was appalled by the primitive conditions. Over the years, other teachers, both nuns and laymen, had tried to adjust to the rugged environment but had departed because the life was too difficult and too lonely. She was determined that this would not happen again.

"Remember," she told the Sisters as she prepared to return East, "you are not here alone. God called you to the religious life and He has called you here to do His work. He will be your only comfort now. You need no other."

The Santa Fe school flourished, the first of many that were to flourish under Kate's direction. Each year more women joined the congregation; each year, as trained and tested teachers became available, they moved out to work in Indian and Negro schools. Most often, Kate had to pay to build the schools herself. This was no problem. Sometimes when the need was great she built the school, then arranged for other congregations to teach there temporarily until her own Sisters were ready. Assuring that her Sisters would be fully ready was most important. Toward that end, Kate took over the supervision of the novitiate for several years. She traveled extensively, digging into local problems thoroughly, then returning to the convent to instruct the novices in the challenges that awaited them in the field.

There were many different problems. On the western plains, sheer boredom could threaten the effectiveness of anyone lacking deep spiritual insulation. Thus Kate taught the novices to seek spiritual restoration in their prayers and religious exercises. Unchanging routine could sharpen the tempers of women who lived and worked together night and day, month after month, year after year. To equip the novices with sincere charity, Kate fostered a love of the congregation's rules and of a nun's vows. In her letters to the missions, she urged the Sisters to love each other, respect each other and obey their superiors. Often on her travels Kate went far off her scheduled route to visit a few isolated Sisters and bring them gifts, displaying her vivid concern for them and the concern she wanted them to have for each other. This was important because the Sisters, however high their motives, were human beings, subject to human weaknesses, and to keep them strong and active Kate had to be strong and active herself. One discontented, recalcitrant Sister in a remote convent could disrupt the whole house and endanger the entire effort. To prevent that required the full attention of the woman whose attitude and conduct were the yardstick of congregation's morale across the country—Kate herself.

There were outside problems, too. In several southern areas there was open resentment against the schools Kate built for Negroes. Attempts were made to close the schools by local laws prohibiting whites to teach in Negro schools, laws that required court action to overcome. Frequently property owners refused to sell to Kate when they learned she planned to build Negro schools on the land, and she had to let others make her purchases for her if she hoped to get any land at all. She was amazed to discover that Catholics could be as guilty of segregation sentiments as other southerners and she used the occasion of a speech she gave at Notre Dame University to make a public issue of it. She also pointed out that northern Catholics were equally guilty. Why was it, she asked, that northern schools so rarely granted scholarships to Negroes? Her bluntness so embarrassed northern educators that immediate steps were taken to correct the situation. In the South, she realized, change would come slower, but she was not willing to wait for it.

Kate's sister Louise and her husband had founded an industrial school for Negro boys at Rock Castle, Virginia, and by the turn of the century it was a thriving operation. Kate visited it and decided that a similar school for girls would be equally important and successful. She bought land across the river from the boy's school and built her own school for girls. In Louisiana, she saw the same inadequate educational facilities for Negroes she had observed throughout the South. In a broad effort to meet the needs, she first opened a chain of elementary schools along the Mississippi delta, and because she lacked the nuns to staff them she hired Negro teachers, few of whom had finished elementary school themselves. Perceiving the future need for higher education of the students, she sent several of her Sisters to Catholic University in Washington, D. C., to earn their master's and doctor's degrees; she even took a few courses herself in the event that she would be called upon to teach. Then she acquired land in New Orleans and built Xavier Academy, a high school and junior college which included boarding facilities for students coming in from the country. The Academy and the better-trained Sisters were ready at the same time.

By 1915, the first students had completed their progression through the junior college. What was needed now was a university. With that in mind, Kate purchased the abandoned buildings of the defunct Southern University, made the necessary repairs and changed its name to Xavier University, which subsequently developed into one of the leading Negro universities in the country. In the South, as among the Indians in the West, Kate specified that though the schools she started were Catholic schools they were to be open to members of all denominations and that no efforts to convert the students, especially the younger ones, should be made unless the student asked for Catholic instruction and had his parents' permission. This was no trick; Kate was sincere in her respect for the religious convictions of others, and although it was understandable that the Sisters should want to convert everybody, Kate assured them they could convert more successfully by personal example than by making conversion a prerequisite to higher education. Out of this attitude evolved a tolerance that was as much an innovation in New Orleans as the university itself.

Kate disliked the word tolerance. "Justice," she often said, "is a better way to put it." On one visit to New Orleans, Kate was delighted to learn that the Xavier basketball team was beating all the schools it played, the only trouble being that segregation sensitivities kept the number of opponents at a minimum. A game scheduled at Loyola University, another Catholic school in New Orleans, had to be canceled for this reason.

"If that game had been played," a Loyola student told Kate, "there would have been a race riot."

"Oh really?" said Kate. "Apparently you people at Loyola are not learning all that you should."

5

Kate was fifty-seven when Xavier University opened its doors. She had been a nun and Mother General of an important religious congregation for almost twenty-five years, years during which she traveled thousands of miles annually on behalf of the American Indians and Negroes. Her work had taken her abroad twice, to Rome: once for the temporary approval of the congregation's rules and again for the final approval. Only few changes were made in the rules as she had written them, among them the name of the congregation; Rome changed it to: Sisters of the Blessed Sacrament for Indians and Colored People. It was a minor change, one that showed how well the rules had been composed. The state of the congregation itself was further evidence of Kate's leadership. Its original thirteen members had increased to almost two hundred, engaged in teaching throughout the West and South. Their success brought requests from bishops in Philadelphia, New York and Boston for help in the large Negro communities in those cities. In most cases, Kate supplied the school buildings as well as the schoolteachers. She also continued to help missionaries outside her own organization. Once she learned that a priest on an Indian reservation was about to mortgage his school buildings in order to get the money to keep them open, and because she knew he would never be able to pay the mortgages, she said: "If you do that, Father, the banks will soon be running your schools. Let me give you the money." She also gave money to other teaching congregations that could not afford to build their own schools. In the same way, she restored shrines, wayside chapels, orphanages, homes for the aged and hospitals, and she and Louise continued the aid to the institutions their father had supported.

Generous, she was not extravagant. Her father had often said, "Be generous, but with prudence." Prudently, then, when a request for funds struck her as worthy she went out to where it came from to see for herself how much was needed and how it could best be spent. She disliked waste. An economic builder, she took it upon herself to change blueprints when she felt they included any useless nooks; when buying land, she watched for convenient forests that could provide inexpensively available wood; she sometimes inspected clay deposits from which bricks could be made; she insisted on using local labor, both because it was cheaper and because the construction would then contribute to local economy. Her convents were sturdy and durable, but plain and practical. Much of the convent food was grown in convent gardens. Kate's vow of poverty led her to make the most use of everything, even stationery. She frequently answered letters on the backs of their own pages. Sometimes she wrote one person on the blank side of someone else's letters, which occasionally caused a little confusion, but saved money. And yet she gave away thousands of dollars every year to missionaries whose needs she knew, and she spent herself with the same steady generosity.

In 1934, when she was seventy-six, her doctors warned against her constant travel and she promised to cut down—next year. She made another arduous trip to inspect the western missions, going all the way to California and traveling by coach because she felt the luxury of a compartment would deprive some Indian or Negro child of needed clothing or food. She was on her way back, in Chicago, when she suffered a mild cerebral hemorrhage, and when doctors insisted that she be hospitalized for rest she said: "I will, when I get back to Philadelphia." But instead of going directly to Philadelphia, she decided to detour to St. Louis to inspect the convents there. On the train she had another attack. This time she submitted to medical demands for a compartment and an accompanying nurse on the trip home. Reaching Philadelphia, she permitted herself to be put into a hospital for several weeks. She realized she would never travel again, and when she was told that even the exertion of walking might prove too much for her, she bought a wheel chair and insisted on being taken back to her convent and to her desk.

Unable to go to the missionaries any more, they came to her, not only to ask for money but to ask for Kate's advice and prayers as well. Nobody was better informed on techniques of the education of Indians and Negroes than she; others were as anxious to discuss ideas with her as they were to discuss finances. Kate's leadership in her special fields was so widely acknowledged that in 1937 the American hierarchy, meeting in Washington, issued a proclamation of gratitude to her for what she had done.

Also in 1937 her terms of office as Mother General of the congregation expired. The congregation's rules had been approved in 1897; Kate had served four ten-year terms, and canon law required that either she step aside or that a special appeal be made to Rome to allow her to remain in office. The congregation wanted to make the appeal, but Kate would not hear of it. She was too old, she said, she was almost eighty, and she was sure she would not live out another term. It would thus be better to put the direction of the congregation into younger hands. Mother Mercedes, Kate's traveling companion, was then elected head of the congregation and in obedience Kate submitted herself to the new leader. Kate was elected vicar general, the second highest office, and continued to serve on the congregation's council. Two years later, Mother Mercedes died and Kate found herself acting as superior of the congregation again for several months until a new Mother General could be elected. This time, Kate refused any office, but she continued to serve as adviser to the council and she continued to supply the funds to support the congregation and its works.

Kate was eighty-three when, in 1941, she celebrated the golden anniversary of her religious vows. "No festivities," she instructed the Sisters. "It's against the rules." But there were festivities nevertheless. Special Masses were held at the many schools she had founded. At the mother house, three pontifical Masses were celebrated, the third by Dennis Cardinal Dougherty, of Philadelphia. Letters and telegrams came from the entire American hierarchy. Pope Pius XII sent Kate a four-page letter, recapitulating her fifty years in service to the American Indian and Negro. Kate endured the whole affair with embarrassed patience.

In 1945, Louise Drexel Morrell died childless, thus putting the entire family fortune in Kate's hands. The fifteen million dollars of the original trust fund remained; despite the great amounts the three Drexel daughters had given away in fifty years, another fortune in interest had accrued. Kate, an eighty-seven-year-old nun with a vow of poverty, was now one of the richest women in the world. Her congregation had come into existence after her father's death and was not a beneficiary of the will. By the terms of the will, Kate herself could not leave any money to the congregation: it would all go to other religious institutions and charities. It would have been understandable had Kate, to safeguard the congregation's future, gone on a building and spending spree, but instead she continued her prudent generosity, using the anticipated needs of the Indians and Negroes as her only yardstick. "God will take care of the congregation," she assured.

She remained in unusual good health. The only sign of her age and infirmity was in her handwriting: gradually she lost her beautiful control of it. But she still wrote regularly to the Sisters in the missions; she had written her own answer to the Pope's letter. When she was over ninety, she still attended Mass every morning in the convent chapel, sitting in her wheel chair. It was only when her strength began to fade and she could not sit erect for long periods or hold her prayer book in her hands that an altar was erected in her room and Mass was said there near her bed.

In 1953, she was elected "Philadelphia's Most Distinguished Lady" and given an Award of Merit by the Catholic women. By now, she was in bed most of the time. Occasionally her mind wandered and she seemed to be talking to someone. Once she removed a shawl from her shoulders and told the Sister with her: "The child is cold, very cold. Put this over him right away." At other times, she said the Rosary over and over, softly, reverently, or she would ask about some Sisters in difficult mission posts. The next year on November 26, her ninety-sixth birthday, she was sitting up in a leather armchair that had been her father's, reading the hundreds of greeting cards that had arrived. She was up again at Christmas, enjoying the many gifts that came.

March, 1955, she caught a cold that developed into pneumonia. On Wednesday, the second, an oxygen tent was placed over her, but the next morning she was so improved that the tent was taken away. She read her missal while Mass was celebrated in her room, she received Communion, then her breakfast was brought to her. She was eating when suddenly she sank back. The oxygen tent was replaced, but it did not relieve her. It was clear to the doctor that she was dying. Priests were summoned and the congregation's superiors knelt in the room to pray. Kate opened her eyes for a moment; she seemed fully aware of what was happening to her and she appeared to be taking a last look around. Then she died.

She had become a legend in her own time. She had done more to improve the lives of the American Indian and Negro than any other individual in the history of the country. Because of her, two neglected peoples acquired dignity and self-respect long before most of the nation was seriously concerned about them. In preparing Indians and Negroes for places of honor in every profession, Kate built forty-eight grade schools, twelve high schools, a university, and only God knew how many country schools whose teachers she personally paid. In addition to founding a religious congregation that attracted over five hundred members in her lifetime, Kate opened three social-service centers and an important mission-study headquarters, and she privately supported scores of institutions for the young, the old, the sick and the unwanted. In the course of doing all this, Kate gave away over twelve million dollars. As important as the money was in the work that was done, there was something else that Kate Drexel gave, without which nothing would have been done at all.

She gave away herself.

Index

INDEX

INDEX